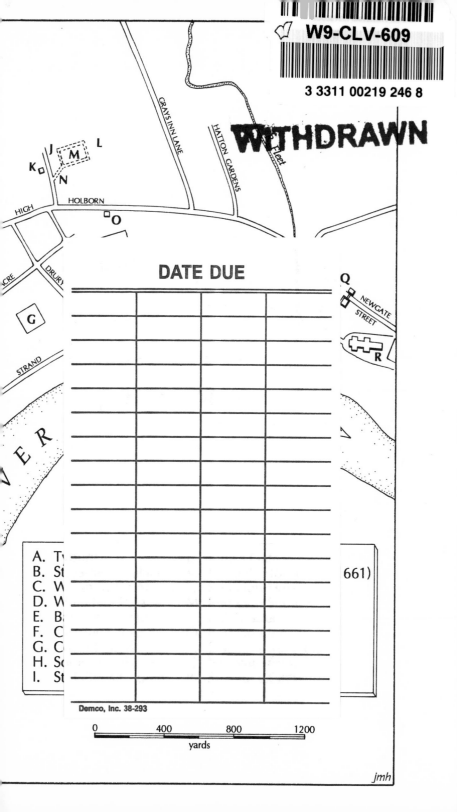

The Death of Oliver Cromwell

The Death of

Oliver Cromwell

H.F. McMains

THE UNIVERSITY PRESS OF KENTUCKY

Publication of this volume was made possible in part
by a grant from the National Endowment for the Humanities.

Scholarly publisher for the Commonwealth,
serving Bellarmine College, Berea College, Centre
College of Kentucky, Eastern Kentucky University,
The Filson Club Historical Society, Georgetown College,
Kentucky Historical Society, Kentucky State University,
Morehead State University, Murray State University,
Northern Kentucky University, Transylvania University,
University of Kentucky, University of Louisville,
and Western Kentucky University.

Editorial and Sales Offices: The University Press of Kentucky
663 South Limestone Street, Lexington, Kentucky 40508-4008

04 03 02 01 00   5 4 3 2 1

Library of Congress Cataloging-in-Publication Data

McMains, H. F., 1941–
        The death of Oliver Cromwell / by H.F. McMains.
            p.   cm.
        Includes bibliographical references and index.
        ISBN 0-8131-2133-7 (alk. paper)
        1. Cromwell, Oliver, 1599-1658—Death and burial.   2. Great
Britain—History—Puritan Revolution, 1642-1660.   3. Murder—Great
Britain—History—17th century.   4. Heads of state—Great Britain
Biography.   5. Generals—Great Britain Biography.   I. Title.
DA427.M38   1999   99-28854
941.06'4'092—dc21
        [B]

In memory of my mother and father
Sarah Elizabeth McMains
and
Howard Webster McMains

$\mathcal{C}$ontents

$\mathcal{P}$reface

The one time I walked through London's Red Lion Square, I did not know it was home to a ghost whom I should like to have met. Seeking an alternate route through Holborn to the old Public Record Office in Chancery Lane, I wandered one morning through an ordinary square just above the high street. The place was undistinguished and did not beckon me to return. Only some years later, while studying the death of Oliver Cromwell, did I find among antiquarian sources that I consulted a curious urban legend that residents of Red Lion Square had claimed for a very long time to have seen Cromwell's ghost. It was easy to dismiss this as nonsense—the square's late-eighteenth- and nineteenth-century residents could, of course, imagine a specter in the famous fogs of those days before clean-air statutes.

I became aware of Cromwell's alleged ghost in a roundabout manner. In Antonia Fraser's *Cromwell, The Lord Protector* there is a description of the funeral of his son-in-law, Henry Ireton, and I wondered why so stern a Puritan should have received in 1652 so elaborate a ceremony. Research into Ireton's demise led to an interesting story that ended with his exhumation nine years later, when the restored monarchy also excavated Cromwell's body from the same vault in Westminster Abbey. I thought to add a paragraph to an essay about Ireton that mentioned Cromwell's death, but I found surprisingly contradictory information. The further I studied Cromwell's death, the more mysterious the puzzle became, and I decided to see how it might be resolved. How curious that in the end the Restoration Parliament ordered the exhumation of four bodies from Westminster Abbey and their display at Tyburn. The authorities not only exhumed Cromwell's body but hauled it from Westminster to Tyburn by way of Holborn, where it lay two nights on the property of the Red Lion Inn. The event was known but unexplained, and the ghost of Red Lion Square gained my interest.

What I found especially intriguing was not the ghostly specter seen by people living in the square but the location of the sightings. It should be recounted that only residents of this particular square, which did not exist until about 1690, reported the ghost. Neighbors in areas that did exist in Cromwell's time—Covent Garden, Lincoln's Inn Fields, or Long Acre, where Cromwell once lived—made no such report. During the English civil wars of the 1640s the City's line of defensive forts ran across Red Lion Fields, as the open land then was known, and yet later residents did not claim to have seen spectral troopers from those days. They claimed to have seen Cromwell's ghost.

I began to see the ghost story as a bit of folklore, an oral tradition that in some way reflected a historical event. Historians in the past two decades have been willing to use such evidence, and I too think it useful. This story—among others, I might note—certainly showed that there was popular suspicion in the aftermath of Cromwell's death. More to the point, it showed that residents of Red Lion Square had memories, passed through the generations, of an unremarked event associated with Cromwell. By the nineteenth century the memories had taken the form of a ghost story best told on foggy nights.

As a result of my investigation I determined to write about Cromwell's lamentable death.

I wish to thank several persons who shared their time and expertise while I carried out this study. When my research first offered suspicion that Cromwell's demise was more complicated than tradition had declared, Mark E. Frederick, M.D., helped sort through several medical issues. Gwendolyn Jones allowed me to consult specialized materials in the medical library at St. Joseph Hospital, Chicago. Eleanor Berman graciously read the chapters concerning Cromwell's illness; she gave me a crash course in toxic metals and the benefit of her considerable laboratory experience. Six anonymous readers commented at length about the manuscript, providing the kind, constructive criticism for which an author is truly grateful. And Robert H. Ferrell thought it important to examine the unexpected death of an important political figure; he read the manuscript several times and suggested improvements in organization and style throughout.

These attentions notwithstanding, I am responsible for the conclusions.

$\mathcal{I}$ntroduction

The pages that follow consider a story long rumored and little credited, that in the mid–seventeenth century the lord protector of England, Scotland, and Ireland, Oliver Cromwell, was poisoned.

On the face of it his murder seems impossible. Such happenings could occur on the Continent, as in the murder of Wallenstein in 1634 by an agent of the emperor, Ferdinand II, but in England such attacks were not the way of politics, the 1628 death of the Duke of Buckingham notwithstanding. Cromwell's lifetime (1599–1658) admittedly was part of a dramatic period in his own land. At one end of the seventeenth century was the Elizabethan inheritance, the Shakespeare plays, the King James Bible, and at the other end the Glorious Revolution, William Congreve's comedies of manners, John Locke's treatises on government. Between occurred the twenty-year era of the civil wars and the interregnum, to use traditional terms, in which Cromwell took so large a part. His death on 3 September 1658 seems, on the surface, to have been natural, although for years royalist émigrés had plotted against his government and his person with agents and invasion plans. His efficient secretary, John Thurloe, knew what his enemies were up to, for he intercepted their letters as readily as, years earlier, Sir Francis Walsingham had acquainted himself with Catholic plots against Elizabeth I. Murder, again, could not have happened.

Historians have asserted that Cromwell's death was natural, even though they are in remarkable disagreement about the precise cause. Thomas Carlyle in his biography described the lord protector's final illness as "a kind of tertian ague, 'bastard tertian' as the old Doctors name it."[1] C.H. Firth referred to "an ague, or intermittent fever," whereas John Buchan wrote vaguely of "a malady which puzzled his physicians, a sickness perhaps as much of the mind as of the body."[2] F.J. Varley's *Oliver Cromwell's Latter End* stated that he died of malaria, which was then called ague.[3] At the conclusion of his four massive volumes, Wilbur Cortez Abbott paid scant attention to the matter, remarking merely that Cromwell "had not been well for nearly a year, he had failed and was failing fast." His death, he wrote, was an anticlimax because financial problems had undermined the protectorate.[4] Christopher Hill wrote in his biography of Cromwell that the protector's health failed at the beginning of 1658, that the "final blow" was the death of his beloved daughter Elizabeth, and that "pneumonia carried off the Protector less than a month later."[5] Lady Antonia Fraser has written at greater length, concluding that perhaps the protector was anemic from malaria and died of septicemia caused by a kidney infection; she did note that the final crisis was so sudden that a few observers suspected poison, but she did not pursue the point.[6] In his detailed study of the Restoration, published in 1985, Ronald Hutton wrote, "As one inconclusive debate succeeded another, the financial position worsened and the Protector's health collapsed. For a long time his illness, low fever, was not considered serious."[7] This, however, is as far as historians and biographers have gone. They have assumed that the cause, whatever it was, was natural and that a statesman's passing, at least in England, could not have been otherwise.

There are two special reasons why scholars have not looked more closely at Cromwell's death. One is an assumption that it was unimportant because his government's collapse was inevitable anyway. Abbott wrote flatly that even had Cromwell lived, "nothing he could have done would have enabled his government to survive." The protectorate's finances were "tottering" and its politics were "almost precarious." This he related without explanation.[8] Also, it has been assumed that Cromwell and his government were "intensely and almost universally hated."[9] In such views the death was inconsequential and restoration of the monarchy in the person of Charles Stuart the only possibility. According to a recent writer, "it is essential to keep a firm hold on the end of the story, and relate events to the king's ultimate restoration."[10]

And yet, nagging questions occur as one traverses this usual explanation for a major change in English politics. It comes to mind that in 1658, although the protector was not universally popular, his death curtailed a trend toward accommodation. The poet Abraham Cowley had been devoted to Charles I, followed the émigrés to the Continent, and had been imprisoned upon his return; nonetheless, he so accommodated himself to the protectorate that after 1660 no royal preferment came his way. John Dryden walked in Cromwell's funeral procession and wrote a lavish eulogy for the protector, yet after the Restoration managed to develop a literary career. They were hardly alone. In England's provinces, one finds a similar ability to adjust to the regime. Warwickshire's historian has made the point that "in the light of the Restoration it is easy to overstate the provincial hostility to the political experiments of the 1650s," though some royalists remained "sullenly hostile or opposed to a non-monarchist England." Months after the protector's death, so this writer says of the regimes of the 1650s, "a fairly broad range of men were willing to accept and work for them in Warwickshire." Not until after a year did "unbridgeable differences amongst previously committed Parliamentarians" make restoration possible.[11] Hampshire's historian found little hatred directed at the protectorate. Objections to the major generals, whom Cromwell appointed to administer the localities, were "muted, if not negligible." Any abuses in that county, which traditionally had a military presence, were also practiced by the monarchy.[12] Kent was the county most alienated from any sort of government—whether of Charles I or Cromwell. Though near London, it was insular. But a study of the county's 179 dominant families revealed that "most of the Kentish gentry, in order to repair the ravages to their estates, acquiesced in an outward conformity to Cromwell's rule."[13] Had Cromwell lived, setting aside the nature of these supposed ravages, it is possible their acquiescence would have become acceptance, especially as nationwide the gentry consolidated its influence under the government of the commonwealth.

Accommodation by mid-1658 was in evidence. Prominent royalists had opposed the regime in 1655–56 less from sentiment for the late king, Charles I, than because of concern about taxes on their estates and loss of power to the major generals. After the Restoration, royalists repeated these fears, turning them into a litany against the fallen government. During the later protectorate their situations were not so dire as they would recount them. Royalists whom the government suspected as dangerous did face a "decimation" tax against their estates and the need to pay security for themselves and their servants. Most of them submitted to government inquiries before Parliament rejected the tax in January 1657. Although the government confiscated some estates, losses of royalist property were more often the result of mismanagement than of taxes and occurred in the middle and late 1650s at a rate consistent with property losses during the entire century. As for the major generals, most of them "never did rule," according to one historian, administering for only about six months and to greatest effect in such matters as regulating weights and measures, an efficiency from which royalists and nonroyalists alike benefited. Parliament also revoked their authority. The leading families tended to consolidate their power during this time of alleged troubles. Many royalists were increasingly able to support the protectorate, if not the protector, "as a bulwark against further social revolution and as a dispenser of firm government."[14] By mid-1658 they, like Cowley and Dryden, simply accepted the protectorate as the established government. One historian has concluded that during the 1650s "too many had made their peace with, and had even served under Cromwell" for the restored monarchy then to seek them out for punishment.[15] An early-eighteenth-century narrator meant as much when he wrote, "The Guilt of the Rebellion [was] so far spread thro' the Nation, that it would have cost too much Blood to make any indifferent Expiation."[16] In fact, restored government would have been impossible without the collaborators. Several members of the judicial bench who in 1660 condemned ten "regicides" fell within the judge's definition of treason because of their collaboration with the protectorate.[17]

With increasing accommodation it is possible that Cromwell could have done something about Commonwealth finances. The bedeviling problem of the protector was the arrears of pay due the army. A month after Charles II's return in 1660 the Restoration's Convention Parliament passed a poll tax and dedicated the proceeds to paying the army, agreeing to additional assessments during the session. By the fall of 1660, most of the army had been paid and was being disbanded. The Cavalier Parliament—which replaced the Convention and then sat for nineteen years, nearly as long as the Long Parliament—passed further grants to discharge Commonwealth debts.[18] But a Commonwealth Parliament led by the protector and supported by increasingly accommodationist sentiment could have developed a similar policy.

This brings us to the real need, the most basic concern, of the royalist émigrés, the one that persuaded them that no time could be lost in seeking the return of the man who would become Charles II. By 1658 royalists resident in England under the Commonwealth increasingly had shown their ability to accommodate to the circumstances of the protectorate. For those who had accompanied the Stuart heir to the throne to the Continent, time was running out, unless somehow they intervened with the protectorate. As G.E. Aylmer observed a generation ago, "the longer the émigrés remained abroad the less likely was their restoration."[19] In the dull summer of 1658, émigrés looked across the Channel and saw a stable government with a powerful leader who himself might soon assume the crown. Whether this possibility would have come to fruition is immaterial, of course, for it was the sensation on which they would have acted. One may well consider that certain émigrés conspired to prevent Parliament's placing the crown on Cromwell's head.

For the émigrés the prospect was not good—even if it might have been glorious for England into the long future. Had the protector lived a few years more, events would have moved differently and appeared just as inevitable as the Restoration. A house of Cromwell might have evolved with a choice of one of his sons, perhaps the capable Henry rather than the older Richard, as his successor. The heirs could have acted as veritable stadtholders on the Dutch model; republicanism might have become stronger, with religion diverse, politics broadly based. The Stuarts would have remained in exile—hunting, dining, plying the French and Spanish courts for money. William of Orange would have stayed in Holland. The Hanoverians would have slumbered in anonymity, sparing the nation a line of monarchs who gloried in the name Briton but by turns were silly, mad, incompetent, and eventually irrelevant.

It is necessary, therefore, to reexamine the manner in which Cromwell died. One might begin by recognizing, as Alison Weir recently wrote in *The Princes in the Tower* concerning the 1483 murder of Edward IV's sons, that it is "unlikely that the truth of the matter will ever be confirmed by better evidence than we already have."[20] There is considerable evidence in published writings of the period. There are the volumes of Thurloe's state papers published in 1742. The collection contains many letters to Henry Cromwell, the lord deputy in Ireland during his father's illness, and they have never been analyzed for medical information. Writers have cited them to support the notion that Cromwell suffered from malaria, and the letters support that he may have had malaria but not that he died of it. Based on this notable collection alone, and there are others, one may describe symptoms and developments in a way that differs from previous conclusions that the protector died of "bastard" tertian ague, intermittent fever, depression, malaria, pneumonia, kidney failure, low fever.

I also note contemporary suspicions about the nature of Cromwell's death. Two observers noted untoward circumstances. One of them was the keeper of the privy seal, Bulstrode Whitelock. Seven years after his death in 1675, Whitelock's diary and records, which according to the seventeenth-century editor were prepared for the author's "memory and private use" and therefore without "temptations to prevaricate,"[21] were published as *Memorials of the English Affairs.* In a record of general matters, he reported that many believed Cromwell had died of poison. Another observer was the Venetian resident, or ambassador, Francesco Giavarina, a man familiar with deception, shadow, and murder, a faithful recorder of events but personally unsympathetic to Cromwell. He had excellent sources at Whitehall Palace and kept apprised of the illness. When he reported the protector's death to the doge and the senate, he indicated a suspicion of foul play.

After setting out the history of Cromwell's illness from contemporary sources, I turn to a diagnosis of his symptoms. Although the evidence is necessarily circumstantial, it indicates the likelihood—I believe the near certainty—of poison.

The next step is to seek signs of skulduggery, to determine whether there was a person who, in the classic formula, possessed motive, method, and opportunity. Motive is not sufficient by itself, for one might see any number of persons with one motive or another; it is necessary for the person with motive to have a method consistent with the manner of death and the opportunity for access to the victim. In the chapters that follow, a culprit emerges, one so obvious as to be difficult to see. The evidence is disquieting. And curiously, the prime suspect confessed to the deed. This fact has been long available, published a century ago from papers that were deposited at the Bodleian Library in Oxford a century and a half before that. The confession, by a man whom the protector trusted, is consistent with the manner of Cromwell's death.

There are accomplices. The confession names Charles II as "privy" to the plot and implicates two unidentified bishops as intermediaries between exiles on the Continent and the poisoner in the protector's court. These men had known and trusted each other since the late 1630s, and thus to conspire they needed only to "breathe together."

Interesting circumstances also concern the exhumation, hanging, and burial of Cromwell's body in 1661, because these events, like his death, are surrounded by unresolved questions.

1

$\mathcal{O}$utward $\mathcal{S}$igns

Oliver Cromwell's death was unexpected. The lord protector had been ill for some weeks but rallied several times and appeared to recover, until 3 September 1658, his last day. There was no public announcement of the illness. There was no private concern for the regime's future until a few days before the end. Hearing of the protector's death, people were surprised, the court unprepared, royalist émigrés jubilant.

Events rapidly followed: Richard Cromwell became his father's successor, and within six months quarrelsome politics prompted him to resign, ending the protectorate. Parliament's attempt to govern a fledgling republic collapsed a year later when Gen. George Monck recalled the Long Parliament elected in 1640 and encouraged it to return Charles Stuart to the throne. The Restoration of the Stuart monarchy occurred in May 1660, when Charles II returned from his travels.

On the afternoon of the protector's death in September 1658, the privy council announced the fact. Issued with the doctors' assistance, the palace's statement was vague and allowed readers to infer malaria as the cause. There were no further statements, and most people accepted the one presented.

The ensuing public events were curious. While Cromwell's body lay in state at Somerset House, the privy council pointedly postponed the funeral by nearly two weeks, without disclosing reasons. They rearranged the display so that mourners saw the lord protector's standing effigy rather than a recumbent one, as previously. Contemporaries, including the Venetian ambassador, recorded knowing that in fact the body had been buried prior to the funeral. The records agree as to location, although confusion has developed that endures to the present. On 23 November a vast procession escorted the hearse carrying Cromwell's effigy through the crowds that lined the Strand and Whitehall. The procession arrived at Westminster Abbey after sunset, and beyond carrying the effigy to an ornate catafalque, there were no ceremonies because—it was said—the Abbey had no candles. No burial was recorded.

Further curious events followed the Restoration of the monarchy. Royal agents in 1661 opened the protector's vault and claimed that they exhumed his corpse, along with that of his son-in-law, Lieut. Gen. Henry Ireton, the protector's successor in subduing the rebellion in Ireland, where he had died. On the twelfth anniversary of Charles I's execution, 30 January, they hanged three bodies on the Tyburn gallows. The final resting places of Cromwell and Ireton and the third body were said to be beneath the gallows, where the executioner threw them into an open pit spread with lime. There were other stories that the protector's body had been buried in any of several locations.

One may ask why contemporaries were generally so complacent about such events. A partial answer is that neither the leaders of the Church of England nor their Puritan constituents had beliefs that gave them reason to question what they heard and saw. In those deeply religious times, popular attention was riveted on the true course to heaven, on the metaphysics of salvation rather than the physics of death. People described the heavenly course, and the world in general, with metaphors and emblems that gave outward form to the inward truths they knew but could not see. Metaphysical poetry described life, love, and death with crisp images and strong lines. Dutch and Flemish flower paintings, popular with English patrons, narrated the resurrection and warned of human frailty but never depicted mere blossoms.[1] Natural events were omens of human fate. Although the century revealed to a few inquirers "the origins of modern science," most Englishmen lived apart from such concerns, dwelling in superstition rather than light.

To understand the beliefs about life and death that flourished in seventeenth-century England, beliefs that made it possible for people to overlook the singularity of their ruler's passing, requires an excursion into the era's remarkable fascination with theology. The religious subtleties of the time now seem barely comprehensible. In the years around 1640 the Church of England and its Puritan members held different views of burial and salvation.[2] Church leaders assumed that the embalmed corpse of a person of rank would be ceremoniously interred, even though they resented Cromwell's royal lying-in-state and placement so near Queen Elizabeth's tomb. They anticipated that on the day of judgment all humanity—except executed and dismembered criminals and traitors—would arise from their graves and account for their faith. Puritans believed that at the body's demise the soul of persons having a covenant of grace, the saints, went directly to heaven, mourners gathering at a later time to hear a sermon to remind them of their mortality; ceremony over the ignoble body was irrelevant to salvation. Although such differences seem minor, they help explain some of the confusions in the death and burial of Cromwell, as well as confusions six years earlier surrounding the demise of Ireton.

In the seventeenth century, life's order and meaning came from what people believed would happen to their bodies and souls. Christianity taught that life was preparation for death and the soul's passage. Death pervaded the culture because life expectancy was short, death in childbirth common, illness routine, ordinary maladies without remedy. The churchman John Donne based his injunction "never send to know for whom the bell tolls" on sounds familiar in villages as well as the metropolis. The Puritan poet John Hall warned "that ere we're aught at all, we cease to be."[3] Contemporaries were in one way or another preoccupied with youthful fulfillment, gathering rosebuds, time's wingéd chariot.

These beliefs traced back, to be sure, to before the Reformation, to the medieval church, which had surrounded death with signs and rituals. Persons who died without mortal sin received purification for their venial sins by suffering in purgatory. Priests controlled a ritual that transferred the dead to this purgatorial afterlife. Without their authority absolution was impossible. The corpse was carried into the church, the earthly image of heaven; a priest offered prayers, administered the mass, and asked absolution. The corpse was interred with further ritual. After purgatory the soul entered heaven. The living could mitigate their ancestors' purgatorial suffering by prayers and deeds. Referring to such deeds, one historian has concluded, "A substantial proportion of the resources of medieval society was thus given over to ensuring the spiritual welfare of its dead members."[4]

As is well known, when in the early sixteenth century the church began aggressively selling indulgences, which granted the dead a release from purgatory, the Reformation ensued in northern Europe. Martin Luther's protest in 1517 included criticism of the church's profiting from these sales. Calvinists and reformers who followed in Luther's wake denied purgatory, the efficacy of individual deeds, and the priest's authority: souls, they said, simply went to heaven or hell by predestination; works availed naught. The result soon was evident, for without purgatory there was no further need for priestly authority.[5]

In England the Reformation did not center on a single scandalized reformer but on the personalities and vagaries of Henry VIII and his three children. The realm seemed securely orthodox in the early 1520s, despite a tradition of Lollard and humanist criticism of clerical corruption: such doctrinal issues as indulgences had not caused irreparable controversy. Henry had even earned the papacy's gratitude as "defender of the faith" for his stance against Luther. Nonetheless, when he could not obtain the annulment of his marriage to Catherine of Aragon, he separated the church in England from papal authority, with no intent to reform doctrine or alter priestly authority.

When Henry died in 1547, church doctrine was largely orthodox. During the reign of his young son Edward, Parliament began to attack priestly authority—much as had John Calvin and the Zurich reformer Ulrich Zwingli—by repudiating purgatory, prayers for the dead, and some ceremonies.[6] One change led to another. The first Edwardian Prayer Book (1549) moved away from the Catholic doctrine of "transubstantiation" and defined communion in Lutheran terms of the "real presence." The second (1552) denied Lutheran and Catholic doctrines concerning communion and accepted the Reformed doctrine of a commemorative service that dispensed with the priest's special authority, although Edward VI died before the book could be promulgated.[7] After Edward's death in 1553, Henry's daughter by Catherine, Mary, led a reversion to Catholic orthodoxy and priestly authority. The English Reformation then received a settlement after 1558 and the accession of Henry's Protestant daughter, the great Elizabeth. Parliament established the queen as the church's "supreme governor" and the second Prayer Book, slightly modified for use in the queen's chapel, as the church's uniform doctrine. The Prayer Book deftly combined Lutheran, Reformed, and even Catholic ideas for the communion service.[8] This compromise of three decades of religious turmoil was the origin of a national church that in one scholar's description was based on "tradition, reason and history—as well as Scripture."[9]

The Elizabethan settlement did not please those church members who came to be known as Puritans. The doctrinal settlement was never in question, although a series of religious problems punctuated Elizabeth's reign, involving Catholics and the appearance of the first Presbyterians. The differences that raged within the church by 1640 arose in the previous century as the faintest of clouds: in the 1560s bishops prescribed uniformity of vestments for priests, some of whom objected to white linen surplices as unbiblical. The dissenting priests and laymen described themselves as "godly people." Other churchmen derided them as "precisionists" and "puritans."[10] The scholar Patrick Collinson has warned that too much can be made of arriving at a "correct" definition of Puritan because "we are dealing with a term of art and stigmatization which became a weapon of verbal finesse but no philosophical precision."[11] The qualities of art and stigma referred to the beliefs of those who emphasized reform according to biblical warrant, sermons over rituals, and intensity of religious experience.[12]

And so change continued. The episcopacy and the priesthood gradually came to have a Puritan tone. It should be emphasized that the term *Puritan* did not include sectaries who at one time or another removed themselves from the church—the Separatists, the Anabaptists, the Brownists, for example—for Puritans remained in the church.[13] Only after the beginning of the civil wars did Puritans divide into groups and sects, of which Presbyterians and Independents were the most important. All of them continued to consider themselves as "the church," even the emigrants to Massachusetts Bay, and each group believed it would lead the English church to godly reform.

The religious settlement broke down after Charles I appointed William Laud in 1633 to succeed the tolerant George Abbot as archbishop of Canterbury, a breakdown that in part contributed to the civil wars. Laud sought to alter the settlement and end the church's Puritan tone. An Arminian, he believed in free will, uniformity, ritual, and vestments. Puritans were outraged by the court-sponsored innovations, the more because Charles I's queen, Henrietta Maria, was a French Catholic. Charles governed without Parliament and used new ways to raise revenue, and his "personal rule" created as much resentment as Laud's innovations. When Laud and the king imposed the Prayer Book in Scotland in 1637, they found little enthusiasm; the Scots resisted, and in 1639 they defeated the king's army. The war's expenses forced Charles to summon a Parliament, and the House of Commons demanded religious and constitutional reforms prior to voting money. The failure of this Short Parliament led to the Long Parliament, and further impasse led to the king's leaving London and raising his standard in 1642.

On the eve of the civil war, the leadership of the church and the Puritans disagreed over many issues of church practice, but not least was disagreement pertaining to the end of life. In church practice death, burial, and salvation were outward events governed by Arminian rites and symbols. The Book of Common Prayer bound ritual, priests, and monarchy—as James I allegedly remarked, "No bishop, no king." After Laud's Arminian innovations, ceremony and symbol carried the faith: "He that is hurt seeks help: sin is the wound; / The salve for this i'th Eucharist is found."[14] Church doctrine based man's spiritual justification upon faith and placed fewer demands on the worshiper than did Puritanism:

> Then, though in flesh my spirit prison'd be,
> She may by Faith ascend to Thee,
> And up be rais'd, till she shall mount to liberty.[15]

Good works were merely outward signs of inward faith, although

Henry Vaughan replied in 1652 to those who questioned "holy conversation and good works" that reward in afterlife "shall be given unto those that serve God in this life."[16] In practice, failure to serve placed faith in earthly doubt, and it was possible for the epitaph of Sir William Strode to assert, "Who dies with works about him, as did he, / Shall rise attended thus triumphantly."[17]

Defining the practical relation between justification and works was as troublesome for the church as for Puritans.[18] The cleric and cavalier poet Robert Herrick wrote that "God will have all, or none; serve Him or fall / Down before *Baal, Bel;* or *Belial.*"[19]

The church retained traditional funerary forms, though in decades prior to the civil wars there was a trend away from elaborate memorials. The antiquarian John Weever lamented that nobles and gentles were either "silently buried in the night time . . . or parsimoniously interred in the day-time." Churches contained "glorious rich Tombes, and goodly monuments to our most worthy Ancestors" from earlier times but far fewer from Weever's own.[20] Funeral services retained the traditional form, such as Anthony Wood described for the bishop of Sarum's funeral at Oxford: churchmen, nobility, and gentry met in convocation, heard an oration, bore the corpse to the church, heard a sermon; there were prayers, an anthem, another oration, and further singing as the bishop was laid in a grave inside the church.[21]

Until the day of judgment—that last of days when the just and unjust, "the quick and the dead," give an account of their faith—body and soul rested together: "What is my Father's House? And What am I? / My Father's House is Earth, where I must lye."[22] Judgment would subsequently be

> A day so fresh, so bright, so brave
> Twill shew us each forgotten grave,
> And make the dead, like flowers, arise
> Youthful and fair to see new skies.[23]

To prepare for heavenly assumption, the dead were sometimes embalmed because at judgment, in the catechism's phrase, the dead will be resurrected "in the fullness of our being." For this reason executioners of traitors and criminals purposely dismembered them and distributed the parts to preclude heavenly assumption. For everyone else, embalming attempted to preserve the fullness of being. Charles I's head was sewn onto the corpse that he might rise "youthful and fair" in the fullness of his being. The bodies of nobles and ranking church-men particularly were apt to be so treated: "Sleepe in thy peace, while we with spice perfume thee, / And *Cedar* wash thee, that no times consume thee."[24]

For the faithful, ritual defined inward beliefs that achieved their salvation. Anticipating the ritual correctness of his own death, the poet Herrick wrote that he would receive confession and the Eucharist,

> And so to travaile hence
> With feet of innocence:
> These done, I'le onely crie
> *God's mercy;* and so die.[25]

In church practice, ritual was a work signifying salvation of the dying and dead; the deceased rested in a grave until judgment of their faith; embalming kept the body unconsumed until heavenly assumption; and a memorial kept the grave from being truly forgotten: "So after death our Flesh, heere dead, and dry'd, / Shall rise immortall, new, and purifi'd."[26]

The church, one might conclude, imagined a world enlightened by divine order and hierarchy. It accepted ceremonial burial of em-balmed corpses and believed faith achieved bodily resurrection and judgment-day salvation. Between death and resurrection they waited in a grave:

> In this securer place we'l keep,
>   As lull'd asleep;
> Or for a little time we'l lye,
>   As Robes laid by;
> To be another day re-worne,
>   Turn'd, but not torn.[27]

For Puritans, however, death, burial, and salvation were far dif-ferent propositions: they were inward moments ungoverned by an-cient ritual. Deeds of confession and unction were unnecessary for saintly persons whose God had predestined their salvation. For a century Puritan theologians had rejected Catholic practices for which they found no spiritual justification. They did not merely simplify old forms; they expunged them: no purgatory, no priest. According to a present-day student, "Once the belief in Purgatory had gone, it no longer seemed necessary to take ritual precautions for the repose of the dead man's soul."[28] The minister did not affect the deceased's predestined salvation; thus, Puritan funeral sermons were exercises for the benefit of the living. Cromwell died believing in his irrevocable covenant with his God: "Yet I beleeve not, he abides faithful."[29] Death separated body and soul, the latter going to its reward. Preservation of the corpse was an irrelevant vanity. Elaborate monuments were idolatrous.

In Puritan belief the soul's preordained salvation and transition to heaven or hell occurred as soon as death separated it from the body.

> So frail a thing he is, so doth he pass,
> That nothing can remain but that he was.
> But thou, triumphant soul! Art elevate
> By thy vast merits 'bove the common fate.[30]

A commentator noted that the soul then departed the body at the moment of death. In his view "fiends" carried a reprobate's soul to the burning "bottomless Lake," where it was a tormented prisoner until judgment day. Meanwhile the "lothsome carkasse" was buried. Separation was eternal: "The Devil hath his soul, the grave hath his carkasse." At the death of a "regenerated man," angels immediately carried "his sacred Ghost" to heaven. At a convenient later time the body "as the sanctified *Temple* of the *Holie Ghost* . . . is by his fellow-brethren reverently laid to sleep." Separation was not eternal, for the body would awaken on the last of days to partake with the soul "of life and glory everlasting."[31] John Milton's vision was that

> When once our heav'nly-guided soul shall clime,
> Then all this Earthly grossness quit,
> Attir'd with Stars, we shall for ever sit,
> Triumphing over Death, and Chance, and thee O Time.[32]

Whether reprobates or saints, Puritans had no reason to embalm the body because they considered it merely "a most loathsome and abhorred spectacle" upon which those that loved it could not look.[33] Puritan sensibility held preservation of mortal remains unnecessary:

> since thy virtues are
> The spices that embalm thee, thou art far
> More richly laid, and shalt more long remain
> Still mummified within the hearts of men.[34]

The body's preservation in an inviolate grave was "unthinkable in a world of change and decay."[35] Pampering "a ruinous, and rotten carkasse" could bring "everlasting misery upon our immortall soules," warned a Puritan theologian.[36]

Puritans thus remembered the soul and did not memorialize the body. They believed that monuments and works resembled the idolatry against which they preached and that such forms were irrelevant to the soul's translation to heaven or hell. The grave was merely where, a poet wrote, "Sleep, sacred ashes that did once contain / This jewel," the soul.[37] In 1644 Parliament, under Presbyterian influence, replaced the Book of Common Prayer with *A Directory for the Publique Worship* and excluded Anglo-Catholic customs that were "no way beneficial to the dead, and . . . hurtful to the living." The *Directory* simply charged the deceased's "Christian friends" to accompany the body to burial and "apply themselves to meditations and conferences suitable to the occasion."[38]

Funeral sermons were ordinary sermons delivered sometime after burial rather than eulogies.[39] The funeral of Cromwell's son-in-law and lord deputy in Ireland, Henry Ireton, occurred at Westminster Abbey ten weeks after his 1651 death, and the Reverend John Owen said near the end of his lengthy sermon that he would not begin a funeral oration but simply list "those fruits of Spirit which we call *Christian Graces.*"[40] At the 1659 Abbey funeral for John Bradshaw, minister John Rowe "wa[i]ved (as his manner is) the vain pomp of Funeral Commedations, and it was the more fitly done, because an hour was too narrow a compass, to comprise the Memorials."[41] Sermons emphasized a suitable text and made only slight reference to the deceased. The 1644 *Directory* did allow for "Civil respects . . . suitable to the rank and condition of the deceased."[42]

The funeral for Cromwell's daughter, Elizabeth Claypole—who died 6 August 1658—was typical of Puritan burial practice. She had lain painfully ill at Hampton Court for several weeks, her father constantly at the bedside. Her body was not embalmed, implying that her father did not want his own so treated. On the evening of the fourth day her "Christian friends" accompanied the corpse on a barge that through the evening drifted down the Thames to Westminster. The protector was too ill at the time to accompany his beloved daughter, and he died three weeks later. After the funeral party landed at Westminster about eleven o'clock, its members carried the body in a torch-lit procession to the Abbey. Several persons spoke, making meditations suitable to the occasion, and interment was completed about midnight.[43]

Puritans persevered in a harsh world that was overwhelming and murky, a life relieved for a few by predestination to an assured salvation. They believed that death ended bodily form and released the soul directly to its reward. They accepted the *vanitas* and ambiguity of existence, seeing in all things their God's intimations of mortality:

> Poor man! What art? A tennis ball of error,
> A ship of glass toss'd in a sea of terror:
> Issuing in blood and sorrow from the womb,
> Crawling in tears and mourning to the tomb:
> How slippery are thy paths! How sure thy fall!
> How thou art nothing, when th' art most of all.[44]

And how did all this affect views of Cromwell's death? The point is that Puritans thought the world a transitory place from which the body's departure was less important than the soul's destination. They accepted what had happened as a divine manifestation from which they drew lessons about the vanity of existence. They did not question the death but evaluated a person's salvation by grace. The manner of Cromwell's passing was not a subject for thought, and in that strangely theological sense his death was the easier for someone to manage, should a person have wished to direct him along the most slippery of paths.

Cromwell's death was a political as well as a theological event, and here, too, the belief of his time readily accepted the public allegories and metaphors that regimes used to represent specific events. The Puritan state buried Cromwell in Westminster Abbey to represent honor and authority; the restored monarchy disinterred him to mark dishonor and illegitimacy. Symbolic staging was more important than material content.

Throughout Europe in the seventeenth century—an era of war and religious turmoil—governments represented authority with art, ritual, and architecture: images defined dominion, ritual controlled populations, architecture validated authority.[45] Medieval Christianity, of course, had asserted authority with art that depicted saints, ritual that regulated lives, cathedrals that overshadowed castles. So, too, seventeenth-century states staged their authority with allegorical paintings, state ceremonies, and royal palaces. Flemish art, French ceremony, and Italian architecture influenced English symbols.

Flemish baroque art gained influence in Caroline England because Anthony van Dyke was Charles I's court painter. The baroque portrait is primarily an assertion of social privilege and political dominion, an icon of power, an illusion rather than reality. It presents naturally rendered sitters theatrically surrounded with emblems of their authority and status. Individuals are portrayed full-length and look disdainfully from positions above eye level. Van Dyke's large-scale portraits of Caroline courtiers abound with a repertory of draperies, vistas, columns, batons, and elaborate dress that reveal their subjects in control of an orderly world. Paintings of Charles I depict regal authority as well as limn a likeness.[46]

Cromwell-period portraits by English artists follow baroque conventions. Robert Walker's portrait of Ireton shows the baton-wielding general slightly above eye level but standing comfortably in full armor before a drapery pulled slightly to reveal an army encampment. Other portraits follow cabinet-scale Dutch examples, which present to the viewer a generation of prosperous, Protestant, and powerful burgers in elegant attire, simple settings, and assured poses. Dress, decor, and demeanor represent power and status as effectively as van Dyke's theatrical devices. Walker's 1649 portrait of Cromwell combines baroque theater with Dutch directness: the baton-wielding general stands three-quarters against a background of clouds while a page ties a sash around his full suit of armor. The best-known Cromwell portrait is Sir Peter Lely's "warts and all" painting. The armor-clad protector is shown half-length against a neutral background, and though at eye level, he looks impatiently past the viewer; dress and demeanor designate his authority. Baroque paintings present an image of their subjects' status: van Dyke's Charles, Walker's Ireton, Lely's Cromwell are symbols of authority foremost, likenesses secondarily.

French ceremony influenced Caroline England because Queen Henrietta Maria was a sister to Louis XIII. Guided by the Italian-born queen regent Marie de Medici and then Cardinal Richelieu, the French court used ceremony to empower the youthful Louis. He was an unregal person whose father, Henry IV, was murdered in 1610 in a Paris street. Louis's prelate-adviser strengthened the monarchy by disguising his weakness and removing him from public view. People saw symbols of the monarch's power rather than the monarch's person. Louis stares down from Juste d'Egmont's state portrait, an aloof image of majesty and authority dressed in armor and posed before drapery and column-carved wainscotting. Henrietta Maria brought French style to England when she married the future Charles I. And Charles favored formality in reaction to his father's informal, bawdy, and weak court. Like Louis and Richelieu, he and his prelate-adviser, Archbishop William Laud, sought order, authority, and ceremony in church and state, contrary to recollections of the great Elizabeth's care "to defend her people from all oppressions."

Puritans included French-influenced ceremony in their criticism of Caroline "oppression," for example William Prynne's 1632–33 *Histriomastix,* a thousand-page jeremiad against the court's love of ceremonial and theater. Whereas Elizabethan drama in the 1590s moved easily between court and playhouse, Caroline masques in the 1630s, lavish entertainments designed for one performance, were performed only at court and flaunted the court's separation from the rest of society. Private palace spectacles replaced Elizabethan public festivals, access to court became limited, and divine right justified authority. Masques were in fact elaborate allegories of divine right and represented the king as a classical god or hero who brought order from chaos. Inigo Jones designed spectacular stage effects giving form to a judge's metaphor in John Hampden's 1637 ship-money case—that the king was "the first mover amongst these orbs of ours, and he is the circle of this circumference."[47] The court understood Prynne's attack as a cut at its ability to govern and charged Prynne with attempting "to withdraw the peoples affections from the King and Governments." Prynne's description of frivolous court masques threatened to reduce Charles's ability to collect the very treasury-filling exactions supporting personal rule.[48]

Prynne's book illustrated the importance of symbols in the rising debate; he attacked signs of power and authority with which Europe's monarchies routinely surrounded themselves. Its author described court theater, but the monarchy heard an attack on its image of divine-right authority. The court convicted Prynne, cropped his ears, and made his attenuated person a symbol of royal power.[49]

Fears about ceremonial were not confined to Prynne, for Catholics among Henrietta Maria's courtiers and the nobility credited suspicions of a "popish" correlation among such elements as divine-right masques, aloof monarchy, personal rule, and Arminianism. For nearly a century English nationalism had been sternly anti-Catholic, and many Englishmen equated Catholicism and Arminianism. A speaker in the 1629 Parliament declared that "an Arminian is the spawn of a papist," and a 1641 pamphlet stated that "*Arminianism* is a bridge to *Popery.*" Laud's Arminian rituals stirred national opposition to outwardly Catholic symbols. In the summer of 1640, there was violence. Parishioners in Essex resisted the introduction of "popish" altar railings, across which Eucharist-dispensing priests administered sacraments; they forcibly regained their "communion tables" and other symbols of Reformed religion. Symbolic "rayles" added to general fear of a court-inspired plot. Charles and Laud may not in fact have cared about doctrinal fine points, but they did seek uniformity based on the church's canons and articles after a latitudinarian period under Archbishop George Abbot.

When the Long Parliament assembled in November 1640, religion became the matter chiefly contended, but it represented many dissensions. Laud's emphasis on symbols over doctrine convinced such leaders as John Pym that there was a connection between Catholicism and royal oppression, whether one existed or not.[50]

Cromwell's protectoral court was smaller, less complex, less a center of culture than Charles I's, but magnificent residences at Whitehall and Hampton Court represented his authority. He received ambassadors in state, attended the 1654 Parliament in a state coach accompanied by the master of the horse leading a decorated horse of state, was twice invested as lord protector, in 1653 and 1657, the second time with ceremony approximating the fourteenth-century order of coronation. Two of his daughters received sumptuous marriage celebrations: Frances's Whitehall festivities included music and dancing and lasted until dawn, Mary's Hampton Court feast was in less state but still appropriate to a royal princess.[51]

In addition to art and ritual, Italian Palladian architecture was an influence on the seventeenth-century state's representation of power. With massive facades, ordered columns, and banks of stairs to overwhelm the viewer, buildings were stage sets wherein governments enacted pantomimes of power. The Banqueting House was a baroque beginning to the Stuart dynasty's rebuilding of Whitehall Palace, although the project did not carry any further. A masterpiece designed and decorated by Catholics Inigo Jones (1619) and Peter Paul Rubens (1635), the Banqueting House placed Counter-Reformation and divine-right symbols at the center of Protestant England, where they intruded upon English sensibility. The army purposely staged the king's execution before this building, the scene of the Caroline court's divine-right masques.

The army drew on symbolic traditions when it enacted the king's execution upon a Palladian stage. The site represented his treason, the method his social rank. All observers placed significance on the place. For the king's opponents the Banqueting House was near the scene of Charles's first alleged act of treachery. A contemporary report described how the platform was close to "the very place where the first blood in the beginning of the late troubles was shed when the Kings Cavaliers fell upon the Citizens."[52] During the evening of 29 December 1641, after three days of demonstrations around Parliament demanding "No Bishops," Charles's lieutenant of the Tower and his troopers drew swords against shouting apprentices and wounded several.[53] An observer in 1649 described Charles as walking from the Banqueting House to the scaffold "with the same unconcernedness and motion that he usually had when he entered into it on a masque night."[54]

Royalists also found the site symbolic, and one, using Arminian metaphor, afterward wrote: "And where's the Slaughter house? Whitehall must be, / Lately his Palace, now his Calvarie."[55] Some royalist engravings depicted the execution from a point opposite the Banqueting House, which became a vast Palladian background for the masque-like mise-en-scène. But the event was not a court masque in which Order rescued the Stuart world from Chaos; it was a grim Elizabethan drama of men and desperate kings.[56]

Manner and place of execution represented the accused's crime and social standing. Common traitors were hanged and drawn and quartered near the site of their treacheries. The 1352 Statute of Treason described the ritualized brutality inflicted upon ordinary persons who acted for the king's death. Henry VIII's 1534 statute broadened treason's definition to include mere speaking for the king's death. Prior to Elizabeth, the Tudor century saw Englishmen executed in the thousands—hundreds for treason, many more for related political crimes. Sir Thomas More described the politics of his day as a king's game "for the most part played upon the scaffold."[57] The game eased in the seventeenth century, but the rules did not. James continued Elizabeth's persecution of Catholics, and forty were executed during his reign.[58] From the death of Strafford to the "bloody assizes," political scores were settled with ritualized public death.

When Charles took the final steps to the scaffold on 30 January 1649, it is unlikely that either Commissary General Ireton or Lieutenant General Cromwell were among the witnesses, although their names were boldly inscribed among the death warrant's fifty-nine. They were nearby, however, when the great political fact and symbolic event of the civil war era occurred. Cromwell was at prayer in a Whitehall Palace chamber with army officers, some of whom at the last minute seemed reluctant to execute the warrant. "Let us seek God to know his mind in it," he proposed, but as he prayed a messenger "whom he had appointed for that purpose" arrived and announced that the king was dead. Some officers were astonished that the execution should have gone forward while they prayed for guidance. Cromwell allegedly said of the king that "it was not the pleasure of God he should live." Ireton may have been at prayer with Cromwell; but, having favored the king's trial and conviction, he was probably in his Whitehall chamber superintending the three commissioners responsible for the execution. After Ireton's personal negotiation with the king had failed, he became distrustful of Charles and would not now have sympathized with the reluctant officers with whom Cromwell prayed. At a gathering in Ireton's room an hour earlier, Cromwell had drafted the executioner's final order. While his father-in-law kept the doubters at bay, Ireton probably bolstered the commissioners' resolve.[59]

The crowd at the Banqueting House in Whitehall could not see the executioner fulfill the order. Black cloth draped the scaffold's railings, troopers kept viewers at a distance, and fifteen people on the platform further obscured the scene. Only persons in upper windows and on rooftops could see the king lie down at the low block. The crowd did see the executioner's ax rise but once and the executioner's assistant lift the king's head high.[60] The army staged the execution with dignity and ritual gravity. People gasped, and soldiers dispersed the crowd.[61] The body was embalmed by an army physician, perhaps the distinguished Thomas Trapham, whom royalists unfairly labeled "a rascally quack." The bishop of London, William Juxon, sought permission to bury the remains among the kings in Henry VII's Chapel, but was denied. Juxon instead arranged burial with few witnesses, in the chapel at Windsor Castle.

The army hoped Charles I would be forgotten, but a dozen years later the execution provided his son's restored government with justification to exhume from Westminster Abbey the bodies of three men important in the 1649 tribunal—Cromwell, Ireton, and presiding judge John Bradshaw—and degrade them in public.

The importance for government was that the monarchy could undo whatever symbols the Puritan state had created. The restored regime

proved extraordinarily effective in erasing Cromwell and his supporters. It virtually obliterated their memory for nearly two centuries.

These symbolic events were arranged for a national audience and
played before the background of London's western suburbs—
Westminster, the Strand, Holborn, Tyburn. London was altogether an
overwhelming and murky place, an appropriate scene for ambiguous
events. Wenceslas Hollar's bird's-eye view conveys the impression
the metropolis made. St. Paul's Gothic bulk dominates Ludgate Hill,
its tower rises unchallenged, church spires pick at the urban sky. On
the south bank stand Winchester Palace and the Clink, on the north
Baynard's Castle and the Steelyard. A jumble of peak-roofed, half-
timbered buildings stretches east to west and spills across the Bridge
into the Southwark foreground. Life here was often difficult. Live-
stock was sold and slaughtered in town, the River Fleet carried refuse
into the Thames, streets were thick with muck. Ordinary residents
swaddled themselves in wool, did not much bathe, and lived with resignation amid the clamor and pollution: "Such a noise, an air so smoky;
/ That to stun ye, this to choke ye."[62] They knew Hobbes's state of
nature because even in the great city their lives were nasty, existence
precarious, death at hand. The place was a medieval aggregation of
wood and compost, soon to endure a final plague and then vanish in
the great fire.

   Suburbs filled the area between the Thames and High Holborn as
far west as Westminster Abbey and St. Giles Church. Beyond lay open
country, except for St. James's Palace. Within the Bars, which marked
city jurisdiction, and clustered along the fetid Fleet's west bank, were
densely crowded houses. Southwest from Temple Bar, buildings had
long since spread down the Strand to Charing Cross and Westminster.
Along the Thames stood religious properties seized over a century
earlier in the Henrician dissolution, and at the river's great bend were
the remains of the old Savoy Palace and the first protector's Somerset
House. The crossroads at Charing, where the road turns to Westminster,
was enclosed with buildings. Houses filled Drury Lane and Long Acre,
where Cromwell once had lived. At Covent Garden, Inigo Jones had

designed a Palladian piazza where the wellborn and titled could dwell apart from the city's natural state.

From Holborn Bar buildings spread along Watling Street's ancient trace. The Holborn high street was a broad way built up as far as St. Giles. Lincoln's Inn Fields had become engorged, but not yet Grey's. One traveler's landmark was the Red Lion Inn, but today Staple Inn's facade survives by the Bar—beyond the fire's limit—to represent the metropolis's seventeenth-century scale. Above the high street, the open expanse of Red Lion Fields allowed wanderers to look north toward the hills of Highgate and Highbury. During the Restoration era the orderly squares of Bloomsbury and Red Lion developed in the area; later the terraces and squares of Georgian privilege spread to the west. Seven Dials was a rural crossroad and St. Giles at the urban edge. Tyburn execution ground was farther out in the country, where Watling Street turned to the northwest and with Roman precision pointed to Chester far away and to Ireland over the sea.

2

*I*reton
Death and Destiny

To prepare for often dismal and short chapters of life, seventeenth-century Englishmen discussed their mortality in sybolic terms, and no Puritan so accepted the *vanitas* implicit in his beliefs as did Cromwell's son-in-law, Henry Ireton. Such devout people as they knew their paths to be slippery, their deaths sure. Even so, Ireton's demise in 1651, when he was only forty, startled contemporaries, who were unprepared for destiny's sudden stroke. They could only understand it as a divine warning of their own mortality.

What is important to the present narrative, however, is that questions concerning Ireton's death and burial curiously rehearse those that seven years later surrounded Cromwell's own. The two men were associated through their adherence to Puritan Independency, their belief in a godly commonwealth, and Ireton's marriage to Cromwell's daughter; Ireton was Cromwell's confidant and adviser, then his successor as Parliament's general in Ireland. When Cromwell learned of his son-in-law's death, he planned the funeral as a vast state occasion to represent the new regime's authority. Arrangements referred to James I's funeral in 1625 and established precedent for Cromwell's own funeral in 1658.[1] Vast processions carried effigies of both Ireton and Cromwell from Somerset House, where they had lain in state, to Westminster Abbey. To all outward appearances their remains were interred in the same vault at Henry VII's Chapel, a presumption that enabled the restored monarchy to open the grave and claim that it removed their bodies for public disgrace at Tyburn. The monarchy sought not merely to expunge the vault of its contents but to stage a pageant "to brand with infamy the memory of rebellion, to give the people a terrible warning by a terrible example."[2]

Before turning to Cromwell's death, it is hence essential to examine Ireton's passing at Limerick in November 1651 and funeral at London in February 1652. As with Cromwell's demise, historians have given contradictory causes—fever of some sort, the plague.[3] Upon examination, it is possible to narrate Ireton's final illness and determine its cause. His burial is less certain, although tradition has assumed it occurred in Westminster Abbey. The lying-in-state and funeral procession were certainly conducted with a traditional funeral effigy, and some observers suspected that his body was not present. The curious anomalies surrounding Ireton's death and burial would be of slight interest had not the restored monarchy so publicly opened "the protector's vault" nearly a decade later and triumphantly displayed a corpse that it alleged to have been his.

Ireton had risen rapidly to prominence. Born in 1611 to a Nottinghamshire family of Puritan bent, he was described as "a Gentleman by birth, a Scholler by education, and afterwards of the Honourable Society of one of the Innes of Court."[4] An Oxford graduate, he studied at the Middle Temple, and after his father's early death he managed the family's property until the outbreak of the civil war. When the king in 1642 raised his standard at Nottingham, parliamentary sympathies led him into the earl of Essex's army. Following the battle of Edgehill, Cromwell appointed him deputy governor of Ely, where he met and wooed the general's daughter. They married in 1646 when he was thirty-five and Bridget twenty-two. Ireton meanwhile had risen through the New Model Army and had become a member of Parliament. In 1647 he was involved in the army's dispute with the Levellers, culminating in the debate at Putney.[5] As devout a Puritan Independent as his father-in-law, he was "a most exemplary Christian in duties of piety and Religion, always . . . seeking wisdom, advise and strength from God on all occasions."[6]

Trained in law, he easily advanced political ideas that were influential, especially with his father-in-law. It was said that "Cromwell only shot the bolts that were hammered in Ireton's forge."[7] He coauthored the Heads of the Proposals, containing generous terms for the army's general council to settle with Charles and contrasting with Parliament's harsh Propositions of Newcastle. Personal efforts by Ireton and Cromwell failed to persuade Charles to accept this constitutional settlement because the king hoped a counterrevolution in London would restore him unconditionally. It did not. Leveller agents confronted the general council at Putney in October and forced a debate over their Agreement of the People. Ireton—gentry lawyer that he was—rejected the document's suggestions that all male subjects should vote and that the king was a "man of blood." Ireton and Cromwell might have arranged Charles's constitutional restoration had not the king signed the Scottish Engagement in November. The Levellers' defeat left the army united to fight the Scots. Charles's dissembling finally prepared Ireton to abandon the monarchy.[8]

Ireton and Cromwell by early 1648 began to consider settling the nation's affairs without the king, whose intransigence led to the summer's fighting. Such army radicals as John Lilburne and John Wildman argued that the king should be brought to trial. In November Ireton presented the general council with the Remonstrance of the Army, which provided a Leveller-influenced rationale for trying the king as "the capital and grand author of our troubles." Parliament's delay led to Pride's Purge on 6 December, and that in turn cleared the way for a trial. Ireton favored trial and conviction but not execution. In debate during early December he argued that power "should not be in the hands of a King, or of the King's peers or commons but in the hands of such as are chosen by the people." Once the trial was under way, he was steadfast for conviction and finally for execution.[9]

Following the execution, Ireton's destiny lay in Ireland, where renewed resistance seemed likely. Ireland had been restless since violence had erupted against Protestants in 1641. Charles's Irish lieutenant, the earl of Ormond, formed a confederacy against Parliament; the king's nephew and the civil war general, Prince Rupert, was at Kinsale, possibly preparing an invasion across St. George's Channel. Parliament organized an expeditionary force in March, appointing Cromwell commander, and in June it named Cromwell's son-in-law second in command.

The army was ready in early August at Milford Haven and other Welsh ports close to Ireland, and Cromwell sailed with thirty-five ships on 13 August. Two days later Ireton boarded the *Charles* at the Haven and sailed with the tide. Indifferent winds left his sixty-ship fleet becalmed offshore overnight, but next morning fresh breezes billowed the sails and eased the little ships toward the Munster shore. Ireton could listen to unfamiliar sounds of the sea and watch St. David's Head become a wisp on the Welsh horizon. Cromwell arrived in the Liffey estuary two days after leaving the Haven, and Ireton soon joined him at Dublin.[10]

Cromwell's Ironsides broke organized resistance in less than a year. On Ireton's advice the general immediately decided to strike north from Dublin to Drogheda on the River Boyne. Ormond might have attacked the still-deploying English army but let his opportunity pass. Cromwell stormed Drogheda in early September, defeated Ormond, and gained the initiative. The well-organized and well-supplied Ironsides subdued the south, taking Wexford and laying siege to Waterford. Other units moved through Ulster, and after a short time in winter quarters, Cromwell resumed his campaign at the end of January 1650 and in May returned triumphantly to England. Ireton remained in command as lord deputy general and completed Cromwell's siege of Waterford, which surrendered in August.[11]

The task in 1650–51 was the taking of Limerick, which proved difficult. The town lay in two parts, the so-called Irish town occupying the south bank of the Shannon surrounded by a mile-long wall, poor and mean, described by an English visitor in 1618 as "but a street of decayed houses." The so-called English town occupied the end of a large island in the river. A drawbridge over a Shannon channel connected the parts. On the island were St. Mary's Cathedral and St. John's Castle, the commercial area along Nicholas Street, "lofty buildings," and open spaces. The Thurmond Bridge crossed the Shannon's broad main channel and connected the island to County Clare. Above the bridge a salmon weir crossed the main channel. Ireton used the weir as a bridgehead, and below the city he built a wooden floating bridge. In the fall of 1650 a siege failed against the "last refuge" of the Irish. This failure along the Shannon prompted the commander to "be earnest with the Lord, to know his minde what he would have his poore servants in the Army to doe." In the summer of 1651 he again invested the city. A careful planner, but an inexperienced tactician, Ireton "thought nothing done whilst any thing was undone."[12] A seasoned commander would have taken the city in less time. Attacks failed during that summer because the Irish, led by Hugh O'Neill, skillfully deterred Ireton's stronger force for four months. Ireton called for Limerick's surrender and offered O'Neill great preferment for yielding the city. According to an unknown Irish chronicler, the governor was "soe honorable, that for a world did not betraye the trust reposed in him." O'Neill answered that he had defended the city for a year and was pledged to do so for another. If Ireton "had the patience to waite upon it till then, as he did see reason, [O'Neill] was willinge to comply with his Lordships desire in any lawfull and honorable attonement." Ireton would not wait, of course. The Irish "dayly waste and burne our quarter," one of Parliament's three commissioners wrote privately, "while the maine of our forces are ingaged in the siege of Limerick." Needing troops elsewhere to fight marauding bands of Irish "Tories," Ireton in August tightened the siege, and the city finally surrendered on 27 October.[13]

The English claimed that a recently received and advantageously deployed battery of cannon prompted the city's surrender. Ireton reported to Parliament that he set the cannon "at a place we had little observed before, God having, as it were, till very lately hid the advantage of it from our eyes." The location was a hill south of the Irish town, which allowed a clear line of fire toward St. John's Gate, a weak place in the wall. Thus, "after the planting of the Battery and some hours short play," the Irish asked for surrender terms.[14]

In fact it was not so much the cannon as a peace faction within the city that opened Limerick to Ireton. Col. Edward Fennell "drew to his partie . . . such inhabitants of both clergie and laytie . . . to all which was Huigh Oneylle a stranger."[15] This faction seized St. John's Castle, and the English guns battered at a vulnerable place in the Irish town wall. After O'Neill saw Ireton's red-coated troopers within the gates, he surrendered himself and his soldiers to the deputy's "mercy and favor." When Parliament received Ireton's siege report and copies of

the surrender articles, it ordered a day of thanksgiving and congratu-
latory letters for the lord deputy.[16]

With the city's fall twelve hundred soldiers surrendered, and Ireton
thought perhaps a dozen persons should be tried for their part in the
siege, including Bishop of Emly Terence O'Brien. The principal charge
against them was that they helped disguise "those bloody Rogues, the
Friers, Priests, and Jesuits," who thereby escaped the city.[17] The court-
martial probably sat in St. Mary's Cathedral, near the house in which
the general had established his headquarters. He eventually exempted
O'Neill from death but hanged seven persons for their "obstinate holding out." O'Brien's real crimes were outrages committed during the
1641 uprising during which Protestants were massacred.[18] His head
was "fixed on a lofty stake, and placed at the top of the King's Fort."[19]
Although generous to O'Neill, Ireton claimed that by executing
O'Brien and six diehards "the terror and sad examples of it may work
upon other places remaining (through God's blessing) as to hasten or
facilitate the reducement of them."[20] Cromwell had followed a similar
tactic after capturing Drogheda.

When O'Brien was condemned, he turned to Ireton and allegedly
pronounced, his voice echoing through the cathedral's dark and stony
interior, "I appeal to the tribunal of God, and summon thee to meet me
at that bar!"[21] His words were a prophecy.

Following Limerick's surrender in 1651, Ireton sought to subdue
territory in County Clare and establish winter quarters. He planned to
move west of the Shannon the next year and establish control in
Connaught, the last region outside English domination. But the weather,
which had been favorable and dry during the siege, turned sharply
cold and wet, and in letters to Cromwell and Parliament a week later,
Ireton referred to winter weather "which had begun with such extremity of wet" at the time of Limerick's surrender. He reported that he
had selected Athloe, fifty miles above Limerick on the Shannon, as
"the most fit place for the head quarters this winter." He arranged to
meet there with Parliament's three commissioners for Ireland.[22]

The arrangement for Connaught's submission would not be
Ireton's to make. Before settling into the winter quarters, he sent Gen.
Edmund Ludlow and part of his now-exhausted army fifteen miles

from Limerick on 4 November to receive Clare Castle's capitulation. The next night Ludlow "took a very dangerous cold" while sleeping in his exposed tent, for the weather was "tempestuous and the [winter] season far advanced." In his memoirs Ludlow recorded the development of his illness, which began similarly to that which soon attacked Ireton. The two men doubtless suffered the same ailment—Ludlow recovered, Ireton did not. On the sixth Ludlow had to pause in his march because he "fell into so violent a sweat," and that evening he was "in a continual sweat." Two days later he accepted Carickgoholt Castle and turned back toward Limerick. On the road he received Ireton's order to return anyway due to "cruel and sharp weather."[23]

Near Inchiquin Castle he met Ireton, who was reconnoitering the area and planning his winter distribution of garrisons. For two days the generals rode the countryside looking for winter garrisons. Inchiquin Castle had no accommodations, so they slept in tents during "tempestuous" weather. On the eleventh Ireton and a party of troopers searched out more territory, but he refused to take along the ailing Ludlow. During that day "there fell abundance of rain and snow, which was accompanied with a very high wind, whereby the Deputy took a very great cold." On the twelfth he and Ludlow rode over difficult ground toward Clare Castle. Next day occurred the frequently told story of Ireton's exonerating the weeping Lady Honoria O'Brien of a charge of hiding goods and cattle. More importantly, he ordered Ludlow to rest and to meet him two days later at his Limerick headquarters. This rest may have saved Ludlow.[24]

Ireton continued reconnoitering, despite foul weather and signs of ill health, and "his last and tedious wet march . . . cost him deere . . . occasioning the fever."[25] When Ludlow returned to Limerick, he found Ireton to be extremely ill. In the version of his memoirs published posthumously in 1698, he referred to the lord deputy's condition: "grown worse, having been let blood, and sweating exceedingly, with a burning fever at the same time."[26] On that Monday, Ireton "took a Purge," and on Tuesday he was again bled.[27] He continued to attend "to the publick business, settling garisons and distributing winter-quarters." Ludlow believed that during the siege he had "totally neglected himself," not removing "his clothes all that time, except to change his linen, that the malignant humours which he had contracted, wanting room to perspire, became confined to his body, and rendered him more liable to be infected by the contagion." He alluded to "contagion" but did not equate it with plague, and there were no visible signs of plague: vomiting, blisters, carbuncles, pain. Ludlow did not remain in Limerick and was not present during Ireton's final crisis. His family was due to arrive from England, and Ireton insisted that he meet them at Dublin.[28] Once there, Ludlow heard of "the sudden Stroke of Death and destiny."

Ireton's headquarters in Limerick following the siege has usually been identified as one of "the tall stone houses . . . in Nicholas Street."[29] These substantial buildings dated from the time of Elizabeth; one was known as Galway's Castle and, later, Ireton's House. It stood in the English town near St. Mary's Cathedral churchyard, and in the late nineteenth century it was next to the early-eighteenth-century Old Exchange. It was a sturdy neighborhood unlike the Irish town across the channel. After the 1651 siege the building's owner, Sir Geoffrey Galway, was one of the seven whom Ireton court-martialed and condemned with Bishop O'Brien.[30]

Local tradition claimed that Galway's Castle in Nicholas Street, Limerick, was Ireton's headquarters, and the unfortunate seven, including Bishop O'Brien, were hanged from one of its gables. A nineteenth-century antiquarian, James G. Barry, wrote that he could not find "sufficient evidence . . . that Ireton ever resided in this house," although he did allow the possibility that it was the site of the executions. As an alternative headquarters he suggested Lord Thomond's townhouse near St. John's Castle. But Thomond's daughter, Lady Honoria O'Brien, had received sympathetic treatment from Ireton a few days earlier, and it is unlikely that the lord deputy would have confiscated her family's house. In 1893 the city corporation pulled down "Ireton's House" rather than leave in place an ancient building associated however briefly with the "scourge of Limerick."[31]

Only hours after the commissioners in Dublin had relayed information to London on 1 December that Ireton was ill, they received "the sad news" of his death from the Limerick headquarters. Next day they sent further letters to the speaker of the House of Commons, the council of state, and Cromwell. To the latter they wrote that Ireton "expired of a fever." Had they suspected plague, they would have said so to Ireton's father-in-law, lord general of Parliament's armies and the Commonwealth's most powerful person. They reported fever. The news did not reach London for nearly a week. Lord Broghil, who had assisted Ireton during the siege of Limerick, wrote to London from Blarney Castle that the news was "one of the worst that I am capable of telling." On Monday, 8 December, the intelligence arrived at Guildhall, London.[32]

Ireton's death in Sir Geoffrey Galway's townhouse was widely reported by seventeenth-century standards, but the cause remained uncertain. After the Restoration, royalists said he died of plague, an assertion that also appeared in two Irish chronicles. The "Hibernia Dominicana" is a Latin chronicle prepared by "the Rev. the Master General *de Marinis,* the other Fathers of eminent wisdom members of the general Roman Chapter of 1656." In a hagiographic section venerating Bishop O'Brien and describing his death at heretical hands, the Dominicans say, "The persecutor Ireton . . . being a short time after dreadfully tortured with plague and phrenzy, openly confessed . . . that the murder of the innocent bishop was now at last fatal to himself."[33] The anonymous "Aphorismical Discovery" claims plague but describes Ireton as "nobly minded" in his last moments and ordering Ludlow to treat O'Neill well.[34] Both scenes are vivid, contradictory, and improbable. A month elapsed between O'Brien's death and Ireton's, too long for plague. Ludlow was not in Limerick when Ireton died. And the writers would not have had access to information from Ireton's death chamber in English army headquarters.

Royalist writers assumed that Ireton died of plague. An early memoirist was Dr. George Bate, who in perilous times managed to be personal physician to Charles I, Cromwell, and Charles II. During the 1650s he attained influence and received outrageous fees for ineffective medical attendance. Of Ireton's death he wrote uncharitably that "this most cruel Pest of his Countrey, died of the contagious Plague." Bate was present at Cromwell's death in 1658, but he had no direct knowledge of Ireton's. His claim is an unreliable rhetorical flourish, but it traced into subsequent royalist narratives. James Heath's royalist 1663 *Brief Chronicle* claimed that Ireton fell ill while returning to Limerick and "died of the plague in that City." A Scottish Presbyterian, James Fraser, wrote that "Iretown . . . died of the plague under the walls of Limbrick." Fraser wrote as if Ireton had died during the siege rather than a month later in a stone townhouse. Sir Philip Warwick claimed ambiguously that Ireton "died at the siege of Limerick of a pestilential fever." Edward Hyde, earl of Clarendon, claimed outright that Ireton "died in Limerick of the plague; which was gotten into his army."[35]

After the Restoration, Puritans were not eager to write their recollections. John Rushworth and Bulstrode Whitelock prepared compilations of documents but not personal memoirs. Several leading Puritans were brought to trial, others fled into exile, and many sought quiet lives. Ludlow was an exile in Geneva for the rest of his life. Using a collection of notes and records and contacts with English nonconformists, he wrote a personal perspective on the era; his severely edited manuscript was sensationally published in 1698 and provided the first inside view of Puritan affairs.[36] After the Restoration, Henry Cromwell lived obscurely in Cambridgeshire until his death in 1674. He had gone to Ireland with his father, risen to the rank of colonel, and become attached to Ireton's headquarters. Present at Ireton's death and at the London funeral, the younger Cromwell possessed much information. He might have succeeded his father in 1658, had he and not his brother Richard been in London when the lord protector died. After the Restoration Henry pitifully and successfully petitioned Charles II to be able "to expiate what he has done amiss."[37] There is no memoir by Henry Cromwell, who was Ireton's close friend, brother-in-law, and later successor as lord deputy in Ireland.

Ireton's death was indeed a curiosity. An eighteenth-century Irish chronicle claimed that "Ireton died in *Limerick* of the Plague, on the 24th of February 1651–52," erroneously stating the 26 November 1651 date. The Reverend Mark Noble elaborated upon Ludlow's account and wrote that "this infamous murder[er] of his sovereign," fatigued from the siege of Limerick, died because "never changing his cloaths, made him so liable to be infected with the plague, that it co-operated to destroy him." David Masson in the next century claimed in his massive biography of John Milton that Ireton "died at Limerick, Nov. 27 [*sic*], of some violent illness, called plague, caught by exposure and fatigue during the siege of that town." The Reverend Denis Murphy, S.J., implied plague by claiming that after Limerick's surrender "Ireton was infected and died." And writing at the time of Irish home-rule agitation in the early 1870s, M.F. Cusack elaborated upon the Dominican chronicle: Ireton "caught plague eight days after he had been summoned to the tribunal of eternal justice [by Bishop O'Brien]; and he died raving wildly of the men whom he had murdered, and accusing everyone but himself of the crime he had committed." The possibility of fever was removed from memory, except that Esmond S. de Beer, noted for his definitive edition of John Evelyn's diary, concluded succinctly in the late 1930s that the plague-death idea is "not supported by the best authorities."[38]

Could Ireton have died of the plague? Fleas carry the toxic bubonic plague bacillus—not identified until 1894—from diseased rats to humans. After a flea bite, incubation in humans is six days; then, the disease runs its agonizing course within another week. Fleas are the disease's agent, and their life cycle is dependent on a warm and moist climate; thus, plague is persistent in summer and abates in the fall. Plague may be transmitted by infected human fleas, which jump from person to person or infest clothing, bedding, or similar freighted goods. According to a modern historian of plague, the victim's symptoms are temperature, headaches, vomiting, pain, and "delirium before sinking into a final coma," a blister at the flea bite that becomes a blackish carbuncle, swollen lymph nodes, and fresh carbuncles on the body called "God's tokens." Plague was a curse that struck the poor primarily because it was the product of squalid wooden and straw neighborhoods where rats bred and fleas thrived.[39]

In 1651 there may have been plague in Ireland.[40] In the summer there were alleged instances of plague in Connaught, and the commissioners in Dublin appointed a day for "a solemn humiliation . . . for the removal of [God's] heavy judgements."[41] During July and August the commissioners reported, "Fifty and sixty died weekly for many weeks past: it now begins to abate." There was disease of some sort in the besieged city of Limerick, at least in the Irish town, and a week before the surrender the commissioners thought the city was "being much visited by the plague."[42] On the same day the council of state in London received Ireton's news of Clare Castle's surrender, they were told that "four or five hundred of Limerick were dead of the plague." Days later Ireton reported to the council that he was settling into winter quarters and "in Limerick there died forty and fifty a day of the plague."[43]

Contrary to these reports, the army's chief physician in Ireland, Dr. Gerard Boate, claimed that "the Plague . . . is wonderfull rare in Ireland, and hardly seen once in an age," whereas malaria and typhus did occur. There were undocumented diseases in the army, and reports indicate that troops had been visited "with the Pestilence, and many afflictions this Summer, in several places." But losses of ill-nourished infantry and cavalry recruits depleted the ranks far more than did disease. It is of interest that shortly before his death Ireton asked Parliament for more supplies of rice as "a great Preservative of the Lives of the Sick." Malnourishment caused many, if not most, of the army's ailments. When on 28 November Parliament ordered two physicians to Ireland, it reacted to accumulating news of illnesses among the army.[44]

If indeed there was plague in Ireland, one must conclude it was not in the army, nor had Ireton's itinerary exposed him. Immediately after the fall of Limerick, Ireton claimed that victory was partly due to "famine and plague" in the squalid Irish town. Indicating that illness was confined there and that it had not spread among his army, he warned Parliament that plague was "still violent among them, the greater indangering your Souldiery here, if God by distinguishing mercy prevent not."[45] The army's encampment was free of plague, which was not as likely in the sturdy English town on its island in the Shannon.

There were of course illnesses in the army. Dr. Boate believed they were being incorrectly reported as plague. He referred to "the Looseness and the Malignant Fever . . . violent Coughs and . . . Stopping of the Breath . . . Lameness of the thighs or *Sciatica*, painful Stanguries, all which . . . might well have been taken for sickness [i.e., plague] reigning in that land."[46] It is also said that an epidemic of plague in 1649–50 had quieted, and by the fall of 1651 plague was not a general problem in Ireland. The army's "afflictions" were most likely illnesses other than plague.[47]

Interestingly, Ireton died at least a month after the weather had turned wet and cold, not during the plague-conducive summer. Though his coming in contact with the requisite bacillus-bearing flea from a diseased rat is possible, it would not have been likely given the weather. More important, perhaps, is that once symptoms appeared, as reported in Ludlow's account, Ireton's illness lasted two weeks, twice plague's characteristic week or less. Furthermore, classic plague symptoms are not mentioned in available references to his "last trial."

Another cause to consider for Ireton's death is influenza. Descriptions of probable influenza epidemics occur as early as Hippocrates in the fifth century B.C. The Italians gave it the present name in 1504, but the English adopted the name only in the mid–eighteenth century. Incubation averages two days, onset is sudden and with general malaise and fever, its effects are usually respiratory, and the course lasts three or so days. In a few cases, usually involving persons over fifty years of age (Ireton was forty), pneumonia can develop and lead to death. According to one authority, "Influenza epidemics have distinctive characteristics that enable us to make retrospective diagnoses with reasonable assurance from historical accounts."[48]

Nevertheless, in Ireland's medical history there is no indication of an influenza epidemic during 1651. The weather in early November was perhaps conducive to influenza, but Ireton's illness developed at a much slower rate than does classic influenza. For the three days after the deputy became visibly ill, Ludlow's account offers no indication that his symptoms were appropriate. From the time of the illness's clear onset (not counting incubation), Ireton lived more than two weeks. Fatal influenza and pneumonia would have attacked more quickly.

The most likely cause for Ireton's well-reported "fever" was typhus fever. Contemporary reports stated that Ireton died of some sort of fever. The council of state received information that he took cold and fell ill.[49] Ludlow's memoirs are consistent with newssheet accounts that he took cold while reconnoitering in County Clare in early November, returned to Limerick, and "fell sick on the 16th of November."[50] A source from Dublin reported death by "a Feavor."[51] An independent report "from Wexford" also said that he "fell sick at Limerick . . . and that he is since dead of a Fever."[52] Days later the news reached an Essex parson who noted in his diary that "this day wee heard that Ireton Deputy generall of Ireland dyed at Limbricke in Ireland No[vember]: 26." Were the news more sensational than death by fever, the gossipy clergyman would have noted the point.[53]

Royalist reports in 1651 were consistent with a death of fever. A week after news reached London, the Venetian ambassador wrote that the Irish commissioners had reported Ireton's death "from a contagious fever." The ambassador added the adjective. The commissioners' words to Cromwell were that Ireton "expired of a fever." Had the commissioners meant plague, they would have said so. Other contemporary royalist sources are equally mute about plague. The royalist agent John King was in Ireland at the time, but his report mentioned "Ireton's death" without citing cause. If King had heard so much as a rumor that Ireton died of the plague, he would have included the information in his report for "his Majesty [Charles Stuart] . . . at Paris." John Evelyn, in Paris, heard the news a month after Ireton's death and noted in his diary that "news came of the Death of that Rebell *Ireton*." His account included no cause for the death. He, too, would eagerly have noted plague had there been mention of it. Yet a few years later he claimed that Ireton "perished of the plage." English exiles in Italy heard "that Ireton is dead" and that Parliament had voted an annual two thousand pounds to his family.[54]

Royalist writers introduced the idea of plague only after 1659, and their reason was political. Plague had symbolic meaning to the well-born, for they did not typically die of its horrors. Like Boccaccio's fourteenth-century Florentine storytellers, they retreated from town to countryside and waited for epidemics to abate. They tended to die of such diseases as malaria and gout, more appropriate to their social standing.[55] Plague killed the urban poor and others unable to retreat from the rat-infested warrens. Royalists alleged Ireton's death of plague so as to disparage a Puritan saint's origins, deeds, and beliefs.

And what does all this say? At this distance, evidence for any diagnosis can never be absolute, but what we know recommends typhus fever. The body louse *Pediculus corporis* carries infection from person to person, especially in overcrowded and unsanitary conditions that armies and prisons provide, conditions different from squalid wooden neighborhoods where rats thrive. Typhus fever was common in colder weather when infrequently changed heavy clothing harbored body lice. Incubation is about twelve days. Patients develop chills and high fever, and the crisis occurs after two weeks. Eruptions may appear on the body but not the face; prostration, coma, and bronchial pneumonia are possible.[56]

Ireton became ill during early November's cold and damp weather, which would have interrupted the life cycle of fleas but not body lice. The deputy had not had a full change of clothes for weeks. The probable incubation and duration of his disease corresponded to that for typhus fever. Both Ludlow and Ireton appear to have suffered similar symptoms: had they been for plague, both would have perished; had symptoms been influenza, Ludlow would have reported the classic symptoms for himself in his detailed account. Reports for both correspond to the symptoms of typhus fever.

While firsthand information for Ireton's final crisis is unavailable, there are passing references. A London newssheet on 16 December described a tender scene: "On his Death-bed he had very heavenly expressions and desired *that the interest of the precious sons of Zion might be preserved.*"[57] The writer seems to have adapted this account from a letter to Parliament by the governor of Dublin, John Hewson, published a week earlier. Hewson's eulogy did not report the death scene; it concluded, "Wee that knew him . . . know no man like minded; most seeking their own things, few so singly minde the things of Jesus Christ, of publique concernment, of the interest of the precious sons of Zion."[58] Henry Cromwell, twenty-three years old, was at the army headquarters. He must have described to the Reverend John Owen what happened; Owen later referred without elaboration to Ireton's "last triall and conflict."[59] Another reference was in the commissioners' letter to Speaker William Lenthall, that by Ireton's death "his gain (we are assured) is very great."[60] These comments derive from sources close to the event and imply an uncomfortable death from some sort of fever rather than a comatose one from plague. Sir Philip Warwick's later royalist memoir described a dramatic but unsubstantiated scene.

Warwick referred to Ireton as a man of blood who "expired with that word in his mouth (for in his raving, as I was told by one that was then there, he cryed out), 'I will have more blood, blood, blood.'" The Irish "Hibernia Dominicana" and "Aphorismical Discovery" contain still different versions of Ireton's final moments. The Dominican writers claim Ireton turned his face to the wall and "kept privately muttering to himself, saying 'I never gave the aid of my counsel towards the murder of that bishop; never; never; it was the council of war did it. . . . I wish I had never seen this popish bishop.'" He died, they say, "Admidst such words, and scourages of conscience, with deep groans, he delivered up his soul to the lower regions." The "Aphorismical Discovery" claims, however, that Ireton "became infected and died . . . and at the pointe of death was so nobly minded that he commanded . . . Ludloe, and the rest of his officers . . . to use all good behavior towards . . . [O'Neill] to send him with his owne corpse into England."[61]

The reports from the newssheet, Sir Philip Warwick, and the two Irish chronicles are certainly unreliable and contradictory. Interestingly, all imply (whatever else they say) that Ireton was feverish in his final crisis, not comatose.

At least three persons other than Ludlow were present during part of the general's illness. Henry Cromwell may not have made a record of the last hours.[62] The important point is that he kept a bedside vigil, something he would never have done if Ireton had been dying of the plague, his body and face marked by plague's "tokens." No account implies the presence of such tokens. Warwick would certainly have mentioned it in his alleged account, had he evidence from a source "that was then there." Known to have been present was Col. Daniel Abbott. But he left Limerick for Dublin on 22 November, four days before the general's death. He reported to the commissioners that Ireton "grew wors and wors every day . . . and was so ill . . . that he could not be admitted to see him" the day he left Limerick. Abbott reported to the commissioners that the deputy "was then very ill of a feavor and that the disease was not then come to the height." This refers to a feverish final condition.[63] Another presence may be inferred, that of Dr. Philip Carteret, advocate general to the army in Ireland and a central if shadowy person to events in Limerick and London, but nothing is known of his testimony. Dr. Carteret was a functionary who possessed Cromwell's confidence, having served as a courier between Parliament and the lord general while the latter was in Ireland.[64] Carteret was one of the Baptists whom Cromwell and Ireton had placed in positions of trust in the Irish administration. Henry Cromwell knew Carteret, if only by virtue of his position at army headquarters. Carteret agreed with Ireton's republican principles and in later years objected to Cromwell's assumption of the title "highness."[65] Most important, Dr. Carteret managed Cromwell's arrangements for Ireton's London funeral. The council of state issued warrants "on his account of the whole charge of the funeral."[66] Carteret was likely to have been at Ireton's headquarters, perhaps as an attending physician. Henry Cromwell made decisions regarding disposition of Ireton's body; Carteret had charge of arrangements. Both men must have traveled with the coffin the army shipped to London and were present in London during the period prior to the state funeral.

What then happened to Ireton's remains? Historians have always assumed that the army carried them from Limerick to London for burial, but as indicated at the outset, evidence is lacking. Nonetheless, in 1652 the Commonwealth staged elaborate ceremonies that presumably culminated with the body's interment in "the protector's vault" at Westminster Abbey. And in 1661 the restored monarchy claimed that it removed bodies from the vault and disgraced them on the Tyburn gallows. With these tableaus of burial and exhumation, puritan and royal governments made symbolic assertions of their respective authority. It is important, therefore, to determine the likely course of events in 1651 immediately following Ireton's death in Ireland.

The idea that the army transported Ireton's remains from Limerick was not supported by contemporary practice.[67] Transporting plague-ridden remains was impossible, and the same was true of those with a contagion. Rules familiar to army leaders advised the importance of immediate burial of a plague body. Regulations dating from Elizabeth's reign and reissued as required afterward stated that each parish should provide a separate burial place. City of London regulations required nighttime burial in the presence of only churchwardens or constables to prevent attendance of mourners so that "no neighbours nor friends be suffered to accompany the Coarpse to Church." Even if royalist allegations of plague were true, fear of spreading illness made it unlikely that in 1651 the army transported the body any farther than the nearest burial ground. It is just as unlikely that the army would have transported the body of a victim of typhus fever. Obviously during the seventeenth century bodies of persons dying of any infectious disease were buried immediately and funerals read at a later time. The Oxford diarist Anthony Wood mentions examples, including an instance of smallpox. The victim was "buried . . . the same day, funerall solemnised the next."[68] Thus, the logic of the time was to bury Ireton's remains at Limerick.

The army could only have carried embalmed remains to London if the leaders had considered transporting Ireton's corpse to the capital, but here again there was a problem: to embalm and transport the body of any victim of infectious disease was unthinkable. So fearful were such diseases that there is but one recorded dissection of a plague-ridden corpse.[69] An unknown Irish writer did refer to "Earthons embalshomed corps [Ireton's embalmed corpse]," but he could not have known what occurred within the English army circle surrounding Ireton's death. Among Puritans who had control of Ireton's body, embalming was also theologically unacceptable, for they held that "thy virtues are the spices that embalm thee."[70] The Anglo-Catholic practice of embalming was irrelevant to both Puritan belief and practical necessity.

If attempted, embalming a body was difficult. It required materials unlikely to have been available in Limerick after the siege. It was also cumbersome. According to one seventeenth-century medical manual's directions, a surgeon opened the body, removed all organs and viscera, and dried the cavity, a difficult and time-consuming process. The manual recommended placing the viscera, brains, and all fluids "into a barrell, and hoope it round, to be buried." The surgeon squeezed blood and fluids from the effluvia, washed and powdered them, and had to place the material "into a barrell pitcht within and without and hoope the barrell well, and then wrap it round with Ceare-cloth and cord it fast, then put it into a bigger barrell also pitcht and hoopt, and send it whither you please." And had all this been possible, there was no assurance it would have succeeded. Were the mass of bodily material not dry, it would putrefy and rupture the hooped and pitched barrel. Embalming really meant the surgeon only attempted to drain the body's fluids through dozens of incisions in the skin and placed cotton soaked with vinegar and "Balme" inside the abdominal cavity before sewing up the unsightly incisions. And all this effort might not work. Embalming the head was especially difficult, for it had to be sawed in half, not merely trepanned. The corpse was anointed with "Venice terpentine," wrapped in waxy cerecloth, and placed in a soldered lead sheet.[71] Unless the body were unburied for a considerable time, the procedure's success was not really known. The embalming of Oliver Cromwell's body in 1658 failed; prior to the state funeral the lead-sheet casing ruptured and produced a ghastly stench. In 1663 the body of Archbishop of Canterbury William Juxon was buried in Oxford four weeks after his death at Canterbury; following the service the corpse was taken from the trestle on which it had been displayed and "because not well imbalmed was put in three coffins."[72]

Ireton's body was allegedly not buried for ten weeks. Embalming was unlikely to have stopped decay and stench, even if proper embalming tools, a lead sheet, adequate soldering, tightly hooped double barrels, and a variety of spices and ointments had been available at Limerick. The soldered lead casing would have borne much stress in its long and tedious journey by a variety of wagons and boats—lifted, handled, carried, hauled. Nothing in the record indicates that a lead-wrapped body within a heavy wooden coffin was transported to London with large hooped and pitched barrels of dried viscera, only that the army carried a ceremonial box from Ireland to London.

It is reasonable to assume, therefore, that of necessity the army buried Ireton's remains near the scene of death. St. Mary's churchyard was only a few paces from the townhouse in which he died, and alternatively it was but a short distance to open countryside. Even if burial had been recorded in some manner, an unlikely occurrence, relevant Limerick parish registers prior to the devastating siege in 1693 do not survive. In any event, given the army's intention to stage a symbolic burial in London, there was no theological reason to mark an Irish grave.

In conclusion, thus far the following is possible. Ireton died from typhus fever and his body was buried in Ireland.[73] During the siege he had not changed his heavy apparel, which protected body lice as cold weather set in. He was probably infected in late October's "extremity of Winter." The disease incubated for two weeks before he "took a very great cold" on 11 November while riding in County Clare during tempestuous weather. Typhus fever symptoms appear suddenly, beginning with such chills as Ludlow described, and the foul weather must have made his "cold" worse. Treatment included purging and bleeding, which he received on two occasions. By the twenty-second he was too feverish to conduct business, but not comatose. He may have had typhus's characteristic body eruptions, but these do not ordinarily appear on the face. Contemporary reports that he died of "a Feavor" are credible. He died on 26 November, fifteen days after the onset of his "great cold," typical of typhus fever and more than twice the time for plague's visible course.

Ireton's death took place during the nasty weather of November 1651, and the cause was the equally nasty typhus fever. Puritans were not so much interested in cause as in the *vanitas* warning implicit in the death of so illustrious a man. In their belief, humanity was simultaneously nothing and most of all, and even the highest personages lived fragile lives at their God's dispensation. They understood a world wherein "slippery are thy paths . . . sure thy fall." When informed of Ireton's death, a Puritan asked, "What will the Lord teach us?"[74] The answer was clear, for the young saint's death demonstrated that "neither Piety, Wisdom, Valor nor Worldly greatness are able to protect a man from the sudden Stroke of Death and destiny."[75] One saint remarked that by Ireton's death "you see the malice and danger of hidden foes we bear about us."[76] The Dublin governor, Hewson, wrote that divine mercies had been many, such as the capture of Limerick, but still "the good Lord teach us to lye low before him, and learn us his minde by all his gracious manifestations."[77]

Puritans were disturbed about the meaning of Ireton's death but consistent in reporting fever as its cause. A Puritan in Ireland wrote to the point: Ireton's "heavenly Father would not suffer him to dye by the hand of the enemy, nor of the Pestilence, whereby many of his deere servants have been called home."[78]

Word reached London six days after dispatch from Dublin, twelve after Ireton's death. On Monday, 8 December, "the intelligence . . . [was] brought to Guild-Hall," indicating that the news had spread across the metropolis. The printer of a newssheet broke open his set form and at the bottom inserted small type, before going to press: "It is certified this day by an approved Letter from *Ireland,* that my Lord Deputy is dead at Limerick."[79]

Parliament did not sit on Mondays, but the council of state did. Cromwell had a full day in which to consider plans with the council before discussion in the House of Commons. Arrangements would reflect the lord general's absolute direction, for Lucy Hutchinson was emphatic in her husband's biography that "Cromwell . . . order'd all things" concerning Ireton's funeral. That Monday, Secretary Bulstrode Whitelock read to the council letters from Ireland concerning the army's condition, Ireton's being at Inchiquin Castle, his taking cold, his death. The final letter stated that a decision had been made in Ireland that "his body was to be carried over into England."[80] The record does not indicate who wrote the letter, but the decision to stage a burial in London was made on the initiative of someone in Limerick. The letter contained information not then reported regarding shipment of a coffin to the west of England for cartage to London. The council appointed the Irish and Scottish committee "to consider what is fit to be done in receiving the corpse of the Lord Deputy of Ireland, which is to come to Bristol, and also for its interment."[81]

As mentioned, the person in Limerick able to make decisions concerning burial of the body was Col. Henry Cromwell. His letter to his father was read in the Commons during the Tuesday session, but apparently no copy was retained. The memoirs of Ludlow, who temporarily succeeded Ireton in Ireland, state that "some of General Cromwell's relations, who were not ignorant of his vast designs now on foot, caused the body . . . to be transported into England."[82] Ireton and Colonel Cromwell were the general's only "relations" in Ireland, thus Ludlow can have only meant the colonel. And Colonel Cromwell played an important part in the army's Irish affairs all through the

1650s, later becoming lord deputy.[83] He was the one individual in Limerick able to make decisions, give orders, and announce to the council of state what would be done without prior authority. He would have known his father's "vast designs" to settle the nation by vesting authority in a single person, designs benefiting from a state burial for a member of the Cromwell family.

The first announcement in London regarding Ireton's interment stated, "His body is appointed to be sent into *England*." An official source claimed that "his Corps is to be brought to *Lindon* [*sic*], to be interred, his lady is there, and as we hear is big with child."[84] When Parliament met on Tuesday, it "received advertisements from their Commissioners in *Ireland* of the death of the late Lord Deputy."[85] Letters were read from the commissioners and young Cromwell. Although many of them were published in the weekly newssheets, the colonel's was not. Parliament made two resolutions approving the council of state's actions the day before, implied in Cromwell's letter. They referred to the council's consideration of "how the Corps of the late Lord Deputy General of *Ireland* may be brought up to *London,* in a fitting Manner." They directed the council to arrange Ireton's interment at state expense, making the funeral public business. Within a day of hearing his son-in-law had died, Cromwell thus set in motion a state funeral for a Puritan saint. These preparations would be appropriate to the question offered by one of Ireton's elegists, "Can such a *Patron* of our *Liberty* / Without a grand *Eclipse,* or Comet dye?"[86]

Later in the day, the Commons received and discussed a bill to settle "certain Manors, Lands, and Tenements" in trust for Ireton's family, similar to one Ireton had disapproved prior to his death. Several days later the house favorably read the amended bill a third time. One of the three trustees named in the act was John Thurloe. It is not clear whether Bridget Ireton ever received the estimated £2,000 pound annual income from these estates.[87]

Cromwell was afflicted by his son-in-law's death. Whitelock described his "great sadness" at the loss of "so able and active, so faithful and so near a relation and officer under him."[88] In a letter the week following, the general wrote, "What is of this world will be found transitory; a clear evidence whereof is my son Ireton's death."[89] There was even a rumor that he had offered Parliament his resignation from his general's commission "now Ireton is dead."[90]

He nonetheless had determined to settle the nation. He had to move ahead with this work. He held an oft-cited conference with parliamentarians and army officers at Speaker William Lenthall's house, and Whitelock described the event under date of 10 December, two days after arrival of news of Ireton's death, but the date is uncertain. Cromwell thought it was time to stabilize the Commonwealth. He told the meeting, "I think it may be done with safety and preservation of our rights . . . that a settlement of somewhat with monarchical power in it would be very effectual." Mrs. Hutchinson believed, as did Ludlow, that Cromwell was ambitious to have government vested in his person; but she believed the republican-leaning Ireton had restrained him.[91] Republican ideas for settling the nation had not developed by late 1651, but before the king's execution Ireton had begun expressing ideas that republican writers would discuss by the mid-1650s. Some theories opposed monarchy as inferior government and single-person rule as fatal to liberty, but the impetus to republicanism came after Ireton's death, from Cromwell's protectorate and the rule of the major generals.[92] Had Ireton lived, he likely would have recommended republican principles to his father-in-law. It is said that his wife "had imbibed from Ireton, so strong an antipathy against the government of a single person, that she could not even bear to hear the title of protector, although it was held by an indulgent father, and a beloved brother."[93] Death hence removed a signal influence from the decade's affairs.

During the winter of Ireton's death and funeral in 1651–52, newssheet essays may have reflected his republican views. In December, as Cromwell discussed a settlement "of somewhat with monarchical power," such republicans as Marchamont Nedham argued against single-person rule. Nedham stated in one essay, "Now . . . it appears, that the Right, Liberty, Welfare, and Safety of People consists in a due succession of their *Supreme Assemblies*." Ireton must have discussed similar ideas with his father-in-law in the late 1640s, without fully forging the bolt, for now Cromwell believed that the state required definition rather than debate. Another of Nedham's 1651 essays pronounced "the form of a *Free-State* (or a *Government by the*

People) to be much more excellent than the [army] *Grandees,* or the *Kingly Power.*" Referring to such chosen assemblies, he argued, "The People thus qualified or constituted, are the best *Keepers of their own Liberties.*" Drawing a different analogy from modern science than did composers of divine-right Stuart masques, he concluded that "as *Motion* in bodies *natural,* so *Succession* in [bodies] Civil, is the grand Preventive of Corruption."[94]

Because Cromwell had decided to settle the Commonwealth with single-person rule, the quickness with which he arranged Ireton's funeral as a state event implies understanding its value to his settlement. There is no indication that he did this cynically, but the funeral served a purpose larger than a saint's burial. Proper ceremony would place the chief mourner at the center of such a function. The funeral assuaged personal grief and served public policy in ways contrary to Ireton's beliefs.

Cromwell determined upon an elaborate state funeral as soon as the news from Ireland reached him. Henry Cromwell's letter must have indicated that the army had buried Ireton and would ship a ceremonial coffin from Waterford to Bristol, thus the reason the letter was neither retained nor published with other correspondence. Parliament during the meeting on Tuesday, 9 December, approved making the funeral a matter of public business. The council of state discussed this on Thursday, providing money "for defraying the charge of the funeral," discussing where to place the corpse once it arrived in London, and considering "all other things relating to that business." The council discussed quartering "the Lord General's regiment of foot" in and around the Parliament to provide security. The question of where to display the putative corpse in state was settled early the following week when the council ordered rooms at Somerset House cleared and prepared. They ordered a ceremonial equipage sent to Bristol to bring the coffin to London.[95]

There were many questions and details for the planners. The council's immediate precedent was the 1646 burial of Robert Devereaux, third earl of Essex and Parliament's commander in the first civil war. That unimpressive funeral was described in verse as having "A gawdy herald and a velvet hearse, / A tattered anagram with grievous verse."[96] The council now wished to stage a sumptuous funeral. They needed to list "gentlemen and others, persons of quality" who would attend and to name pallbearers, the chief mourner, and assistants. They thought the mourner's honor should go to the lord deputy's brother, John, one of the sheriffs for London. Council sought to provide the panoply of a state burial, suitable to Ireton's "rank and condition."[97]

While the council proceeded with arrangements, there was apparently acrimonious debate in the House of Commons over some aspect of the proposed funeral. In the week after receiving word of Ireton's death, the Commons debated "the manner of the . . . funeral" and took several votes, indicating objection to some point. The matter of greatest disagreement was probably Cromwell's intention to bury the coffin in Westminster Abbey. Some who knew Ireton's mind must have argued that he would not have approved, but Cromwell prevailed and the Commons authorized burial.[98]

In mid-December 1651, one first catches a glimpse of Ireton's coffin. Near England's western coastline, an Irish troopship reported sailing in the Severn estuary, "in the midst of which came in that sad spectacle, [the ship carrying] the corps of that venerable person, the late Lord Deputy of *Ireland*." The captain presumably sent notice of this arrival to Bristol's mayor. On 17 December the ship anchored in the King Road, "a commodious Haven" at the Avon's mouth four miles from Bristol. The coffin was received "with all the decent ceremony that this place could affoard."[99] Ceremonial at Bristol anticipated the council of state's preparations at London.

The coffin was taken from the ship to a black-cloth-draped longboat, placed under a canopy, and brought up the Avon to a landing at Beck. Covered with velvet, it was carried to the castle accompanied by the mayor, the aldermen, the common councilors, the city governor, and military officers, "all in their Formalities." Completing the procession was "a multitude of Inhabitants." To salute "the Corps of the much honored and much lamented the late Lord Deputy of Ireland," salvos were fired from the castle and fort cannon. This ceremonial was "as much as could be done in so short a time," an observer at Bristol reported to the council of state. The coffin lay at the castle for several days while the city arranged for departure on Christmas eve.[100] There was no public viewing of the coffin during the time at Bristol Castle.

To carry the coffin from Bristol to London, the council of state ordered "a chariot and six horses, with other requisites."[101] The coffin departed Bristol on this velvet-draped chariot and in another procession. The city governor and military officers rode ahead. After it came two draped chariots "hanged thick with Scoutchions" to proclaim the deceased's importance. The procession included the mayor's sergeants and a sword-bearer behind the wagons, the mayor and aldermen "in their black Gownes" and on horseback, and the sheriffs and two hundred citizens on horseback riding in pairs through a military guard "in the mourning posture, with their Drums covered with black," together with eight hundred local militiamen and five hundred soldiers from the garrison. The parade wound though the city to Lawford's Gate, where "there was at parting three Vollies of shot, after two Murderers placed for that purpose, and then all the great Guns in Castle and Fort." City officials left the procession, but sheriffs, the governor, officers and "many others on horse back" accompanied the chariots for the rest of the first day of the journey.[102]

For six days the spectacle paraded across England toward the capital. All the way "my Lord Generals Regiment of Horse" marched with the chariots. As the procession neared London, "many honourable persons" joined. And on the evening of 29 December the coffin arrived at Somerset House accompanied by a now-large procession of military guards and others. The council of state had as yet announced no date for the funeral, but with Parliament's approval the council had made plans for interment in Henry VII's Chapel at Westminster Abbey.[103]

Funeral arrangements were not complete until the end of January 1652, when the coffin was placed "for a time in state at *Sumerset House*." Over the gateway an escutcheon carried the motto "Dulce est pro patria mori," which royalists in their post-Restoration memoirs gleefully translated as "It is good for his Country that he is dead."[104] On 27 January, a month after the coffin arrived from Ireland, announcement was made that "the Figure or Effigies of the late Lord Deputy of Ireland is now set up."[105] Also "divers Elegies . . . sacred to his Memory" were published. One concluded, "Heap yet new honours on Him: let Him have / All that's his due: Pomp presses not the grave."[106] Asked another, "Is Ireton dead, and yet the heavens not beare / In such a *publicke* loss an equall share?"[107]

In the London ceremonies that followed lay no indication that Ireton's remains were present. Puritan theology did not require glorification and preservation of the body; it emphasized salvation. Contemporary accounts do not refer to Ireton's body, only to the coffin and the effigy. The lying-in-state, funeral procession, and Westminster service all were conducted with an effigy.

Two persons with views inside the Commonwealth suspected the disguise. Mrs. Hutchinson did not believe Ireton or Cromwell a match for her dear husband Thomas, but her memoirs of the dashing colonel contain opinions from within the Cromwellian elite. Of Ireton's funeral she wrote: "But God cutt him short by death, and whether his body or an empty herse was brought into England, something in his name came to London, and was to be by Cromwell's procurement magnificently buried among the Kings at Westminster."[108] Lucy does not say whether or not she observed the procession, although her husband did. Ludlow seemed to go further. As Ireton's temporary successor to the Irish command, he was in a position to know. In his *Memoirs* he claimed Cromwell's "relations . . . caused the body . . . to be transported into England." A few lines later the text refers to the London funeral and observes oddly that if Ireton "could have foreseen what was done by them, [he] would have made it his desire that his body might have found a grave where his soul left it."[109] But Ludlow's original text may have said more, for the published version is highly suspect. Following his hairbreadth escape from England after the Restoration, he lived in exile and wrote a manuscript from which others published an unauthorized text after his death. The original apparently did not survive. The 1698 publication—source of Firth's "standard" 1894 edition—is heavily edited, almost to the point of removing Ludlow's hand. The editors drastically rewrote, deleted vast amounts of text, and in other incalculable ways altered the integrity of Ludlow's recollections. The 1698 publishers "did not merely cut and reorder the manuscript. They completely rewrote it." According to a modern writer, "There is not a single sentence in the *Memoirs* . . . in which Ludlow's text is accurately reproduced." A fragment of the original manuscript does survive for the 1660–62 period. First published two decades ago, it was unknown to Firth. From it Ludlow's deep religious faith, political cynicism, and access to sources, all edited out of his published memoirs, are fully apparent. One must read it carefully. Referring to the 1661 exhumations of Cromwell's and Ireton's bodies, this original manuscript covering later years makes passing reference to Ireton's burial, confirming Mrs. Hutchinson's suspicions: "the wise providence of God so ordered it that his body being interred in Ireland. . . ."[110]

A comparison to the ceremonial for Ireton is perhaps the 1663 funeral of Archbishop Juxon of Canterbury, buried at some remove from the place of death. Anthony Wood, the Oxford diarist with love of ceremonial, described the funeral. There is no doubt that Juxon's remains were embalmed (with difficulty), carried to Oxford, and buried a month after death. Wood referred to the "body" many times and described it lying under a drape of cambric sheet and black velvet on a trestle in the Chapel of St. John the Baptist—under a canopy, surrounded by symbols of authority, a gilded miter resting on a velvet cushion at the coffin's head, a gilded crosier, banners bearing arms, escutcheons. The funeral was elaborate, and a rich procession carried the body to the grave.[111]

Ireton's lying-in-state lasted only a week prior to the funeral. Mourners first walked through three rooms in Somerset House, each draped with black velvet and symbols of authority and status. In the fourth was the effigy. Walls and ceiling were covered in black velvet. A fringed black velvet canopy hung above the effigy, which was "richly apparelled in a suit of uncut Velvet." In each of the effigy's hands were symbols of Ireton's military command, mace and sword. The effigy lay on a velvet-covered bed, next to a suit of armor, and at its feet other symbols. When mourners came into the room, they "were not to be permitted to continue any time but only to passe along into another Room where the back stairs were."[112]

On 6 February, the Venetian ambassador reported, "they gave a sumptuous funeral to Lord Ireton." Mourners were to be at Somerset

House by eight o'clock in the morning. Among gathering black-cloaked mourners, Colonel Hutchinson was an obvious exception. Cromwell may have slighted Ireton's cousin by not sending him an invitation to join the official mourners. Mrs. Hutchinson related that the colonel "putt on a scarlett cloake, very richly laced, such as he usually wore" and entered the close-mourners room. Both London sheriff John Ireton and Cromwell attempted to soothe his ruffled feelings. The lord general and the sheriff understood that the colonel wore bright attire "publickely to reproach their neglects."[113]

The coffin was carried "in great pomp to Westminster Abbey." An observer thought it "very solemne and magnificant." John Evelyn was an observer of "the Magnificent Funeral of that arch-Rebell *Ireton*" and wrote a hostile but full account, which began with description of regiments of horse and foot soldiers, a "good part of the Army" having been brought to London. Following were the official mourners, led by Cromwell and composed of members of the House of Commons (whom Evelyn called "Mock-Parliament men"), the lord mayor, aldermen, and common councilors of London. Afterward came forty gowned poor men; horses, including Ireton's charger covered "with embroidery and gold on crimson *Velvet*"; heralds dressed in newly embroidered coats with the "States badges." The mace and sword of Ireton's Irish command were carried in black scarves and preceded the black-draped chariot pulled by six horses carrying the coffin. The covering pall was held by walking mourners. Lastly, soldiers beat cloth-covered drums in slow, muffled time while others carried reversed arms. The procession marched down the Strand "in a very solemn manner."[114]

When the procession reached Westminster, the effigy was taken from the chariot at the western gate and carried through the nave to Henry VII's Chapel. Mourners filed into the chapel to hear the funeral sermon. The "pulpitt and quire" were hung with black velvet drapery.[115]

John Owen, Dean of Christ Church, Oxford, delivered the sermon on a text from the book of Daniel, "But go thou thy way till the end be, for thou shalt rest, and stand in the lot at the end of the dayes." The sermon followed Puritan expectation. The Oxford diarist Anthony Wood described it later as "not without some Blasphemy," so seriously did the century take these matters.[116] Published as *The Labouring Saints Dismission to Rest,* its dismissed saint was the prophet Daniel. "This deceased Saint" possessed several qualities: wisdom allowed him "to look after the name of God, and the testification of his will," it permitted him to consider "what *Israel ought to do,* in every season," and Daniel loved his people, as did "our deceased friend." All his undertakings were *vicit amor patria,* for how else did he carry so many burdens to the end of his days but for the benefit of "*Jerusalem,* and the prosperity thereof"? And the prophet possessed righteousness "in the administration of that high place whereto he was called."

Owen said that the Bible's great prophets—Moses, Daniel, John the Baptist—had each his season, yet "they must go their ways *to rest.*" Referring to Ireton's early death, he said, "God oftentimes suffers not the choicest of his servants to see the accomplishment of those glorious things wherein themselves have been most eminently engaged." The reward was the service; consolation for listeners was that "God hath better things . . . in store," and Ireton now enjoyed "the glory of that eternall Kingdome that was prepared for him before the foundation of the World." Only at the end did Owen reflect upon the effigy. He commended the courage, faithfulness, industry, and impartiality wherein Ireton "walked before the Lord, and the Inhabitants of this Nation." He committed the audience "to him, who is able to prepare you for your eternal condition."[117]

Cromwell ordered William Wright, "graver in stone to the Protector," to prepare a monument. When Wright petitioned the council of state for his £120 fee and a further £52 to erect the tomb, he hoped his work displayed "the well-deserving fame of the said late lord deputy." The council did not charge these fees against the funeral but paid Wright from its contingency fund. Under supervision of Cromwell's chaplain, Hugh Peter, the marble tomb was apparently in place by the spring of 1654.[118] It was an arch covered with Ireton's arms and the words "Dulce Pro Patris Mori." Peter wrote a Latin epitaph, concluding, in translation, "Irreparable Loss! He dyes, and dying, steers / His Course to *Canaan,* through a Sea of Tears."[119] Like the funeral, the tomb was a "pompous and expensive" vanity of which Ireton would have disapproved. Ludlow believed the lord deputy "erected for himself a more glorious monument in the hearts of good men . . . than [in] a dormitory amongst the ashes of kings." He reflected Puritan belief that embalming and preservation were unnecessary.[120] Those who despised Ireton noted that Cromwell had given him "that vain glory, which himself had often declared against."[121] And republicans and radicals thought the spirit of Antichrist had appeared in "the vain pomp at the funeral of Lord Ireton [which] was very offensive to many."[122]

Thus they "solemnized the Funeral of the late Lord Deputy" and "magnificently buried among the Kings" the purported mortal remains, the loathsome and ruinous carcass, of that Independent who believed the dead descended "into a pit of carions and confusion."[123] There was, of course, no interment.

3

$\mathcal{C}$romwell

Ivit ad Plures

O liver Cromwell died nearly seven years after the passing of his lamented son-in-law, Henry Ireton, in faraway Ireland. The lord protector had done much during his lifetime. His great achievement during the 1650s had been to stabilize the nation after a decade of civil turmoil. In 1653 he dramatically dismissed the Rump Parliament, whose members had been elected a dozen years before, and summoned the Nominated Parliament, also called the Barebones. This Parliament of saints attempted radical reform, but conservative gentry members finally voted to return their commissions. Army officers had anticipated this possibility and prepared the Instrument of Government, under which Cromwell became lord protector of the Commonwealth of England, Scotland, and Ireland.[1] The Instrument did not become "the constitution," however, and by mid-1658 it seemed possible that Parliament would grant Cromwell a king's title in final settlement of the nation's affairs.

The protector possessed an inherited longevity and a strong physical constitution. He died at age fifty-nine, above average for the time but less impressive than his mother's age at death, which was about eighty-five. Four of his children also lived to advanced ages: Henry died at sixty-six, Mary at seventy-two, Frances at eighty-three, and Richard at eighty-six. Four years before Richard's death in 1712, he was "so hale and hearty, that . . . he would gallop his horse for several miles together."[2] The protector's life did not reveal inherited illness or disability. He was not subject to ailments or injuries common to persons who survived infancy. He did not suffer disability from accident or warfare. He may have been bothered by kidney stones and possibly some malaria. He was as susceptible as anyone to infectious disease. And he was at risk during military campaigns. Given the signs of generally good health, Andrew Marvell well wrote of him: "So have I seen a Vine, whose lasting Age / Of many a Winter hath surviv'd the rage."[3]

Physical strength such as Cromwell's was the seventeenth-century's best preservative of life. Medical practice at the time divided between the established Galenists in the Royal College of Physicians, who thought illness the result of an imbalance in bodily humors, and a few Paracelsians, who thought illness treatable with chemical adjustments that were easily applied and endured. Paracelsus (1494–1541) developed laudanum to relieve pain, and he argued for simple and natural remedies.[4] Nonetheless, studies of disease at that time were generally descriptive taxonomies and offered cures that were little more than traditional folk remedies. Medical attendance could be as fatal as disease. A doctor let Ireton's blood in 1651, a standard treatment that probably weakened him and hastened death. Left alone he might have recovered, as had Ludlow. Parliament sent Dr. Laurence Wright and Dr. George Bate to Edinburgh to attend Cromwell in 1651. The general was convalescent when they arrived. He believed at the time that "the Lord . . . hath plucked me out of the grave," not the doctors.[5] They collected outrageous fees anyway. In the summer of 1658, at Hampton Court, his daughter Elizabeth lay dying from uterine cancer and doctors recommended she take the waters at Tunbridge. Her brother-in-law, Gen. Charles Fleetwood, concluded, "The truth is, its beleeved the physitians do not understand hir case."[6]

Throughout Cromwell's career his enemies of course sought signs that death would remove the presumed author of their troubles. In 1646 a royalist heard hopeful rumors. He was optimistic about the king's military prospects because it was "agreed uppon from all parts, that Cromwell is either dead or soe desperately sicke of the bloody fluxe, that he is for the present uselesse, and must be soe long if he recovers at all."[7] In 1651 Parliament and the army heard that Cromwell had fallen ill in Scotland, and they sent Wright and Bate to attend him. Royalists heard the same news and thought it to Charles Stuart's advantage that Cromwell "is in a very weak condition, which it is supposed may dishearten the English soldiery very much."[8] His recovery meant "there is not any fear by the blessing of God but he will be enabled to go into the field when provisions come."[9]

During the Scottish campaign of 1651, he suffered illnesses that produced rumors of his death.[10] In mid-February he fell ill with dysentery, from which he did not recover for weeks.[11] The first of May he possibly had a kidney stone attack but was soon "well and chearful."[12] A week later, weakened by this event, he may have suffered "five fits of an ague" in three days, although five ague fits in so short a time seem unlikely. According to a published report, "his lips brake out . . . which is a good sign of recovery." This was "the third relapse since his first sickness which was contracted by a winter's march." These references may be to further dysentery rather than ague. An observer thought that Cromwell at age fifty-two was unmindful that "he is grown an old man."[13]

He possibly had several kidney-stone attacks in the mid-1650s, but evidence is inconclusive. In late 1653 he suffered an "indisposition" that kept him from court for several days. This may have been a stone.[14] In 1654 he may have had another. Dr. Bate claimed that "being much troubled with the stone, he used sometimes to swill down several sorts of Liquor, and then stir his Body by some violent Motion . . . that by such Agitation he might disburden his Bladder." He described how Cromwell once rode in the coach box to agitate his body but during the ride fell to the ground and received injury. Bate's story carried an apocryphal rather than medical purpose.[15] The Dutch embassy reported the accident but not the stone. It said Cromwell and some courtiers took dinner in Hyde Park, and afterward he had "desire to drive the coach himself." The six-horse team became unruly and the postilion could not rein them in. Cromwell was "flung out of the coach-box upon the pole," his foot tangled in the tackling, and as he was dragged along the ground a pistol in his pocket fired. For all the danger he was not injured. At Whitehall doctors let blood, doubtless inflicting more harm than had the accident.[16]

A year later he underwent "a course of physick" because he "hath bin troubled with severall fits of the stone." The attack was reported as displaying a "violent and dangerous colick"—severe pain and gas.

Cromwell's physicians brought in Dr. James Moleyns, a royalist and lithotomist at the hospitals of St. Bartholomew and St. Thomas. He held license from the College of Physicians "to administer internal medicines in surgical diseases." He applied the medicines and treatments described as "a course of physick," and a week later Cromwell seemed recovered.[17]

His infirmities were routine, but Cromwell carried a Puritan's sense of imminent mortality and in his early fifties wrote, "I grow an old man, and feel infirmities of age marvellously stealing upon me."[18] Then in 1656 he was bothered by "an angry knott in the nature of a boyle that is broke out unhappily by the side of his neck; he is very well in health."[19] In August 1657 the Venetian ambassador reported that he rested at Hampton Court, as he usually did in late summer: "a slight purge being ordered by the physicians, and to drink some medicinal waters not far from that spot." The ambassador thought his health "has not been entirely satisfactory for some time past, as he is subject to frequent catarrhs which weaken him considerably." Thus he had cold and sinus problems, and physicians occasionally were present.[20]

During August 1658, however, the protector's health collapsed. He suffered a month-long series of medical events, which occurred in five episodes. Unlike the preceding problems, these events were serious.

In setting out what brought Cromwell to his death, it is necessary to relate the unhappy episodes in detail, the first of which began weeks earlier than historians have generally assumed. One often reads that the illness began two weeks prior to his death on 3 September, as the palace announcement of his death stated, but in fact he fell ill on the last day of July. On 16 July he had traveled to Hampton Court, ostensibly "to enjoy the weather." His daughter Elizabeth was desperately ill, and there was no hope for her recovery. His health was normal, except for stress from being constantly at her beside, and this caused him to have inadequate food and sleep. Near the end of July, his secretary, John Thurloe, wrote to Henry Cromwell that Elizabeth's illness was "a great afflication to hym." An absence of comment about the protector implied the sufficiency of his health.[21] On 30 July he held public audience and private discussion with the Dutch ambassador, Willem Nieuport.[22] His health deteriorated immediately thereafter, and the onset of illness, at first ordinary gout, can be reasonably dated to the evening of this meeting or the following day. It quickly became more serious than mere gout. Charles Fleetwood wrote to Henry Cromwell, his brother-in-law, on 3 August that the protector had been "for these 4 or 5 dayes very indisposed and ill" and referred specifically to "his paynes and distemper."[23] At about the same time Thurloe wrote to Gen. George Monck in Scotland and reported that Elizabeth then seemed in "a hopefull way," whereas the protector had recovered from "a fitt of the collick," an attack of abdominal pain.[24] Charles Harvey, Cromwell's valet, wrote in a similar manner that the lord protector first fell ill "a little before the Lady Elizabeth died," which was 6 August, and suffered under "bodily distempers, forerunners to his sicknesse, which was to death."[25] Harvey thereby confirmed that Cromwell was ill at the beginning of the month with symptoms similar to those that he had at his death in early September. Another of Thurloe's letters to Henry also dated the illness to the beginning of August, noting that as Elizabeth's health failed, the protector developed "the sickness," and when she died he "at the same tyme lay very ill of the gout, and other distempers." In the seventeenth century "sickness" referred to vomiting and diarrhea. Despite evident and worrisome "other distempers" prior to Elizabeth's death, doctors made no diagnosis, other than perhaps gout, for Thurloe noted merely that if the illness were "from some other cause, I am unable to say."[26]

Cromwell's distress became more serious during the period of grief following his daughter's death, when the second episode of illness began. By 10 August, when Elizabeth was buried, he was so ill that he was unable to be carried on the gentle downriver journey for her midnight interment at Westminster Abbey. He remained bedridden at Hampton Court; the court's mood was "sad and sorrowful." Thurloe described his pains as though the gout had moved "into his body," and noted that he was dangerously and violently sick. Fleetwood wrote more descriptively that he "hath bine very much indisposed, troubled with paynes in his bowells and backe, and could not sleepe."[27] The situation was so serious by the next day that "wee had some doubts of his recovery, the greatness of his distemper of the goute and other distempers, with the sorrow for the death of his daughter, having deepe impression uppon him." Bulstrode Whitelock recorded that on the twelfth "The Protector was ill at *Hampton-Court.*"[28] Newssheets did not refer to the illness—which was never publicly reported—but remarked that "His Highness was not present" at the privy council's Hampton Court meeting on 13 August.[29]

A week after Elizabeth's funeral he seemed to be nearly well. A report to the army commander in Scotland, General Monck, said, "hee is pretty well recovered," and the writer thought the brush with death would cause Cromwell to resolve "something of settlement" in the succession question.[30] Thurloe and Fleetwood also noted that the illness had eased. On the morning of the seventeenth he felt well enough to go horseback riding for an hour.[31] Dr. Thomas Clarges wrote to Monck, his brother-in-law, "His Highness is well recovered of a great distemper too much like that in Cannongate."[32] This reference to the Canongate in Edinburgh is ambiguous, but the letter verified that Cromwell had fallen ill of "a great distemper" by the beginning of August and had recovered by 17 August.

The protector showed ravages of this physical distress, and yet, as George Fox reported, he had so recovered that he was able to go horseback riding. The evangelist met him in Hampton Court Park while the protector was "abroad for an houre" on the morning of the seventeenth. Fox often had corresponded and visited, and Cromwell always considered his presence "good news." He had traveled to Hampton Court to speak with the protector about the Friends' suffering: "I met him riding into Hampton Court Park; and before I came at him, as he rode in the head of his life-guard, I saw and felt a waft (or apparition) of death go forth against him; and when I came to him he looked like a dead man."[33] Fox spoke of the Friends, and the protector invited him to visit the palace the next day, indicating a sense of recovery. Fox's account implied that although Cromwell had visibly deteriorated, he had enough vigor to go riding.

The first recorded consultation with physicians was "after Dinner" during that same day, when observers thought he had recovered. The consultation did not amount to much. It nonetheless was a curious exercise. Bate briefly mentioned the event in *Elenchus Motuum*

Nuperorum in Anglia, his account of the 1650s first published in 1661. One of the doctors—probably Bate, who told the story—merely "felt his pulse, said that it intermitted." If the examination were really so cursory after two weeks and two near-fatal episodes it was inexcusable even by standards of the day. According to Bate's report, Cromwell "suddenly started" at news of an irregular pulse, "looked pale, fell into a Cold Sweat, almost fainted away, and orders himself to be carried to Bed, where being refreshed with Cordials, he made his Will." The response was disproportionate to the finding.

The consultation nonetheless revealed symptoms. Cromwell displayed irregular pulse, lightheadedness, swooning, sweating. The doctors must have given their patient a more thorough examination than the irresponsibly lax consultation that Bate reported. He implied as much by saying that Cromwell made a will for his private affairs that evening, hardly the action of one who has been told merely that he had an irregular pulse. The protector did not sleep "the greatest part of the night" because he was restless from back and bowel pains that had occurred periodically since the turn of the month.

During that night ministers prayed for recovery, an indication of relapse. Bate said nothing of treatment in his later account, and he ridiculed the ministers. Speaking with another doctor the next morning, he said, "Our Patient will be light-headed," curiously predicting a symptom. The other doctor replied, "Don't you know what was done last Night? The Chaplains . . . have prayed to God for his Health, and all have brought this Answer, *He shall recover.*" Bate was contemptuous of the ministers and blamed them for the doctors' seeming indifference: "These Oracles of the *Saints* were the cause that the Physicians spake not a word of his danger." Clarges also referred to the "private Thanksgiving beforehand for his undoubted recovery." He also noted that the ministers' confidence amused the doctors, who were therefore "less regardful of his Condition."[34]

When "one of his Physicians" visited the patient—again, one infers Bate—during the morning of the eighteenth, the protector asked why the doctor looked sad. The doctor replied to the effect that "it becomes any one who had the weighty care of his Life and Health upon him." Cromwell began saying, "Ye Physicians . . . think I shall die," but someone ordered the room cleared except for the doctor and Cromwell's wife, whose hand he held. "Go on chearfully," he told the doctor, "banishing all sadness from your looks. . . . Ye may have skill in the Nature of things, yet Nature can do more than all Physicians put together; and God is far more above nature." He still believed that his God, not the doctors, guarded his grave.[35]

Despite apparent recovery on the seventeenth, even riding horseback for an hour, by the next morning Cromwell had entered the third medical episode with the recurrence of back and bowel pains. Fox returned to Hampton Court that afternoon, but Cromwell was sick, and Charles Harvey, "who was one that waited on him, told me, the doctors were not willing I should come in to speak with him. So I passed away, and never saw him more."[36] Fleetwood wrote his brother-in-law that "the lord was pleased upon thursday last [19 August] to let his distemper return." Friday, 20 August, Cromwell appeared better again, his pains having remitted. Saturday morning, three weeks after he first fell ill, Fleetwood and Thurloe thought he might have fallen into "a fitt of an ague." Fleetwood reported that he "hade a very sore second fite upon saturday [21 August], whic[h] is now turned into a tertian ague." It is important to note that prior to this point no one had described the illness as ague—that is, malaria. Monday night, 23 August, he had a mild fit, after which he rested well.[37] Some observers suspected that whatever the nature of Cromwell's distemper, the "illness change[d] to a tertian ague."[38] He may indeed have exhibited some malaria at this time alongside existing symptoms, but the second episode had begun three days earlier, on the eighteenth, with the return of alarming pains. The episode distressed him enough that, probably on Monday, he spoke with his family about his "danger" and their abiding "upon the Covenant," and he discussed his estates with his stewards.[39]

On 24 August, Tuesday, Cromwell traveled from Hampton Court to Whitehall because the doctors advised it was an "intervall day" between malarial fits and "the change of aire" would benefit recovery.[40] Such advice was as helpful as recommending that Elizabeth take the Tunbridge waters for uterine cancer. That night in Westminster he had another fit, "somewhat more favourable" than the previous attack, followed on Wednesday by a "good intervall" that gave hope his ague "was very much upon the decreasinge." On 26 August he was well enough to see at least two persons on important matters. He had an unpleasant interview with Thomas Fairfax about his son-in-law, the duke of Buckingham, arrested and imprisoned in the Tower, whom Cromwell was unwilling to release. He had a pleasant visit with Bulstrode Whitelock, whom he "kindly entertained at dinner." Whitelock, who favored one-person government, reported that the protector "discussed privately with me about his great Business," implying not only the protector's expectation of recovery but also of receiving Parliament's grant of kingship.[41]

The fourth episode of illness began Thursday evening, 26 August, and lasted until 1 September. After his dinner with Whitelock, Cromwell's health again collapsed: first he suffered an ague that began "very favourablye" with a mild cold fit, but the subsequent hot fit was "very long and terrible." Doctors feared he might then succumb. An alarmed Thurloe started writing a dispatch to Henry shortly after midnight, by which time the protector fell into "a breathinge sweate, which we hope he will come well out of."[42] Francesco Giavarina, the gossipy Venetian ambassador, wrote the next day that Cromwell "is now suffering severely in mind and body, unable to attend to the many affairs which require decision." Only one item of public business was noted—a warrant conferring a baronetcy upon one William Wynham of Somerset, issued in Cromwell's name.[43]

Richard Cromwell wrote anxiously on 28 August to his friend John Dunche in Berkshire. Since his father's illness began he had not "Opportunity or Desire to set Pen to Paper." His greatest fear was uncertainty, for the doctors could not provide him with a diagnosis: the illness "hath put the Physicians in a Nonplus." He was confused and referred both to "this Fit of Ague" and separately to "this dangerous Illness." He had little confidence in the doctors, believing "the Goodness of God . . . shall save him . . . the Spirit of Prayer is poured out for him."[44]

By Saturday the latest display of ague revealed additional symptoms similar to the earlier two episodes. Clarges reported, "The temperate condition of his health ebbs and flows," a general description

consistent with ague, while at the same time "his repose being obstructed with intervalls of restlesse paine."[45] Thurloe described this to
Henry as "a double tertian, haveinge 2 fitts in 24 houres . . . which doe
extreamley weaken hym, and endanger his life." He probably referred
to restlessness and pain when saying that during Sunday and Monday
he "hath scarce beene perfectly out of his fitts." Thurloe was confused. He reminded Henry that early in August Cromwell had suffered "a general distemper of body"—another allusion to the kind of
pains he had consistently displayed. Thurloe was reluctant to assume
the worst but noted the doctors' hopes "mingled with much feare."[46]
Giavarina did assume the worst, writing, "On Saturday, Sunday and
Monday he was exceedingly bad."[47]

On Monday another of Cromwell's sons-in-law, Thomas Belasyse,
Viscount Fauconberg, wrote Henry in cipher "of H. H. condition, which
all the physitians have judgd dangerous, more then ever." According
to Dr. Clarges, Cromwell suffered sharp pains and a sore throat, and
he wrote to Henry that the protector's "violent sicknes . . . fils me with
sad apprehensions." In his correspondence Clarges also referred to
"double tertian ague" for the first time, a diagnosis inconsistent with
the symptoms mentioned.[48]

By the end of August concern for the succession was becoming
apparent. Fauconberg did not believe that the protector had named a
successor "that I can learn." Army officers met, ostensibly to pray for
recovery. Secretary Thurloe gathered rumors that "the cavaliers doe
begin to listen . . . and hope their day is comeinge, or indeed come, if
his highnes dye." He presciently believed that if Cromwell died the
regime risked becoming unstable because of "our own divisions . . . if
his highnesse should not settle and fix his successor." Thurloe claimed
Cromwell had written a letter "directing it to me" and naming a successor. Before Cromwell left Hampton Court, he sent John Barrington,
clerk of the green cloth, to Whitehall to find the paper in his desk.
Barrington could not locate it. Bate told a similar story and concluded
curiously that Cromwell "had either burnt it himself, or some body
else had stole it." Thurloe indicated to the family that he would be
willing "to press him in his intervals to such a nomination."[49]

On Monday afternoon, the thirtieth, the great tempest occurred that was later interpreted as a harbinger of Cromwell's death. Celestial omens marked earthly events for seventeenth-century Englishmen as for the ancient Romans they admired. James Heath's royalist *Flagellum,* a hostile 1663 biography of Cromwell, noted with disappointment that in 1599 there had been "neither Comet, nor Earthquakes . . . pointing out, that the Scourge of the *English* Empire and Nation was now born."[50] After Cromwell's death Marvell thought the storm indicated "Heav'n it self would the great *Herald* be." Typical of the time, he believed that

> A secret Cause does sure those Signs ordain
> Fore boding Princes falls, and seldom in vain.
> Whether some kinder Pow'rs, that wish us well,
> What they cannot prevent, foretell.[51]

The storm caused much damage in southern England. Anthony Wood recorded at Oxford "a verie terrible raging winde, which did much hurt, especially in tearing of tre[e]s." Edmund Ludlow, who was in Essex traveling to London, described a west wind so strong that "the horses were not able to draw against it." He stopped overnight at Epping, resumed the road to London next morning, and arrived at midday.[52] The poet Edmund Waller wrote with license, conflating the days of the storm and Cromwell's death:

> His dying groans, his last breath, shakes our isle
> And trees uncut fall for his funeral pile;
> About his palace their broad roots are tossed
> Into the air.—So Romulus was lost![53]

Others also imagined Cromwell had died during the storm, but Anthony Wood's antiquarian instincts prompted him to write in his journal that this was not so. "This I set downe," he wrote when noting the storm's passage, "because some writers tell us that he was hurried away by the Devill in the wind before mention'd."[54]

By the evening, after the storm, Cromwell seemed near death. The Venetian ambassador wrote simply that "on Tuesday evening he was given up by the doctors."[55] Fauconberg added a postscript—also in code—and told Henry that the protector was "now beyond al possibility of recovery."[56] Fleetwood also wrote to Henry that Cromwell was "under a very great distemper, called an ague, but mostly his heate gave us the sadde apprehension of danger." Like Thurloe and Richard Cromwell, he suspected that the illness was an ague but was confused by inconsistencies among the symptoms. He, too, thought were was little reason for hope.[57]

Anxiety at Whitehall Palace appeared on Tuesday when General Ludlow arrived in London, his trip delayed by the storm. He traveled on personal business related to his mother's illness, but Cromwell was allegedly suspicious and asked Fleetwood to inquire about the reasons. The protector was at the time recovering from the previous evening's distemper, so it was probably Fleetwood who suspected Ludlow of "a design to raise some disturbance in the army." He requested an interview, and Ludlow met him on Wednesday and "assured him, that as it was not in my power to cause any commotion in the army, so neither was it in my thoughts." Suspicions eased and Fleetwood turned conversational, telling Ludlow that Cromwell had been ill "but that it was now hoped he was recovering." Indeed, he had improved dramatically by the time Fleetwood and Ludlow spoke on Wednesday. Ludlow's memoirs, as published in 1698, do not contain further detail.[58]

Death had seemed imminent on Tuesday, but the next day, when Ludlow saw Fleetwood, the patient had improved markedly. The Venetian ambassador reported that on Tuesday night the doctors had given him up, but "all of a sudden he became better, slept well . . . and the fever which should have recurred in the morning [Wednesday] was very slight." Thus, the mild ague that Cromwell had probably displayed since 21 August abated and no malarial fever occurred on Friday, when tertian ague would have recurred. Fleetwood observed that Cromwell had some "slumbering sleepes, his pulse better, his water good all this day." Fleetwood was hopeful: "His return will be, if the Lord restore him, as life from the deade." The Venetian ambassador observed, "The improvement has certainly been sudden, unexpected and extraordinary."[59]

The protector felt improved, as implied by a prayer that Harvey included in a pamphlet published the following year. Harvey wrote out the prayer, which he said the protector offered "two or three daies before his end"—that is, during the period of recovery on Tuesday night or Wednesday. In previous days, according to Thurloe, he had "scarce been perfectly out of his fits" and was thus unable to pray. The prayer began characteristically, "Although I am a miserable and wretched Creature, I am in Covenant with thee, through Grace." He continued ominously that although many had set upon him a high value, "others wish, and would bee glad of my Death." At the prayer's conclusion he said, "give us a good night, if it be thy pleasure." He was well enough to wish to feel better.[60]

Clarges reported to Monck that Cromwell rested during Tuesday and Wednesday and the ague subsided. The sore throat and "the sharpness of his fitts are abated, so there is good hopes of him recovering"—except, he added oddly, "some unexpected accident happen."[61]

The brief fifth and last medical episode began Thursday night. On Wednesday observers had reported dramatic improvement and expressed hope for recovery. So suddenly did the fatal crisis occur that on the afternoon when Cromwell died, the Venetian ambassador—who had generally excellent sources of information—was still writing of improvement and recovery. Malarial fever had not recurred on Wednesday, thus it was an unlikely factor at the time of death; there were pains and sore throat, though his water was good all day. But during the night of 2 September serious nonmalarial symptoms suddenly reappeared and caught the household by surprise. Clarges's prediction came true: "some unexpected accident" reversed recovery.

There is meager description of the final crisis. Harvey referred briefly to "the very night before the Lord took him." His pamphlet, published in 1659, prior to the Restoration, sought to affirm the protector's state of grace rather than narrate a medical record. Nonetheless, it provided information. He had been with Cromwell during the entire illness, and he reiterated that Cromwell first fell ill prior to Elizabeth's death, then mentioned his moving to Whitehall. Harvey's text emphasized the final Thursday night and Friday, implying a dramatic and noteworthy change in the protector's condition. He said that at one point Cromwell began to speak the words, *"Truly God is good, indeed he is, he will not—"* but did not finish the thought. Harvey assumed the conclusion would have been "hee will not leave mee." Cromwell spoke in this vein during the night but "with much chearfulnesse and fervour of spirit in the midst of his pains." This reference indicated recurrence of the violent abdominal pains that had accompanied the onset of each episode.

Harvey reported Cromwell's saying that he was willing to be of further service "to God and his People, but my work is done." "He was very restlesse most part of the night, speaking often to himself. And there being something to drink offered him, hee was desired to take the same, and endeavor to sleep, unto which hee answered, *It is not my design to drink or to sleep, but my design is to make what haste I can to bee gone.*" Restlessness and pessimism indicated further pain, and the offer of water implied possible fever. As morning broke, Cromwell used "diverse holy expressions, implying much inward consolation and peace" but also "some exceeding self-debasing words . . . judging himself." The previous assumption of "chearfulnesse . . . in the midst of his pains" probably represents Harvey's attempt to cover the protector's depression, which he indicated elsewhere. The Venetian ambassador understood that Cromwell became "so much worse about mid-day." Harvey's pamphlet reported Cromwell's final thoughts as "taken from himself on his deathbed, speaking of the Covenant." The protector's thought drifted but dwelt on his belief that "Faith in the Covenant is my onely support, yet I beleeve not, he abides faithful." Harvey did not cite dying words because Cromwell entered an unconscious state of syncope.[62] Quiet death was implied in the official announcement issued that afternoon: "His most Serene and Renowned Highness *Oliver,* Lord Protector, being after a sickness of about fourteen days (which appeared an Ague in the beginning) reduced to a low condition of Body, began early this morning to draw near the gate of death, and it pleased God about three a clock afternoon, to put a period to his life."[63] At the lying-in-state, an inscription suspended over the bier said that he died "with great assurance and Serenity of Mind, Peaceably in his Bed."[64]

And so the great man died. Thurloe wrote to the lord deputy of Ireland, Henry Cromwell, that "it . . . pleased God to put an end to his dayes" and that it was not possible to express "what affection the army and all people shew to his late highness. . . . A great man is fallen in Israel!" Marvell wrote, "He without noise still travell'd to his End, / As silent Suns to meet the Night descend." Cromwell's chaplain, Hugh Peter, preached the following Sunday on the text "My servant Moses is dead." There were less charitable reactions. Bate wrote coldly that "he yielded up the Ghost in the Afternoon not (as it was commonly reported) carried away by the *Devil* at Midnight, but in clear Daylight." An Essex parson noted in his diary merely that "Cromwell died. people not much minding it." The Venetian ambassador was suspicious: "The death of Oliver came, we may say, unexpectedly."[65]

With the protector's death it was necessary to secure Richard's succession, and this business was dispatched quickly. The protector's intent regarding the succession was ambiguous, to contemporaries as well as to historians, but Thurloe claimed to Henry that "His highness was pleased before his death to declare my lord Richard successor."[66] Henry was a member of the army and perhaps more capable than his older brother, but there was a question about the succession—did the Instrument allow the protector to designate a successor? At Whitehall it seemed important to establish Richard as protector as quickly as possible.[67] Several days later Thurloe wrote again, saying that "it hath pleased God hitherto to give his highnes your brother a very easie and peaceable entrance upon his government." He added, "there is not a dogge that waggs his tongue, soe great a calme are wee in." Thurloe was in fact worried about "some murmurings in the army" because Richard was "not generall of the army, as his father was."[68] Dissatisfaction among officers prompted Richard to speak to them at a meeting on 18 October. He said God had raised him to the protectorship, and he sought to allay their complaints.[69] Three weeks later he "had debate with certaine feild officers" about arrears in pay, one of the aggravating issues.[70] Given such concerns for the army, the Cromwellians thought it necessary to do "right to the memory of that great person, so beloved of all, in the solemnity of his funerall" lest a cabal attempt "to rule themselves, or set all on fire."[71]

The afternoon of Cromwell's death, the council of state ordered his doctors to embalm the body and "fill the same with sweet Odours," which they did the following day.[72] Just a few weeks earlier, Cromwell had buried his daughter unembalmed; thus, the council disregarded the protector's likely preference for himself. Dr. Bate described the procedure. After lining the abdominal cavity with spices, they wrapped the body in layers of cerecloth and sealed it in a lead sheet, which they placed in a wooden coffin. But they only partly embalmed the body, for they did not completely drain its fluids, an essential step.

Arranging the funeral took more time, for like Cromwell's ceremony for Ireton in 1652, his own burial served a purpose: it was a pantomime bolstering the protectoral regime. Pageantry arrayed the procession with regal solemnity, giving dignity and authority to the protectoral mantle that Richard had assumed. Ireton's ceremonies became a precedent for Cromwell's own. An effigy was placed in state at Somerset House, where "still though dead, greater than death he lay'd."[73] On 23 November spectators crowded the Strand and Whitehall as a vast procession carried the effigy for "dismission to rest" in the same Abbey vault allegedly containing Ireton's body. The crowd was enormous. Persons were said to have traveled to London "as far as from the Mount in *Cornwall,* and from the *Orcades.*"[74] The ceremony presented viewers with coffin and chariot, pomp and circumstance, signs and symbols. As in Ireton's funeral, spectators did not see the corpse nor witness interment. The funeral served its larger purpose. On 14 September the council had issued "Orders about removing the body of his late Highness" from Whitehall Palace.[75] During the night of 20 September the "Corps . . . was removed . . . in private manner" to Somerset House. A large party of household officials—lifeguards, halbardiers, "and many other Officers and Servants of his Highness," including two heralds—accompanied the hearse drawn by six horses. The transfer was "private" in that it was not announced, but the procession's movement up Whitehall and the Strand could not have passed unobserved, even at so late an hour.

Arrived at Somerset House, the body was presumed to rest "for some daies more private, but afterwards will be exposed in State to public View."[76] This wording implied that the body was in condition to be exposed, that is to say, it had not corrupted. Nonetheless, it was wrapped in a lead sheet and placed in a coffin, and thus only the coffin could be "exposed." After the coffin had arrived at Somerset House, the new protector and the council issued a declaration inviting people "to observe a day to seek God by prayer and humiliation in reference to his late dispensations in taking away his late Highness."[77]

Funeral plans included displaying an effigy placed above the closed coffin, as in the 1625 funeral for James I.[78] Within a week of Cromwell's death, there were arrangements for "an effigies of wax made to represent his late Highness."[79] The effigy was "curiously made to the life, according to the best skill of the artist . . . viz. Mr. Symons." The head was carved in wood and "covered or enamelled with wax; and that according to nature." The body was carved in wood by "Mr. Phellips (being caruer to the house and surveyor)."[80] Funeral preparations took longer than anticipated. The Venetian ambassador, who wished to appear in state for the funeral, thought "much time is required for arranging everything required for the magnificence and pomp they intend to give." It was reported that "black velvet is bought all London over to hang in Whitehall and Somerset House."[81]

On 7 October the council set the funeral for 9 November and a few days later announced that "the Corps . . . is to be exposed at Sommerset-house . . . with the Representation of his person in Effigie."[82] A correspondent wrote, "All our courtiers are preparing for the greatest funerall that has been seen in England" and added, "Much honour is performed to the corpse which lies at Somerset House."[83] A few days later public announcements dropped reference to Cromwell's "Corps" and stated that only "the Representation of the person of his late Highness in Effigie" would be presented for public viewing.[84]

At Somerset House a coffin was displayed with the effigy. An account of the lying-in-state described how mourners passed through three rooms—presence chamber, privy chamber, withdrawing room— each decorated with velvet and displaying symbolic chairs of state. In the fourth "the Body and Effigies do lie," but the account made no further reference to a body or a coffin. It described the elaborate effigy displayed on a bed of state enclosed by railings, surrounded by velvet draperies, illuminated by eight burning tapers in five-foot-high silver candlesticks. The effigy was vested with symbols of authority and wore "the Regall Cappe of purple Velvet."[85] Within the railings stood bareheaded men in mourning who held black batons; outside were others "whose office it was to receive people in, and turn them out again." In dim saffron light, which flickered faintly around the black-velvet-draped room, mourners could not see clearly the object before them. Many probably assumed it to be the corpse. These descriptions of the effigy date from mid-October, when the staterooms were first opened to the public. For several weeks there were "multitudes daily crowding to see this glorious but mournful sight."[86] A London correspondent noted at the end of October that "His Highness's effigies has lain in state to be seen."[87] Peter Mundy, world traveler and diarist, went through the state mourning rooms at this time and in the fourth room saw the coffin, "which was of pretious wood, ritchly garnished with iron worcke, all guilt." And he saw the royally attired recumbent effigy and "the rest of the ornamaments, as trophies, banners, scutcheons, etts., all very ritch and excellent workmanship." Mundy described the coffin in which Cromwell was buried and "wherein I thincke hee was at that tyme."[88] He wrote this diary entry later, and it reflected information circulating by mid-November that there had been a secret burial prior to the funeral.

When Mundy went through the mourning rooms at Somerset House near the end of October he saw both the recumbent effigy and the coffin enclosing Cromwell's remains, but in early November the coffin was secretly removed, the funeral postponed, and the recumbent effigy placed "standing upright in his Robes of State."[89] The effigy was "removed to another inner room" and placed on a dais, "only now his purple velvet [cap] was changed for a crown."[90] Sir John Burgoyne noted sarcastically to a member of the Verney family, "The old Protector is now gott upon his legs again in Sumersett House, but when he shall be translated to the rest of the Gods at Westminster I cannot tell."[91]

The reason for removing the "pretious" coffin from Somerset House was that the body had putrefied. Bate stated in his memoirs, first circulated prior to the royalists' exhumation of Cromwell's body in January 1661, that doctors wrapped the corpse in layers of cerecloth and lead sheeting. As he described the result, the corpse "purged and wrought through all, so that there was a necessity of interring it before the Solemnities."[92] Poorly embalmed and wrapped in a soldered lead sheet, it had decayed until gas pressure ruptured the sheet's seams. The Reverend John Prestwich, a follower of Cromwell, wrote that the corpse, "although thus bound up and laid in the coffin, swelled and bursted, from which came such filth, that raised such a deadly and noisome stink, that it was found prudent to bury him immediately, which was done in as private a manner as possible."[93] According to another account, "His Body, for the Stench, was buried privately."[94] Realizing that the putrefied corpse could no longer remain at Somerset House, council on 3 November announced the funeral's postponement from the ninth to the twenty-third.[95] The French ambassador reported the funeral "which was to have taken place tomorrow [9 November] . . . has been postponed to another day not yet fixed."[96]

On the night of 10 November the body and the "pretious" coffin were removed from Somerset House, carried through St. James's Park, and buried at Westminster Abbey. Although removal and burial were never part of the record, many people knew they had occurred, and there can be no doubt—subsequent speculation notwithstanding—that the body was buried in the Abbey. According to a Verney family letter, "My lord protector's body was Bered last night at one o'clock very privittly."[97] The French ambassador wrote prior to the funeral, "interment last week at one o'clock in the morning; his effigy however was still left exposed in the same place where his body had been."[98] An agent notified General Monck, in Edinburgh, "The corpes of his late Highness were on Wednesday last removed from Somerset House, and passing through James's Park were carryed to Westminster, and there interred in the vault in Henry 7 Chappell."[99] Even an observer of the procession on 23 November noted as a matter of fact in his diary that upon the hearse lay "not ye Body, for that was buried before, but the effigies."[100] The Venetian ambassador reported later that the funeral contained only an effigy, "his actual body having buried privately many weeks ago."[101]

The council delayed the funeral for two weeks after the secret burial—until Tuesday, 23 November. When it made this decision,

Thurloe informed Henry and added an uneasy note about the army: after the funeral "wee shall begin busines, if troubles do not begin before."[102]

Preparations included setting rails along the Strand, decorating Westminster Abbey with black velvet drapery, and building a large canopied platform in the Abbey's eastern end on which to display the effigy.[103] Description of the vast funeral on 23 November refers neither to coffin nor body, only to an effigy. The effigy was "taken down from his standings, and laid in an open chariot, covered all over with black velvet." Gentlemen carried "the effigy out of the hall at Somerset House" to the hearse.[104] The procession passed down the Strand and Whitehall, "lined with rayles, and the rayles were lined with armed Souldiers."[105] Standing outside the railings were musketeers dressed in new red coats with black buttons and holding ensigns wrapped with cypress. They "made a lane, to keep off spectators from crowding the procession."[106] The French ambassador thought the ceremony little different "from ordinary proceedings of this nature; its magnificence consisted in the number of mourners, who walked from Somerset House to Westminster."[107]

John Evelyn watched "the superb Funerall of the *Protectors*" and described the procession, the hearse, and the elaborately caparisoned horses. He saw "*Oliver* lying in Effigie in royal robes . . . like a King."[108] Abraham Cowley was another "Spectator of that Solemnity, the Expectation of which had been so great." Although friends insisted he go with them, he later feigned a disinterest in the protector that he had not demonstrated at the time. After the Restoration he wrote an essay, once considered a model of English prose, which described the funeral in cadences as measured as the muffled procession-pacing drums:

> There was a mighty Train of black[-clad] Assistants, among which too divers Princes in the Persons of their Ambassadors . . . ; the Herse was magnificent, the Idol [i.e., effigy] crown'd and (not to mention all other Ceremonies which are practis'd at Royal Interments . . .) the vast Multitude of Spectators made up, as it uses to do, no small Part of the Spectacle it self. But yet, I know not how, the whole was so manag'd, that, methoughts, it somewhat

represented the Life of him for whom it was made; much noise, much Tumult, much Expence, much Magnificence, much Vainglory; briefly, a great Show, and yet, after all this, but an ill Sight.[109]

Cowley wrote that the procession was long and "very tedious." But it impressed other spectators who "saw the solomnities of funerall of Oliver Cromwell."[110] The knight marshal and fourteen mounted attendants cleared the way for eight poor men in gowns, the protector's servants and others, military commanding officers, commissioners of all sorts, the protector's doctors, judges and barons, relatives, ambassadors, lords commissioner, "grandees in close mourning . . . in divisions, each division being distinguished by drums, trumpets, standards, banners, and horses"; the hearse, banners and arms; lords and nobles; the elaborately caparisoned "Horse of Honour"; and finally the protector's halbardier guard and a horse troop.[111] After the hearse walked the chief mourner, General Fleetwood, Cromwell's son-in-law, who had married Ireton's widow Bridget. He held this honor because "this procession being assimilated as much as possible to the ceremonials of royalty, the new Protector could not mourn in public, for his Father, and Henry Cromwell was still in Ireland."[112]

Before the procession left Somerset House, the "ambassadors had some dispute with the envoy of Sweden" over precedence, and the funeral did not reach Westminster until after dark. It was explained that there were no ceremonies in the church because "there was not a single candle in Westminster Abbey to give light to the company and conduct the effigy." From the Abbey's western door "Gentlemen" carried the effigy through the nave to Henry VII's Chapel where they "placed it in that Noble Structure which was raised there on purpose to receive it, where it is to remain for some time, exposed to public view." Because of the darkness "there were . . . neither prayers, nor sermon, nor funeral oration, and after the trumpets had sounded for a short time, every one withdrew in no particular order."[113]

After the funeral Thurloe again wrote sadly to Henry Cromwell that everything had been honorably solemnized, "but alas! It was his funeral." He mentioned attempts "to blowe the coale amongst the souldiers," but all passed without incident and "in great order."[114]

For many years there was speculation over the place of burial, although the record is clear that he was buried in the Abbey. Stories abounded—his corpse was sunk in the Thames near Greenwich, buried at Windsor in place of Charles I, at Newburgh Hall in Yorkshire, at Narborough near Huntington, in the field at Naseby. Such tales suggest doubt about the funeral and an obfuscatory intent—"his friends cannot unfortunately agree amongst themselves in what way the body of the protector was disposed of." A century later the Reverend Mark Noble studied the Cromwellians and concluded reasonably that the protector "always meant to be buried in Westminster Abbey, or he would not have laid those he most loved there." He argued that Cromwell believed the future would regard him as a great ruler and did not anticipate a Restoration. The protector and his family "must have supposed it much more for his honor, that he should sleep with kings."[115] His reputation seemed secure, burial in the Abbey appropriate for his life's achievement.

Following death, his work met with literary adulation. Andrew Marvell, poet and the protector's Latin secretary, did not waver, even though he became a member of the Convention and Restoration Parliaments. "As long as future time succeeds the past, / Always thy honour, praise and name shall last."[116] John Dryden, who would trim his admiration—he probably walked in the funeral procession—to the winds of Restoration, wrote an effusive panegyric. He may have regretted this verse, written prior to the Restoration; his benediction indicated the willingness in 1658 of all but extreme royalists to accept the protectorate:

> His Ashes in a peacefull Urne shall rest,
> His Name a great example stands to show
> How strangely high endeavours may be blest,
> Where *Piety* and *Valour* joyntly goe.[117]

Abraham Cowley did not entirely condemn Cromwell, whatever he wanted people to think in later years. The procession left him in a pensive mood when he returned to his chamber, "Where I began to reflect on the Whole Life of this Prodigious Man, and sometimes I was filled with horror and Detestation of his Actions, and sometimes

I inclin'd a little to Reverence and Admiration of his Courage, Conduct and Success."[118] Restoration was not in Cowley's thought that melancholy evening. His reverence and admiration would only have increased with the protectorate's survival. Honor, valor, and success had indeed earned Cromwell burial among the kings in Henry VII's Chapel at the eastern end of the ancient abbey.

Cromwell may not have been as concerned with earthly adulation and especially where his remains were buried as were the royalists who exhumed them. In 1652 during Ireton's "solemne and magnificent" funeral, the Reverend John Owen's sermon addressed the Puritan sensibilities of the chief mourner, Oliver Cromwell. Speaking over Ireton's effigy, Owen emphasized the Puritan belief that physical remains were unimportant compared with the soul. He said of Ireton what Cromwell believed of his own mortality—that "Dismissed Saints rest in the bosom of God."[119]

4

An Unexpected Good Accident

Histories of the civil war and the Restoration have seen Cromwell's death as a step in the protectorate's inevitable collapse and considered the cause of the lord protector's demise as unimportant, uninteresting, or unworthy of investigation. He was the demon that haunted royalist nightmares, and royalist historians quickly set forth the themes of Cromwellian usurpation, Stuart legitimacy, constitutional redemption.[1] Mixed monarchy was thought to be England's glory, and for J.H. Plumb's eighteenth-century "Venetian oligarchy" it was the fortieth article of faith. Cromwell's death later became an antiquarian matter, reduced to the piquant display of a skull alleged to have been his. The investigations of why the protector died have gone no further.

The council of state did not announce during August that the lord protector was ill, nor did it determine the reason he died. Tradition has tended to accept the cause as ague, and historians have also assumed a variety of other causes. The afternoon of his death the council announced simply that Cromwell had died after an illness, possibly malaria, lasting about fourteen days.[2] This statement is the origin of the idea that Cromwell suffered a two-week illness. Dr. Bate's *Elenchus Motuum Nuperorum in Anglia,* first published in Latin in 1661, also implied that Cromwell died of an ague. In 1663 the royalist James Heath's *Flagellum* asserted that "the disease was a bastard Tertian which appeared not at first of any danger, but after a weeks time it began to shew very desperate symptoms." Eighty years later, publication of Thurloe's *State Papers* seemed to offer the tradition qualified support: in letters written between 21 August and 1 September, such observers as Thurloe, Fleetwood, and Richard Cromwell mentioned ague. But Cromwell already had been ill for three weeks. In the revival of Cromwell's reputation that began in the mid–nineteenth century, Thomas Carlyle praised a great Englishman and, taking his lead from Bate, wrote that Cromwell suffered from "a kind of tertian ague, 'bastard tertian' as the old Doctors name it."[3] At the same time W. White Cooper collected medical notes pointing to malaria. In the twentieth century F.J. Varley's *Oliver Cromwell's Latter End* described malaria as the cause.

Ague was an ailment common in England, and people blamed it on bad air, "malaria." Although malarial fevers were mentioned in Bede's *Ecclesiastical History* and Chaucer's tales, the Italian word did not come into use until the 1740s, and parasitical infection was not discovered for another century and a half. The mosquito subgenus *Anopheles maculipennis atroparvus* thrives in damp lowlands and carries either the parasite *Plasmodium malariae* or *Plasmodium vivax*. Female mosquitoes inject humans with these parasites, which invade red blood cells, multiply, break down cell walls, and release toxic byproducts into the bloodstream, causing malaria. New organisms invade other blood cells and repeat the cycle. Seventeenth-century observers thought ague appeared in predictable cycles—quartern *P. malariae* every seventy-two hours, tertian *P. vivax* every forty-eight. Not until the middle of the nineteenth century did malaria begin to recede—drainage reduced swampy lands, improved forage crops increased the animal populations that mosquitoes preferred, and effective quinine treatment was available after 1820.[4]

European forms of malaria in the seventeenth century, one should add, did not generally cause death. The usually fatal malaria is *P. falciparum,* the African type, which was unlikely to have affected seventeenth-century Englishmen. Although malaria was a common complaint, it was not "one of the great killing diseases." Neither *P. malariae* nor *P. vivax* was virulent enough to be a widespread cause of death. The old and the weak were the most likely victims.[5]

In the seventeenth century, malaria was one of the many diseases that, as Fleetwood had commented about his sister-in-law's cancer, "physitians do not understand." Doctors could not explain ague but described it as occurring when "the Blood . . . being too sharp and burnt, does not soon . . . ripen the nutritive Juice . . . but perverts a great deal of it into a Nitrosulpherous Matter, wherewith . . . [the blood] falls a fermenting. From the flowing of that nitrous Matter, which obtundes the Heat . . . a Cold is caused with a shivering: Afterward, the vital Spirit . . . begins . . . to be kindled in the Heat, by the burning of which, an intense Heat is diffus'd throughout the Whole Body: Afterward its Relicks being several . . . are sent forth by Sweat." They more accurately described symptoms. Patients exhibited "a breaking forth of the Lips, a *Jaundise,* and a *Phlegmon* suddenly raised in any part of the Body." In some patients "Pushes have broke out all over their Body, as though they had the Small-pox." With deeply settled fever, patients would be weak, thirsty, and feverish; they would have no appetite, a weak pulse, and "ruddy Urine . . . very full of Contents."[6] Malarial outbreaks occurred in spring and fall.

Remedies varied. A cure's objective was "that the Minera of the Disease be extirpated, and that the febrile Matter be eradicated out of our Body without any remaining fomes or fear of a Relapse; wherefore we diligently insist on Vomits and Purges." If that did not work, "the whole business is committed to Nature." Remedies were hit-and-miss applications of herbal medicine. A new remedy appeared during the 1650s, but applications of the Peruvian bark were uncertain and dangerous. Inert bark was ineffective, an overdose of correct bark lethal. In 1655 a London alderman named Underwood may have died from an improper dosage. This line of inquiry did not produce treatment until quinine derived from Peruvian bark became available a century and a half later. A textbook case of the time indicated that the whole business was in fact best committed to nature. A "certain noble Youth" fell into a tertian fit. He vomited "yellow and greenish Coler . . . was sorely troubled with . . . Heart-burning, a Heat and a Drought." His doctor bled eight ounces and injected "an emollient Clyster." He prescribed a thin diet and every evening an "Opiate" composed of "Conserve of Roses vitriolated half a Dram, Diascordium a Scruple, and every Morning a Scruple of Salt of Wormwood, in a spoonful of the Juice of Oranges." Treatment failed. The doctor prescribed another recipe that caused the patient to purge ten times; he bled another six ounces and induced another purge. The patient "grew perfectly well."[7] The salient points about this case are merely that a youthful nobleman could afford expensive orange juice and survived despite outlandish treatment.

After 1660 Dr. Thomas Sydenham did important work to define symptoms, but he did not produce a remedy. Of a dead patient he could only say "*ivit ad plures,*" he is with the majority. His lectures and writings were influential in Restoration England, and John Locke studied with him. Sydenham observed that agues "begin with a vigor and horror which is succeeded by heat and that afterwards by a sweat . . . the patient is troubled . . . with reaching to vomit and great sickness with thirst and a dry tongue." Autumnal agues "come in shoales, their fits upon severall persons agree in the same day and hower." He concluded that in 1661 and other years "quartans and autumnall tertians . . . first appeared about midsomer." From such data he developed ideas on conditions likely to give rise to ague.[8] Everyone in Stuart times was familiar with "successive stages of the ague-fit." Doctors had a vocabulary to describe afflicted persons, and ague was one of the most recognized complaints.[9]

And yet the explanation of ague for Cromwell's death is unsatisfactory. For one, his general health was such that although he might well have taken ill of an ague, he would not have died from the varieties known in the seventeenth century. This was not African malaria but English ague. His month-long illness did not reveal symptoms limited to those so familiar in Stuart times. Episodes were irregular. They began unexpectedly. They produced fears of eminent death. Except for the last of the protector's five episodes, each led to nearly full recovery.

Consider the lord protector's first two medical episodes, in which descriptions of his illness were unrelated to the vocabulary of ague. Observers frequently referred to his "sickness" and to "gout, and other distempers" that moved "into the body" as life-threatening "paynes in his bowells and backe." Ague-like fevers run in cyclical hot and cold "fits" based on the infecting parasite's life cycle, but observers did not report cyclical fits or other appropriate symptoms. As he was at low-lying Hampton Court, ague ought to have "come in shoales" and affected others, but other cases were not reported. Doctors might have induced "Vomits and Purges" and let blood, and observers would have reported "pushes" and "Phlegmons," yet the record contains no references to treatment. Bate never made a straightforward diagnosis but after Cromwell's death laconically dismissed the distemper as "one, and sometimes another." He avoided saying Cromwell suffered from ague or anything else. Harvey specified that the first-episode symptoms, not ague, were "forerunners to his sickness, which was to death." As late as 28 August, Richard Cromwell reported "Physicians in a Nonplus." After four weeks the doctors would have been certain if the illness were the malaria so familiar to the seventeenth century and would have diagnosed it for the protector's son. The cause of death must be related, therefore, to the cause of the illness that he displayed in early August and which no observer described in the well-known vocabulary of ague. They did describe severe attacks of abdominal pains that were debilitating, life-threatening, undiagnosed—and not ague.

The third episode ran from 18 August until 26 August and probably did include indications of ague. It began with the return of the debilitating abdominal pains displayed earlier. Only on 21 August did Cromwell's anemic body begin to exhibit some putative symptoms of ague. Fits occurred approximately in forty-eight-hour cycles, indicating the *P. vivax* parasite. And yet there was doubt. Whitelock noted ambiguously after visiting the protector on 26 August that Cromwell was ill, "as some thought of an Ague."[10] Despite the possibility of ague, no observer reported treatment consistent with contemporary practice. If he exhibited occasional ague since about age thirty—as Bate implied—it would not have been the cause of death. Bate merely claimed that during the embalming process he noted internal conditions consistent with "the Disease that for a long time he had been subject unto." This ambiguous claim is not a diagnosis, does not stand for clinical evaluation, and certainly does not name the disease.

The fourth episode began during the night of 26–27 August, when severe symptoms renewed fears for the protector's life, and lasted until 31 August. Cromwell's fits of ague seemed more serious. He was restless with pain. The doctors were "in a Nonplus" on 28 August. Were the illness simply ague, they would have given a clear diagnosis to his son for one of the century's most identifiable illnesses. Thurloe, Fleetwood, and Richard Cromwell perhaps sensed that ague did not quite explain an illness that had begun some four weeks earlier. On 31 August the patient revived suddenly, and his "water [was] good all this day" rather than full of ruddy contents. On 1 September fever did not recur according to the *P. vivax* cycle, and a day later he improved so dramatically that he was thought to be near recovery.

The final episode lasted a short time, the night of 2–3 September, for he collapsed overnight and died the next afternoon. There was no indication of ague. He was in a state of syncope at the time of death rather than in a "shaking fit" typical of those who died of ague. The Whitehall announcement confirmed the dramatic revival on 31 August and syncope on the third by describing how he "began early this morning to draw near the gate of death." It said that two weeks earlier his illness "appeared an ague in the beginning," but the beginning had occurred a month earlier. The council did not refer to the appearance of the illness in early August or its appearance at the end.[11]

The embalming failed to confirm ague as the cause of Cromwell's death. The privy council met on 3 September and ordered "the Physicians and Chirugians . . . to embowel and embalme the Body of his late Highness, and fill the same with sweet Odours." The doctors did not perform this duty until the next afternoon.[12] The embalming was unsuccessful and the body required burial prior to the funeral. Furthermore, the council had ordered a procedure contrary to Puritan belief, contemporary practice, and Cromwell's wishes.

Bate in his history mentioned the embalming. This is sometimes incorrectly termed an autopsy, but the procedure did not seek a clinical determination of the cause of death.[13] In his account he might have provided unambiguous medical information by the standards of the day, but he did not. "His Body being opened; in the *Animal* parts, the Vessels of the Brain seemed to be overcharged; in the Vitals the Lungs a little inflamed; but in the *Natural,* the source of the distemper appeared; the *Spleen,* though sound to the Eye, being within filled with matter like to the Lees of Oyl. Nor was that Incongruous to the Disease that for a long time he had been subject unto, seeing for at least thirty years he had at times heavily complained of Hypochondriacal indispositions."[14]

He wrote elliptically that what he saw was not incongruous with unspecified "Hypochondriacal indispositions" of which Cromwell allegedly had complained for years. His reference to indispositions (given in the obvious plural) has been misinterpreted in the years since to mean ague, even though the statement did not claim Cromwell died of any one of these alleged and unnamed indispositions. It is clear, therefore, that the protector's physician did not make a diagnosis based on the best medical evidence before him.

Bate implied portentously that there was minor inflammation in the brain ("Vessels . . . seemed to be overcharged") and lungs ("a little inflamed"). This signified no more than a low-grade fever at the patient's death. Fever accompanies many if not most pathologies. In the event of death from ague, inflammation and hemorrhaging in these tissues would have been so pronounced as to preclude such restrained descriptions as "seemed . . . overcharged" and "a little inflamed." These references have little significance.

Of the spleen the doctor made two claims: the organ was "sound" and it was filled with unctuous substance. In death from ague the spleen would not typically appear sound; it would be enlarged and the surface tissue thickened, even adhering to nearby tissues. For death to have occurred, the spleen would probably have enlarged and ruptured. Rupture could explain Cromwell's collapse on 3 September, but Bate was clear that the spleen was sound and had not ruptured. Reference to unctuous matter may be to a small amount of hemorrhagic substance that is typically released by parasitized blood cells and collects in the spleen.[15] Assuming these limited observations to be credible, they do not confirm ague as the cause of death but do allow the possibility that Cromwell had exhibited ague at some time during his life.

Bate offered no information about Cromwell's repeated abdominal pains. Those troubles have been detailed earlier. The pains recurred throughout the illness, but in his book they apparently had no place. The protector's Oxford-trained physician might have been more helpful than the oxymoronic conclusion that Cromwell died of "Hypochondriacal indispositions."

There was, then, an extraordinary imprecision about Bate's explanations for the cause of Cromwell's death. He was in a position to have influenced the Whitehall announcement, which practically speaking said nothing when it declared that he died of an illness lasting two weeks that "in the beginning" appeared to be ague. A few weeks later the inscription suspended at Somerset House above his bier expanded this claim: "Died Sept. 3, 1658, after fourteen Days Sickness of an Ague, with great Assurance and Serenity of Mind."[16] The Whitehall confusion had become the official conclusion. Bate's *Elenchus Motuum* claimed that Cromwell "was taken with a Slow Fever, that at length degenerated into a Bastard tertian Ague" but died of an unnamed malady not incongruous with unnamed long-term indispositions. Unnamed indispositions do not equal ague. If Bate meant ague, he was capable of saying it. Imprecise hints of ague had become the diagnosis.

It is sometimes said that Cromwell died of renal failure. He had a possible history of kidney stones, and some have thought an attack might have caused his death. Pascal wrote that "the royal family was doomed . . . if it had not been for the tiny particle of sand which got into his bladder."[17] In 1651 the protector reportedly had an attack of "gravel." Bate in 1654 implied a kidney stone attack when relating the coaching accident in Hyde Park. But the point as he eventually made it in 1661 was apocryphal and defamatory, not medical: "God Almighty thought it not fit that this Plague of *England* should thus expire." Cromwell had another attack in 1655, and the doctors summoned a noted lithotomist. During August 1658 the Venetian ambassador made two references to stones. On 20 August he reported that Cromwell's gout "has recently been aggravated by the stone." A week later, "the gout and stone . . . was ceasing" but turned into "a tertian ague."[18]

It is possible that the medical episodes in August involved kidney-stone related events, for conditions causing gout can lead to formation of stones. His tendency to form stones is impossible to determine, but if he were predisposed, he might well have developed at a much younger age a stone sufficient to have caused urinary blockage, septicemia, and death.

If he had stones, they were small, uncomfortable, and passable. For August there is an absence of firsthand references to kidney stones. Giavarina did not indicate the source of his report, and letters by Thurloe, Fleetwood, Fauconberg, and Clarges simply did not mention this identifiable problem. Bate did not mention stones in his history. No observer except Monck, writing from Scotland, mentioned "colick," a possible reference to general abdominal pains as well as to stones, nor did the medical narrative move in a manner consistent with stones. It is also significant that the doctors did not summon a lithotomist, as they had three years earlier. Bate would certainly have reported evidence that related to kidney stones and supported a conclusion of natural death, if such evidence existed. His diagnosis is incomplete, unclear, and evasive. He cited the spleen as "the Source of the distemper," although he reported it as sound, and made no reference to the kidneys. Furthermore, Fleetwood's 31 August letter had reported that Cromwell displayed an ague and, looking for good signs, noted "his water good all this day."[19] Seventeenth-century doctors particularly examined a patient's water. Four days prior to death, ague would probably have yielded cloudy water and kidney stones bloody water. During the embalming, doctors disemboweled the body and thereby had access to the internal organs. If within the space of one month he had succumbed to a kidney-stone-induced infection or renal failure, they could have found evidence, if not the stone itself.

If the protector did not die of ague or renal failure, there was another possibility, not often talked about, to which one comes with care. That was, of course, poison. Contemporaries were mindful of it, for Whitelock wrote in his diary that "some were of Opinion that he was poisoned," and the Reverend John Prestwich observed that Cromwell's disease "appeared to be that of poison."[20] They said little more in those troubled times. In subsequent years biographers and other scholars have not considered this possibility. In the 1930s F.J. Varley marked out a generally accepted position: "The sudden manner in which the patient collapsed after the shortlived rally preceding death might have led to the circulation of an absurd rumour that the patient had been poisoned." The medical evidence, "such as it is," he opined, "is sufficient to dispose of this rumour."[21]

Detection of poison is awkward without modern forensic investigation, and one cannot go back to Cromwell's era and determine absolutely what happened. Poisoners also perform their deeds in secret. Historians can cite the extant documents, and all the circumstances seem to lie on the side of the rulers, who tend to document their legitimacy rather than record misdeeds.

But poisoning was a common circumstance in early modern Europe. Renaissance and baroque princes employed food tasters and—one may infer—poisoners. When Marie de Medici married Henry IV of France in 1600, an entourage of poisoners and astrologers accompanied her from Italy, plunging the country into a confusion that lasted through the century. By the time of Louis XIV's reign, poisoning had become such a menace that the king established a special court and forbade the sale of poisons to anyone except persons known to apothecaries. His dining ritual at Versailles culminated in a ceremonial tasting and a long royal lifetime of cold food.[22]

In this regard an intriguing possibility in poisons was arising at the time Cromwell died so unexpectedly. From time immemorial vegetable poisons had been well known. But if Cromwell was poisoned, the individual who accomplished the task probably used a metallic poison. The Greeks and Romans knew of metallic poisons, and by the sixteenth century some metals—it is very interesting—were thought to have curative powers. Debates arose between followers of Galen's vegetable pharmacopoeia and Paracelsus's metallic remedies. Paracelsus applied mercury to the treatment of syphilis and emphasized the curative powers of metals: "In all things there is a poison, and there is nothing without a poison. It depends only upon the dose whether a poison is poison or not. . . . That which redounds to the benefit of man is not poison; only that which is not of service to him, but which injures him, is poison."[23]

The Galenist faculty in the University of Paris prohibited the use of metallic remedies because of their dangers.[24] The German scientist Joannes Jacobus Wepfer treated dogs and goats with Peruvian bark and other poisons to observe the effect. He corresponded with Locke as to whether poisoned animals died in convulsion or syncope.[25] Richard Mead made inquiries to understand "Mechanical Considerations in Accounting for those surprising Changes, which *Poisons* make in an Animal Body." He began, he said, "entertaining myself at Leisure Hours with Experiments on Vipers, and other Venemous Creatures; Examining now and then the Texture of . . . Malignant Substances."

He cited authorities and experimental data. Despite their curative potential, he concluded that metallic compounds were dangerous. He wrote in his book of 1702 that compounds "of a *Mineral* Nature are the most violent and deadly, the greater Gravity and Solidity of their Parts giving to these a Force and Action surpassing the mischief of *Vegetable* Juices."[26]

Among the era's best-known metallic poisons were antimony, mercury, and arsenic. Exposure to them might be categorized as acute or chronic—high concentrations for a short term or low concentrations over a long term. Poisoners calculated that acute doses acted quickly but suspiciously, whereas chronic doses were slow and insidious. Exposure was typically by ingestion, although individuals preparing such potions had to avoid inhaling fumes, especially from mercury. In more recent times, of course, the common form of exposure has been inhalation in industrial settings. The symptoms of the above-mentioned poisons when ingested held similarities because the body absorbs them through the gastrointestinal tract, and they can cause abdominal pains, gastric distress, and toxic accumulations.

It is possible that antimony caused the protector's early symptoms. An ingested dose would account, in part, for the violence of his gastrointestinal distress in early August. The Romans understood antimony's effect: they induced vomiting by drinking wine from a *calices vomitorus,* a goblet made with an alloy of antimony. Observers wrote that Cromwell first fell ill of the gout, and one may infer he was presented with a remedy that included antimony. It is absorbed slowly and produces abdominal irritation. He then displayed sickness, a word that referred to gastrointestinal distress, and "other distempers." The body would excrete a single dose within a day, leaving a residue. From the intestinal tract antimony would be absorbed slowly and concentrate in the heart, liver, and thyroid. Long-term exposure would produce toxic accumulations, cardiac problems, and skin discoloration.[27]

If Cromwell displayed symptoms of antimony at the beginning of his illness, it was unlikely the cause of his death a month later. He did have an irregular pulse on 17 August, possibly induced by a residual amount of antimony, but the length of his illness was insufficient for accumulations to cause cardiac failure. Observers of his final days would also have noted cardiac problems, and he would probably not have died in syncope but in "apoplexy." Dr. Bate's report of the embalming did not refer to the liver. As for thyroid problems, there was no evidence. Although antimony may have been present in the first dose, it did not cause his death: an acute dose would have caused suspicion, and chronic doses acted slowly over an extended time.

Mercury deserves attention as a possible poison employed during August. An early-seventeenth-century writer described it as "the hottest, the coldest, a true healer, a wicked murderer, a precious medicine, and a deadly poison—a friend that can flatter and lie."[28] Mead described it as the most deadly of mineral substances and provided details for its effect. Mercury poison was "no other than a Mixture of *Quicksilver* with *common* Salt," produced at Venice and distributed throughout Europe. Anyone with apothecary or medical training could have produced it. Mead summarized the symptoms as "violent Gripping Pains, with a distension of the Belly, Vomiting of a slimy, frothy Matter, sometimes mixt with Blood, and Stools of the same, an intolerable Heat and Thirst, with cold Sweats, Tremblings, Convulsions, *&c.*" He concluded that "the Saline Particles do impart to the *Mercury* this Malignant Quality" because they are "as so many sharp Knives or Daggers, Wounding and Stabbing the tender Coats of the Stomach, and thus causing excessive Pains, with an Abrasion of their Natural Mucus." William Ramesey in 1663 described "intollerable pains in the stomack and bowels, gripings, and erosions, a general indisposition of the whole body."[29] And consider Benvenuto Cellini's reaction following ingestion of a mercury-laden sauce: "I felt as though my stomach was on fire. . . . During the night I got no sleep, and was constantly disturbed by motions of my bowels. When the day broke, feeling an intense heat in the rectum, I looked eagerly to see what this might mean, and found the cloth covered with blood."[30]

Mercury was less familiar than other poisons and acted more rapidly, reasons a poisoner might have considered its use. Chronic doses of inorganic mercury were absorbed through the gastrointestinal tract and accumulated in organs, especially kidneys. The victim displayed abdominal pains, nausea, diarrhea—Ramesey's "gripings, and ero-

sions," Cellini's "motions" and heat. The poison could produce gingi-
vitis, salivation, oral soreness, perspiration; it could lead to restlessness and depression. The symptoms of mercury poisoning resembled
those in Cromwell's medical narrative. During August observers noted
such symptoms as abdominal and back pain, indisposition, gastrointestinal distress, sweating, interrupted kidney function, and depression.
Individually nonspecific, together they indicate the possibility of mercury. Observers noted sharp bowel pains consistent with the language
of Mead, Ramesey, and Cellini that described stabbing sensations and
"gripings, and erosions, a general indisposition of the whole body."
Before ague masked the problem, observers referred to Cromwell's
"sickness," a word in the seventeenth century that denoted nausea,
vomiting, diarrhea—"gripings, and erosions" rather than merely feeling unwell. Observers mentioned his sickness as "violent." Modern
authorities state that mercury's effects appear within a few hours and
last for several days, causing "intense pain, which may be accompanied by vomiting."[31]

The protector's illness lasted long enough for chronic applications of mercury. Prior to August there were no reports of poor health.
On 30 or 31 July, while his daughter lay dying, he exhibited routine
gout, followed in a short time by severe abdominal pains and gastrointestinal sickness. A mixture that included mercury as well as antimony would explain these symptoms. Harvey said that Cromwell
was "under bodily distempers, forerunners to his sicknesse, which
was to death." Cromwell was thought near death, then recovered dramatically, the pattern that appeared in the later episodes, which were
also irregular in occurrence, violent at the onset, and caused fears the
patient was near death. The last episodes were closely spaced, which
implied that the poisoner had adjusted doses to produce maximum
effect with minimum suspicion. It was the poisoner's good fortune
that after three weeks, malaria in Cromwell's weakened body masked
the poison and provided a diagnosis for those who sought one.

The possibility of mercury in Cromwell's body appears in
Fleetwood's letter of 31 August, which recorded the protector's "slumbering sleepes, his pulse better, his water good all this day." The date
of the letter is important, for it was when the protector made another

dramatic recovery from a near-death episode. Fleetwood was so surprised at the improvement in sleep, pulse, and water that he declared, "His return will be . . . as life from the deade." The Venetian ambassador similarly reported, "The improvement has certainly been sudden, unexpected and extraordinary." Several points may be ventured: Cromwell's kidneys had not functioned properly the day before, and perhaps for some days prior; function returned as another dose of poison abated; and several weeks of exposure to poison had not fully damaged the delicate kidney tissues. Cromwell's good water on 31 August was consistent with mercury. Short-term exposure can cause oliguria, the secretion of small amounts of urine, but generally not anuria, the failure to secrete. Renal injury, according to modern authorities, "follows long-term exposure to inorganic mercury" and injures the glomerulus, the kidneys' network of filtering capillaries.[32] Cromwell must have had a relatively brief exposure to the poison, for its short-term effects could be responsible for temporary suppression of urine. The doses were sufficient by the fourth week to begin suppressing urine but not strong enough or long-term enough to damage the kidneys. As poison was excreted from his body by 31 August, kidney function likely resumed, allowing "good water all this day" and other signs of recovery. His water would have appeared clear to seventeenth-century observers, who were unable to measure the chemical indications of mercury.

Arsenic was another possible agent, for since the Middle Ages it had been "the poison of choice." Borgia Italy and Bourbon France had many victims.[33] Whether poisoners used acute or chronic doses of the tasteless substance depended on their willingness to risk suspicion. An acute dose of arsenic poisoning acts rapidly, but its effects are obvious; discomfort may begin within twelve hours, or much less if there is no food in the stomach. Chronic arsenic "impairs vitality slowly and progressively," sometimes requiring years because effects are cumulative, and its gastrointestinal symptoms are "so gradual that the possibility of arsenic poisoning may be overlooked."[34] Chronic doses were difficult to detect, making arsenic an appealing agent to persons with sinister motives. Doses carried through the gastrointestinal tract and blood to the liver, the kidneys, the lungs, the spleen, the intestines, and eventually the skeleton. Symptoms could eventually include a burning throat and difficulty swallowing, "garlic" breath, vomiting, diarrhea, suppression of urine, and long-term decay of kidney tissues.[35] The popularity and availability of arsenic suggest that a skilled poisoner in 1658 might have considered it. The poisoner merely required access to the victim for several months, if not years, to administer doses that eventually induced a natural-appearing death. Not until a century later, in 1752, did doctors in Britain testify during a capital trial and help convict a defendant charged with using arsenic in chronic doses.[36]

Chronic arsenic requires many months to be effective and thus cannot explain the thirty-three-day duration of Cromwell's illness. In modern industrial settings an acute exposure to a large dose of arsenic can produce some motor dysfunction in ten days, whereas a chronic exposure may not appear for "a period of years" and even then may be difficult to ascertain. Given the protector's good health in mid-1658, the display of gout on 30 July was the first occasion when a poisoner might possibly have acted. A skillful series of chronic doses starting then would not have begun taking effect for weeks, or even months, because such doses worked "slowly and progressively." The first effects of arsenic can include inflammation of vessels in the kidneys and an increase of protein in the urine, neither condition discernible in the seventeenth century. Given enough time it can induce anuria. Arsenic will begin to accumulate invisibly in the victim's hair in perhaps two weeks and form deposits under the fingernails in six. Unlike the insidious onset of arsenic-induced symptoms, the protector's illness began suddenly, with severe pains, gastrointestinal violence, expectations of death. This implies a primary agent more toxic than arsenic.[37]

Although arsenic was not the likely agent during August, descriptions of the final episode indicate the distinct possibility of a single massive dose of arsenic. Ingestion of such a dose of arsenic can produce shock, fluid loss, convulsion, and coma. Cromwell's kidney function was suppressed toward the end of August, yet the significant point is that four days prior to death it was noted "water good all this day." Dr. Bate's report on the embalming was specific in claiming the spleen as "the Source of the distemper," though describing it as "sound," and he did not mention the diagnostically significant kidneys or the presence of decayed tissue. Cromwell's emotional stress in the last episode, the suddenness of his collapse—the very suddenness that Varley discounted—and the final period in syncope imply a massive dose of arsenic on the night of 2–3 September. Observers did not refer to arsenic's characteristic "garlic" odor because the time between administration of that dose and the patient's death was only a few hours.

A further consideration—beyond antimony, mercury, and arsenic—is the presence of toxic metals in the environment. The households of the gentry and the nobility included minuscule amounts of toxins that tainted food, such as lead in pewter, pottery, and glassware. In the seventeenth century people did not tend to die from this exposure, which nonetheless could have affected their general health in the presence of other problems. The protector was physically exhausted when the gout occurred, because he had neglected food and rest during his daughter's illness, and any lead ingested from the environment could have accentuated the effects of gout, malaria, and poison.

To recapitulate: The pattern of symptoms indicates that on 30 July or thereabouts Cromwell fell ill of the gout, for which he received a remedy that contained antimony, probably mixed with some mercury.

Two days after Elizabeth's death on 6 August, his distemper became more serious, for he could then have received a dose of mercury alone, which increased the symptoms. He suffered further pain and gastrointestinal distress. The debilitating illness raged for about five days. On 10 August he was bedridden, unable to travel by barge to his daughter's funeral at Westminster. Death seemed imminent. After the thirteenth he began to recover, and on the morning of the seventeenth was so well he went horseback riding for an hour. During this time no treatment was recorded, no diagnosis made, no reference to ague or kidney stones.

During the evening of 17 August he received another dose of mercury. That afternoon he had consulted with doctors, who found an irregular pulse; he swooned and perspired. A physician "refreshed" him with more "Cordials." The following morning a physician even predicted a symptom, that he would become lightheaded. He suffered sickness and pains similar to those earlier. On 21 August his body began to exhibit *P. vivax* malaria when the pain "turned into a tertian ague." He began what one now would describe as a series of malarial fits, occurring late on the night of the twenty-second, late on the twenty-fourth, and late on the twenty-sixth. These were consistent with the era's vocabulary of ague. In the fever interval during the day of the twenty-fourth, he made an ill-advised trip from Hampton Court to Whitehall and on the twenty-sixth discussed politics with Whitelock.

The next likely poison-induced episode, again with mercury, followed the malarial fit of 26–27 August, when he relapsed from an apparent recovery. Alarming symptoms appeared and continued several days. They resembled prior episodes but were more serious. The doctors were unable to provide the protector's son with a diagnosis, observers were perplexed, and all again expected death. On 31 August he appeared beyond recovery, then improved suddenly as poison abated and ague failed to return; he regained kidney function. On 2 September he appeared weak but apparently in a recovery so pronounced as to seem miraculous. At this singular moment, Dr. Clarges—be it noted—wrote to General Monck that the protector was recovering, unless "some unexpected accident happen."

The poisoner must have administered the final dose during the evening of 2 September, and it would have differed from previous doses in that it probably contained a massive amount of arsenic, enough to push the protector over the edge. Overnight the patient's health collapsed. He became depressed, lightheaded, feverish, sleepless with pain; he had a sore throat and thirst caused, one senses, by arsenic-induced fluid loss. On the morning of 3 September he began "to draw near the gate of death," and he died in syncope during the afternoon— "unexpectedly."[38]

Analysis of the death, thus, raises the probability that someone with access to Cromwell possessed medical knowledge of antimony, mercury, and arsenic and understood that a careful combination would do what he desired. Antimony at the beginning, he knew, would quickly produce an ambiguous "distemper" that would weaken the protector. During most of August the more likely agent was mercury, which was not easy to detect. Then, at the end, the poisoner seems to have re-sorted to a massive dose of arsenic, insuring that the protector would not recover.

Royalists possessed clear motive, present opportunity, and assured method to encompass the lord protector's death. Routed in the midcentury turmoil—whether it was rebellion, revolution, or civil war—the exiles sought nothing so much as restoration and revenge. Oliver Cromwell was the villain in their misfortune, usurper of their position, traitor to their divine right. As lord general he had defeated and judged a king. As lord protector he governed a powerful maritime republic. As king he would have placed Charles Stuart at further re-move from the throne.

After nearly a decade, England in 1658 was adjusting to the new regime, and the royalists in exile feared their day was passing. One of Charles Stuart's secretaries of state, Sir Edward Nicholas, wrote from Bruges a year prior to Cromwell's death that "all letters from England affirm that Cromwell is now absolutely master of all England and secure against all intestine opposition."[39] His mastery was easier as the protectorate became settled—social hierarchy, bicameral Parlia-ment, single-person rule, secure land titles. Many who were pro-nounced royalists in 1661 had fed eagerly enough at the Cromwellian trough when the protectorate was not "the interregnum" but England's once-and-future government. Men who sought political careers acted accordingly. Restoration England was awash with royalists who, not long since, had been collaborators with the protectorate, such as Sir Orlando Bridgman, who presided over the trials of Charles I's judges.[40] Nicholas concluded that trusting in mere fate was insufficient for re-venge and restoration, for he wrote Sir Edward Hyde in 1657, "There will be little hope for the K to do much good in order to his Restora-tion untill that villain be knockt in the head."[41] Sir Edward did not turn phrases casually. The court-in-exile long conspired to effect "Restoration," but its resources allowed little more than merely "breathing together."

The exiles considered various tactics.[42] The Venetian ambassador reported in February 1657, a year and a half before the protector's death, that Charles Stuart "had many devices and high hopes of bringing off some important stroke against Cromwell" but awaited money promised from Spain.[43] Early the next year he reported in cipher that "a trustworthy person has informed me in confidence that his Majesty is only waiting for the breakup of the frost to cross the water with an adequate body of troops and make a descent upon this kingdom."[44] Weeks later, John Stapley of Sussex supposedly confessed to Cromwell that "24 leading men in the county . . . had conspired . . . and declared that they would defend the Stuart cause."[45] Such rumblings concerned the regime but in fact represented an improbable threat. Royalists at Brussels hoped Spanish funds would allow invasion, but Nicholas at Bruges concluded that "I cannot hope, much less believe, we shall be enabled to attempt anything this spring from these parts."[46] Hyde wrote in April, "The King cannot satisfy himself of one plan that can be depended on in any place of England." At the same time he asked English agents to advise Charles "if any extraordinary change takes place, such as the death of Cromwell."[47]

Rather than descend from without, the émigrés could more easily consider encouraging disorder from within. Giavarina reported rumors that Stuart agents "sojourn secretly in these realms in great numbers . . . seeking for means to reduce the present rule in England to disorder."[48] Should the regime falter, Charles could then represent order and legitimacy and invade by acclamation. But Thurloe collected intelligence, intercepted correspondence, and apprised the council of state of the exiles' activities.

There was the possibility of assassination. Nicholas urged Charles Stuart "to set a good price" on the heads of Cromwell and his leading commanders because he believed that their assassination would weaken the regime.[49] The government denounced alleged royalist conspiracies against the protector. Two men "armed with great muskets loaded full with ball" had supposedly prepared in 1657 to ambush Cromwell's coach on its way from Whitehall to Hampton Court, "killing all those inside." Cromwell habitually took precautions by personally ordering the route his coachman traveled, and the men waited along the wrong road. The government arrested three Frenchmen for allegedly placing "bombs and other fireworks" in Whitehall Palace and attempting to kindle the area near Cromwell's rooms. During the confusion caused by the ensuing nighttime fire they might have murdered the protector. Royalists replied that "the conspiracy has been made up by the [protectoral] Court itself to cast odium on the name of the king." This may or may not have been true, but Stuart agents' activity gave color to such allegations. Giavarina wrote in May 1658, "The last conspiracy was no sooner discovered than they began to devise another."[50]

Open assassination was unlikely because an attack similar to Ravaillac's murder of Henry IV in a Paris street was all but impossible. To emphasize that point the government publicized the alleged plots in early 1657. Cromwell increasingly lived in seclusion either at Hampton Court or at Whitehall, and lifeguards traveled with him between the two. The evangelist Fox described how guards surrounded the coach and prevented anyone from approaching. Bate claimed Cromwell "never was at ease" and was suspicious "of all Strangers, especially if they seemed joyful," and reported that he traveled "wearing Armour underneath his clothes, and Offensive Weapons . . . never coming back the steight publick Rode, or the same way, or never passing but in great haste and with speed."[51]

The exiled court doubtless was in a quandary. It did not have sufficient resources to mount an invasion. It could not hide conspiratorial activity from Thurloe's intelligence service. It could not assault Cromwell's person because of security. Their projects seemed so futile that a few weeks before Cromwell's death a royalist lamented, "When I looke on our cause, there still comes some motion to hope, but then the persons and actions lay all in the dust."[52]

Everything became urgent by the summer of 1658, for exiles feared that during the forthcoming session Parliament would place a monarch's crown on Cromwell's head. The kingship question had long agitated protectoral politics. As early as 1651, Cromwell had urged a settlement "somewhat with monarchical power in it." Perhaps he had made Ireton's funeral a state event in order to emphasize his own leadership. During the previous sitting Parliament seemed ready to bestow the purple, had the protector agreed. Royalist memoirist Philip Warwick was among those who feared the kingship question was near resolution, referring sarcastically to the ministers who during August

1658 prayed for Cromwell's recovery, "so necessary to divers things, then of great moment to be dispatched," meaning the kingship.[53] Despite the émigrés' sense of urgency, their plots had proven ineffective, and in the summer of 1658 they seemed powerless. From their viewpoint at the beginning of that summer, events moved without them, and prospects for their return to power and station receded rapidly. And yet, though one might believe them capable of hiring roadside assassins and placing incendiaries, could they have maneuvered an agent close to the lord protector? Could Charles Stuart have successfully reached around the protectoral court's formidable security and left no trace? It has all seemed unlikely.

The suggestion of a royalist conspiracy causes discomfort, perhaps because it taints the Restoration's central institution and the idea of constitutional redemption. The official record does not admit the suggestion, though one would hardly expect otherwise. Such a dramatic plot seems appropriate to nineteenth-century historical fiction. The idea was unthinkable to the Restoration generation, which placed its faith in monarchy's legitimacy and tacitly agreed that the lord protector had to have died of natural causes.

Yet something in the medical record appears amiss, and a search for the possibility of conspirators can begin in the records of Charles Stuart's secretary of state in exile, Sir Edward Nicholas. His papers do not attaint him of plotting to knock Cromwell in the head, but significantly the surviving collection is not complete. The papers fall so curiously and obviously silent in mid-1658 that Sir George F. Warner, who in 1920 published the volume containing correspondence for 1657–60, commented on the point in his preface. Correspondence falters following a short letter to Nicholas from the earl of Ormond, dated 24 August 1658 and written from Hoogstraten in the Netherlands, where Charles was hunting. Ormond was another dispirited royalist: "Our condition is most sad, and the more that there appears no visible way out of it." The collection then reveals a possibly informative lapse. Warner noted: "Any letters which Nicholas may have received relating to his [Cromwell's] illness and death have not been preserved, and the first intimation that he was dead is in a letter from Sir A. Hume [dated 14 September 1658 at The Hague]. . . . The only letters during the rest of 1658 are from the King himself. . . . After an interval the correspondence begins again in March, 1659, and from this point it is fuller and of increasing interest."[54] The absence of letters from late August and September prompted Warner to assume the exiles' reaction when they heard the protector had died: "The news that the most formidable obstacle to royalist hopes was removed by Cromwell's death on 3 September must therefore have been welcome." Warner's understatement notwithstanding, exiled royalists did not rely on tardy intimation. Cromwell's illness was not made public, but neither was it a secret, since rumors did circulate. Nonetheless, during the time that illness and death were removing "the most formidable obstacle" to restoration, the papers of Charles Stuart's secretary and confidant are curiously silent.

The surviving "intimation" letter in Nicholas's correspondence at least offers insight to the exiles' expectations and their preoccupation with an "accident," by which they meant assassination rather than an innocuous incident. Sir Alexander Hume served at The Hague as chamberlain to Charles's sister, the princess of Orange, and was connected to the exile network. Using polite obfuscation, he earlier had urged Nicholas to encompass the protector's death: "The Royall party in England ar indeed in a very sad condition and haue cause enough to fear worse, unlesse God in his infinite mercy preuent it by some unexpected good accident for the King."[55] Warner did not doubt that Hume referred to assassination.[56] In the 14 September 1658 "intimation" letter, Hume assumed that Cromwell had died unnaturally: "Wee are now in great expectation to hear what this late great accident will produce in England. God send us to hear something that may be comfortable."[57]

Nicholas's papers indicate that murder was much in the secretary's mind, for prior to the "late great accident" he urged Charles to offer bounties to assassins. He had a revealing correspondence in 1656 with a royalist agent in Paris, Thomas Ross, who relayed a proposal from England. Although Ross's letter was not preserved, Nicholas reiterated its contents in his reply. He wrote from Cologne, where Charles Stuart had taken his household. He said he had acquainted Charles with "the contents of most of your letter" but omitted "that particular

concerning an offer." According to Nicholas's reply, which used two
code names for the protector, Ross had relayed "an offer made . . . by
a gentleman of estate and interest with Mr. Jackson *[Cromwell]* to put
Norton *[Cromwell]* out of possession, he hauing (you say) infallible
ways and means to effect it, if he haue approbation and encouragement from Mr. Hall *[the King]* to under take it."

The "gentleman of estate and interest" was not identified. Sir
Edward claimed he would not inform Charles of the proposal, but his
reply to Ross implied he did. He first said Charles need not be informed because anyone "that will undertake such a charitable business will do it principally out of conscience and honour for the goodness
of the deed." Nicholas then used a telling passive-voice verb that referred to Charles Stuart: "I am assured," he wrote carefully, "no man
that shall effect so glorious a work can possibly fail of an ample and
honourable reward." Only Charles could have offered such assurance
to Nicholas. He ended with a pledge of secrecy and "encouragement
for any person that hath a real inclination to perform so charitable a
deed in so seasonable a time."[58] Charles must have given the trusted
Nicholas assurances similar to those he gave his brother James: "Whatever rewards you shall think necessary to promise to any man who
shall do signal service, I will make good."[59]

Edward Hyde acquiesced in Nicholas's offering bounties to those
who might knock Cromwell in the head. Nicholas had written him in
1657 that the only arguments against such a policy were more "fond
fancies . . . than solid reasons."[60] Hyde replied, "You and I shall never
differ in opinion what should be done with or against Cromwell," add-
ing that some thoughtful men may "dissent from us in the particular
you mention."[61] Hyde's papers become as suspiciously sparse as
Nicholas's during the following summer. A surviving letter, written to
Nicholas's son in mid-August 1658, is especially curious because it
eschews Hyde's usual concentration on high politics and avoidance
of personal banter. He wrote at the time Cromwell lay ill and included
a sentence that appears frivolous: "Tell Lady Nicholas that the stills
are up, and they spend their time wholly in making strong waters."[62]
His uncharacteristic words may simply mean what they say, the result
of a sudden interest in domestic distillery, or they may imply acquies-

cence for plans then in motion and phrased to avert suspicion were the letter intercepted.

Nicholas wrote several letters to Hyde in early September. On the first of the month he mentioned "Cromwell's illness" and rumors that "many believe he may now be dead." Three days later he reported Cromwell's move to Whitehall, which had occurred on 24 August, and further rumors that he may "die shortly." Cromwell's habit of rebounding into recovery during August makes Nicholas's speculation interesting. He also expressed the hope, in light of his knowledge that there would be no Spanish subsidy for an invasion, that Cromwell "may say something on his deathbed to the City and the army that may be a means to bring his Majesty home in peace." Two days later he mentioned that "Cromwell's physicians are said to affirm that he cannot live till spring." And by 8 September he certainly knew that Cromwell had died.[63]

Nicholas understood the advantages of quietly encouraging a person to undertake "such a charitable business" as assassination. The idea was simple, inexpensive, and easy to disavow. And who might need encouragement? For one man to effect "some unexpected good accident for the King" required no more than an agent concealed in the protectoral court. It is interesting that at least two such persons were present in Whitehall Palace the afternoon the lord protector died— royalists with clear motive, household members with present opportunity, physicians with assured method.

The ambitious, ubiquitous, and unscrupulous Dr. George Bate is the person on whom suspicion falls for the lord protector's death. The case for his involvement must be circumstantial, but it is not easy to dismiss. The indictment rests on anomalies in his career, the tenor and detail in *Elenchus Motuum,* prescriptions in his pharmacopoeia, his medical "diary," his Restoration rewards, contemporary rumor, and finally, his previously disregarded confession to the deed.

Bate was "a concealed royalist" during the 1650s, according to the well-informed Oxford diarist Anthony Wood, as well as "a most noted physician of his time." Born in Buckinghamshire about 1609, Bate had received a bachelor of medicine degree from Oxford in 1629. He began to practice near Oxford "among precise and puritanical people, he being then taken to be one of their number," a phrase indicating that he observed as much as attended them. In 1637 he became a doctor of medicine. Then abandoning the cover of "precise and puritanical," he became Charles I's physician when the court was at Oxford. In 1640 he moved to London and "closed with the times for interest sake." He became physician at Charter-House, fellow of the College of Physicians, and by 1651 the concealed royalist was physician to General Cromwell, and he "did not stick . . . to flatter him in an high degree," as well as other Commonwealth dignitaries.[64]

Bate was no ordinary physician. Access to Charles I required commitment to the royal person and cause. His move to London "for interest sake"—prior to the outbreak of war—implied his placement as a royalist agent in the Puritan-inclined city. Later involvement with Commonwealth and protectorate affairs also implied his royalist agency at the center of the new regime. Historians have noted that at the time spies and conspirators were often doctors or apothecaries, either as legitimate practitioners or quacks. Such men had a naturally secretive air because their profession relied on closely guarded remedies and pharmacopoeia; they might easily be abroad in London at all hours and were able to gather information from vulnerable patients.[65] Bate fitted the pattern all too well. In 1648 his political sentiments were published as *The Royal Apology;* revised and enlarged, the *Apology* in 1651 became the first part of *Elenchus Motuum Nuperorum in Anglia,* a royalist narrative of the 1640s. Whether Cromwell knew of this authorship is unclear. On the one hand, Norman Moore speculated in the 1880s that the protector accepted Bate's medical service because in the *Apology* "Bate praises Charles I with the warmth of a client, and Oliver perhaps thought that a man so grateful to one patron would appreciate another."[66] On the other hand, Cromwell once said, "The State, in choosing men to serve them, takes no notice of their opinions, if they be willing faithfully to serve them, that satisfies."[67] Cromwell was confident of the regime's future, diffident to his doctor's past.

Elenchus Motuum Nuperorum in Anglia is a crisply written Latin narrative that was not published in English until the reign of James II, well after the author's death. Its guides were royalist political sympathy and Arminian religious sensibility. Referring to Cromwell's death, the author wrote, "Behold the perfidiousness of Mortal Men, and a wonderful instance of Divine Providence, which presides over, and alters Humane Affairs and Governments, as it seemeth Good to the Almighty!" Many details and observations reveal an insider's familiarity with the protectoral court. The author feigned a judicious posture but consistently found the king's opponents flawed, ambitious, disorderly.

Norman Moore wrote, "There is nothing in the 'Elenchus' to make its author respected among contemporary politicians."[68] Perhaps. But for Cromwell's death the book is invaluable because Bate inevitably provided incriminating information. The book attainted "perverse men . . . and crafty Promoters of publick Debates" for the midcentury crisis. They disrupted "the old customs . . . that made *England* for many Ages past to flourish." It maintained that "*Britain* was never in a more flourishing condition" than before the civil war, but some persons "could not repress the insolency and wantonness that sprung from so great prosperity." The author dated the crisis to a time after "we had been unfortunate in some foreign expedition," which resulted in moderate but lawful "impositions." The king finally refused to call new Parliaments "so the heats and Animosities might be allayed." Hence the crisis, as Bate saw it: "Crafty and restless men [spread] their poyson over all *England . . . That Religion was ruined, the publick Liberty opprest, and the Laws in danger of being subverted.*" These restless schemers capriciously disrupted the golden age of Stuart monarchy, "those halcyon days of Peace and Tranquility."

Bate's interpretation surely characterized the royalists. They had believed the execution of a Stuart monarch impossible, and Charles's death was the one event they would not forgive. Revenge shaped their ideas, defined their politics, inspired their actions. They could not admit Charles I's failures as king. They could not understand honest opposition. They could not abide Cromwell, whom they held responsible for the trial and unanimous guilty verdict. When describing the court president, John Bradshaw, reading the sentence, Bate wrote in biblical cadences: "Then was his *sacred Majesty* hurried away by the Souldiers to be by them (most like to his Saviour) scoffed at before he suffered."

The book's iconography paralleled the fashions of baroque art—martyred saints, *ecce homo,* Christ's scourging. The army brought Charles before the people at the Banqueting House as a mortal. In Bate's devout view the king "most humbly resigned his sacred head to his Maker to be struck off by a masked Executioner; which was quickly done at one blow. So fell Charles and so with him expired the Honour and Soul of *Great Britain.*"

According to Bate, death did not end Charles's ignominy. After Charles's head was sewn to his body, Bate alleged that Cromwell opened the royal coffin "and *with his fingers severed the head from the shoulders*" in order that he might "glut his traiterous eyes with that Spectacle." Royalists charged that the army gave Charles's body to "a rascally Quack Physician" for embalming and sought "to blacken his Memory amongst men."[69] Cromwell "was not unworthy of Government, had he not invaded it by Villainy, Fraud, Treachery, and the Blood, not only of others, but of his own Prince."

This grand indictment subjected Cromwell to due punishment, and Bate knew the methods by which royalists sought to extract it. He knew that "Royalists in England . . . cast about all ways how they might restore the King to His ancient Dignity, and by shaking off the Yoke of Tyranny, recover at length their own Liberty." He knew the details of conspiracies "by faithful Messengers, by Cyphers and Characters, by Signs and dumb language of Fingers, [to] exhort, animate, and stir up Parties against Cromwell." He approved "various Colours and Pretences" to appear obeisant while "jumbling affairs, and Plotting," for he disguised himself with various colors to appear obeisant.

The author was well informed about methods of protectoral intelligence and security. He knew how information was gathered from the mails, by questioning messengers, by spies, "*Evedroppers,*" and double agents. He knew Cromwell "never was at ease" and was wary of unanticipated circumstances. He knew the protector "took particular notice of the Carriage, Manner, Habit and Language of all Strangers, especially if they seemed joyful." He knew details of Cromwell's security—armor underneath his clothing, carrying several offensive weapons, varying his routes. He alleged that Cromwell did not sleep in the same room, used rooms with more than one exit, and posted guards at all doors. He knew that outsiders would likely fail to reach the protector's person.

Bate's account of Cromwell's illness was oblique to other records because he disguised the narrative. From other sources it is absolutely clear that a week *prior* to the death of his daughter Cromwell fell ill of gout and then immediately displayed debilitating pains and sickness that were not gout and left him bedridden. Within the week he was thought near death. Bate revised the story. He erroneously claimed that "shortly after" Elizabeth's death, Cromwell was taken with a slow fever that eventually became a "bastard" tertian ague: "For a Weeks time the Distemper so continued without any dangerous symptoms, (as appearing sometimes one, and sometimes another kind of distemper) that every other Day he walked abroad." This was inaccurate and deceptive. He moved the onset of the illness to a later time in August. Cromwell's symptoms were in fact dangerous, alarming, and violent. Bate described the debilitating pains as merely "Slow Fever." He implied but did not state a malarial diagnosis, despite reference elsewhere in the book to how "men in an Ague after a burning heat, fall presently into a shaking cold." He used an imprecise diagnostic idiom, for "Bastard Tertian" implies symptoms that are not actually ague. He compressed chronology to imply a connection between the onset of the "Slow Fever" and ague, although three weeks separated the beginning of illness and the probable ague. He claimed that Cromwell "walked abroad" every other day, an outright fabrication. He omitted references to the painful, life-threatening, and undiagnosed first-episode distemper that so alarmed other observers. Bate wrote shortly after these events, and his inaccuracies surely were disingenuous disguises thrown over Cromwell's medical condition rather than excusable time-fogged recollections.

In his book Bate reported several matters occurring on 17 and 18 August. Cromwell met with his doctors, who observed an irregular pulse, sweating, lightheadedness. Carried to bed, and "being refreshed with Cordials, he made his Will, but onely about his Privat and Domestick Affairs." He did not sleep "the greatest part of the Night," despite (probably because of) these so-called cordials. In the morning he prayed with his wife, a physician predicted "*our Patient will be light-headed,*" doctors thought death near, and Bate claimed that he was in "danger." Bate did not report these incidents in chronological order but separated the taking of cordials from sleeplessness by nearly a full printed page of dense text. Other observers referred to sleeplessness in connection with the presence of pain; Bate disassociated the putative poison-related cordials from the pains they caused.

The account omitted Cromwell's subsequent third episode and references to ague. It jumped to the fourth episode, noting Cromwell's move to London but emphasizing events of 30–31 August. He reported that the doctors consulted with each other "in the Chamber of the aforementioned Doctor [possibly Bate himself], who at the time was troubled with a grievous *Head-ach,* and an *Imposthume* in his ear." The latter information seems gratuitous but excused Bate from the sickroom so another doctor could independently describe Cromwell's serious condition. The second doctor, therefore, sat with Cromwell through the night and reported "how ill he had been in the last fit, they all conclude that he could hardly out-live another." Bate omitted the apparent recovery on 1 September. As a result of "this Sentence" by the doctors, the privy council met with the protector on 2 September "that he would name his Successor." Cromwell was "in a drowsy fit" and answered "out of purpose." His senses were clouded but "he answered, *Yes*" when asked if Richard should be his successor. "The Day following . . . he yielded up the Ghost about three of the Clock." Bate wrote the last words with a brisk Arminian flourish.[70]

Elenchus Motuum described the author's motive and opportunity; his posthumously published pharmacopoeia revealed his probable method. He did not make his medical secrets known during his lifetime, of course, for professional success depended on an illusion of skill. Medicine had few generally accepted treatments, and physicians experimented with their own remedies. Bate kept Latin records of his prescriptions, as useful for his apothecary as for himself, and did not imagine that some years later they would be published in full. In the later seventeenth century collections of remedies became a publishing staple. Medical progress was available to only a few persons in the larger towns, leaving even landed gentry medically isolated in times of crisis. There was a market for the pharmacopoeia and an even larger market for medical books in English that reasonably literate persons could use. Bate may have thought his papers private, but after his death James Shipton collected and published his "*Arcana and Prescripts.*" The book sold well, even though in Latin, and Shipton prepared a second edition with a hundred more of Bate's prescriptions. The two editions sold six thousand copies, making it a remarkably successful book for its time. William Salmon in 1694 expanded it and issued a thousand-page English translation, *Pharmacopoeia Bateana: Or, Bate's Dispensatory.* Bate's translated original recipes were accompanied by Salmon's directions for preparing the compounds.[71]

Bate used mercury in many of his remedies. His recipe for "Mercurius Prœcipitatus albus, white Precipitate" is an interesting example in light of Cromwell's gout because "it is used in the French-Pox, Dropsie, Gout, Yellow Jaundice, &c." Salmon added extensive directions for variously precipitating the mercury salt and warned of its danger. When trying to produce a very white precipitate, he advised dissolving quicksilver "in a Vessel whose mouth is very large, so that the red Vapours of the Sp. *N.* may vanish more easily." Full doses should be given only if the compound of crystals had been fired to destroy "most of its Acid points." He warned, "This Precipitate . . . ought to be given only to Persons of a strong Constitution." If administered externally "it ought to be used with Caution, because *Mercury* is an Enemy to the Native heat, Nerves, Bones, &c. and therefore may at long run prove of ill consequence." Bate's routine medical doses of mercury were not lethal, of course, but they were high enough to have provoked distress in almost any patient.[72]

Another of Bate's medical records has recently come to light, a "medical diary" for the years 1654 to 1660. The small leatherbound book is not a diary as such but a ninety-eight-page alphabetical list of patients and his consultations with them. Bate obviously transcribed the original notes and organized them shortly after the Restoration. It is unlikely that he continued seeing patients after about the beginning of 1661, because his own health began to deteriorate.[73] The diary is neatly written, without corrections, in a consistent hand and ink, not erratically jotted day by day. There is no surprise in the omission of his most famous patient, the lord protector, whom he had attended since 1651. Bate purposely made this orderly arrangement of his patients' records, save for one of them.[74]

Bate's "diary" contains notes for consultations in August 1658 while he also attended the lord protector. He saw "Lord Rich" on the eighth and the tenth, "Sir Thomas Reinall" on the ninth, and "Mrs. Rolles in threadneedlestreet" on the twelfth. These were prominent persons, typical of Bate's patients in general. The whereabouts of the first two cannot be verified for the days mentioned, but a reasonable inference is that they were with the protector in Hampton Court. Robert, Baron Rich was a member of a prominent family, notwithstanding his pleading remission for a parliamentary fine. His father was the Puritan and parliamentarian earl of Warwick who was bearer of the sword of state during Cromwell's 1657 inauguration as lord protector and whose death in early 1658 elevated Baron Rich to the title. His son also served in the inauguration, married Cromwell's youngest daughter, Frances, in November 1657, and died three months later. The baron's health was precarious, and he died several months after the protector's demise. Sir Robert Reynolds (not Thomas, as miscopied into the diary) was an MP and Cromwell's solicitor general. Cromwell knighted his son, a valiant colonel in the wars who had married Henry Cromwell's sister-in-law. He died in 1661 and was adaptable enough to have received a knighthood from Charles II. Mrs. Rolles was the widow of a prominent lawyer and judge, a professional colleague of Whitelock's, and a resident of the City, where Bate attended her.[75]

The implication for the protector's medical narrative is at least curious, if not ominous. Bate saw the first two patients, doubtlessly at Hampton Court, on 8, 9, and 10 August, days when Cromwell, also at Hampton Court, displayed increasingly debilitating symptoms from a second dose of poison, probably mercury administered on the eighth. On the tenth Cromwell was unable to attend his daughter's burial at Westminster; he was assumed to be near death. The attack lasted about five days altogether. On the twelfth Bate was away from the Hampton Court sickroom attending Mrs. Rolles in the City, and during this absence Cromwell began to recover. Bate perhaps assumed the protector would die following the dosage of mercury administered on the eighth and absented himself to avoid suspicion, should it arise. A further inference is that the émigrés had pressed him to act quickly, consistent with their motive to prevent Parliament's bestowing the kingship. During Bate's absence, Cromwell nearly recovered and on 17 August went horseback riding. Dr. Bate meanwhile returned to Hampton Court, and the protector saw the doctors; then during the night of 17 August Cromwell fell into another round of debilitating pains. Bate's next recorded consultation was 6 September, two days after he assisted in the unsuccessful embalming of Cromwell's body.

Following the Restoration Bate received extraordinary royal favor, as did other conspirators in the plot to return Charles Stuart. In July 1660, two months after returning to England as Charles II, the king appointed Bate to "the office of First Physician in Ordinary" with a yearly fee of one hundred pounds.[76] Even if he had been one of the distinguished physicians of his generation—which he was not—this appointment immediately after the Restoration for one of Cromwell's doctors was curious. Bate obviously possessed bona fides of some sort to be physician to the king despite seemingly loyal service to the lord protector, attendance at his death, and embalming his corpse. Charles would not have appointed a politically untrustworthy physician, even to a sinecure.

Bate's access to influential persons extended to his family. Placing him in a network of loyalists was a telling petition to the king just a month later from "Matthew Bate, brother of Dr. Bate, his Majesty's principal physician. For presentation to the Rectory of Marsh-Gibbon, co. Bucks. . . . Certificate by Rob. Bishop of Oxford, and Drs. Sam. Bolton and Rich. Owen, in his favor."[77] The otherwise obscure Matthew Bate attracted support from highly placed churchmen. The diarist Anthony Wood also knew "Mr. Bates (brother to Dr. Bates)" and recorded having dinner with him.[78]

Anthony Wood's familiarity with George Bate's brother draws attention to a previously disregarded entry in his diary. The voluminous diary at the Bodleian Library is a collection of material that Andrew Clark skillfully edited in the 1890s. The writer recorded information in various forms, including notations in the margins of yearly almanacs and jottings of news and observations on blank sheets that he placed between the almanac's printed pages. Wood's interests were ranging, for he knew virtually everyone connected with Oxford, and he paid attention to ceremonies, music, deaths, and the university's graduates.

The provocative and disregarded diary entry is jotted on a sheet inserted into Wood's 1663 almanac, between May and June: "Jun. 1 or 2, Dr. Bates died at London of french pox and confessed on his death bed that he poysoned Oliver Cromwell with the provocation of two that are now bishops, viz. . . , and his majestie was privi to it."[79] This remarkable entry reports news Wood heard in June 1663, perhaps from Matthew Bate. It is in Wood's hand and consistent in form with other notations on the interleaved sheets. On the same sheet he recorded the death that month of Thomas Baltzar, the well-known violinist who was born in Lübeck and not Sweden, as some thought. He jotted down the confession because he knew Matthew Bate and collected information about authors and churchmen educated at the university. He had no reason to fabricate such a notation in his private papers nor record a mere slander against his friend's well-connected brother. Wood included the information in his massive *Athenae Oxonienses,* first published in 1691, four years before his death: "Upon the Restoration . . . he got in with the Royal Party, (by his Friends report that he by a Dose given to *Oliver* hastened him to his end) was made chief Physician to K. Ch. II and a Member of the *Royal Society.*"[80] Wood might easily have omitted this but did not. If it were false, there were many people to gainsay it. None did. Bate's royalist friends believed the protector had died of poison, as did Whitelock and Prestwich. By printing the story about an acquaintance's brother, a story that had currency, Wood indicated that he also thought it credible. There is no reason to doubt Wood's record nor Bate's confession.

An objection might be that Bate did not die in 1663 but in 1668 at his house in Hatton Gardens, Holborn. He was buried at Kingston upon Thames next to his wife Elizabeth. A memorial table referred more to her than him, identifying him as "Car. 2 medici primarii."[81] He was not visible during his last years. According to a private letter in mid-1661, "It is credibly reported Dr. Bates is dead, but how true I know not."[82] The rumor was not true, of course, but it was consistent with his having serious health problems some two years later. Placed alongside Wood's diary the 1661 rumor is sufficient to indicate that soon after the Restoration Bate's health began to fail. The date of Wood's diary does not invalidate the confession made at a moment when Bate thought he was dying; if anything it makes credible his confession that he poisoned the protector with Charles II's knowledge.

It is interesting that Wood's diary connected "two that are now bishops" with the murder, information that on the surface seems unlikely until its circumstances are considered. Wood refused to name the bishops, even in the privacy of his diary, implying that he was more shocked by episcopal than royal involvement in murder. Despite his dramatic ellipsis, it is possible to adduce the names of two men who became bishops after the Restoration and prior to 1663 (hence "*now* bishops") and who were connected to Charles Stuart, Edward Nicholas, and George Bate.

In fall 1660 the church received five new bishops. Many of Charles's early appointments and rewards recognized the recipients' participation in the Restoration enterprise, and one may consider that possibility here. On 23 October, four "reverend and eminent Persons" were publicly confirmed at the old church of St. Mary's-le-Bow: Gilbert Sheldon, George Morley, Robert Sanderson, and Humphrey Henchman. The weekly newssheets called them "Persons of such known prudence, learning and piety that the Church of *England* may promise to her self happiness and settlement in their several Jurisdictions." These four and George Griffith were consecrated five days later at Henry VII's Chapel in Westminster Abbey.[83]

Two of the five, Sheldon and Morley, were extraordinarily close to Charles I and his son, and the newssheets that described the appointments all but gave the game away. Gilbert Sheldon, privy councilor and the new bishop of London, had been warden of All Souls College, Oxford, and "heretofore Chaplain and Clerk of the Closet to his late *Majesty,* now Dean of his Majestie's Chappel-Royal." In 1663 he became archbishop of Canterbury. Sheldon's interests were as political as theological, for he employed his own agents, opposed nonconformity as a form of rebellion, and practiced the black arts of double dealing. According to the recent historian of Caroline espionage, there is evidence for the "involvement of Sheldon in this rather murky sphere of life."[84] He was close to the Nicholas family. His installation on 3 November 1660 as bishop of London was at St. Paul's Cathedral—and the ceremony was by proxy. According to the public newssheets again, the archdeacon of Canterbury conducted the ceremony wherein he "install'd that most worthy and reverend Dr. [Matthew] Nicholas, Dean of St. Paul's, (brother to Sir *Edward Nicholas* . . .) who was this Lord Bishop's Proxy."[85] Matthew Nicholas had on 10 July 1660 been appointed dean.

George Morley, the new bishop of Worcester, had been "Dean of *Christ-Church* in *Oxford,* who since the Murther of King *Charles* the *First* left this Island, and devoutly followed the service of his Majesty."[86] In 1662 he became bishop of Winchester. As a member of the household in exile, Morley vowed "never to return till . . . the crown and the church were restored."[87] He necessarily had close contact with Nicholas. Twenty years earlier Sheldon and Morley would have known each other while in service to Charles I at Oxford, and they must have known the king's physician at Oxford, George Bate. Morley's familiarity with Bate was acknowledged in the preface to *Elenchus Motuum,* where Bate stated that while writing the book "it was several times seen by the Reverend George [Morley] Lord Bishop of *Winchester.*" Another advisor for Bate's book, incidentally, was Dr. Richard Owen, who wrote one of the letters in support of Matthew Bate's petition.[88]

Sheldon, Morley, Edward Nicholas, and Matthew Nicholas had long and varied careers, but in the summer of 1658 they agreed on the necessity of "some unexpected good accident for the King." They literally "breathed together," silently, beyond Thurloe's observation.

Wood's diary hence recorded credible information that cannot be disregarded. The pattern of evidence favors accepting Bate's confession in 1663 as given in a near-death crisis from which he partly recovered. Present with the protector, he could easily have administered the fatal antimony, mercury, and arsenic as part of a conspiracy that reached to Charles Stuart. Wood's diary notation in fact encompassed the major participants: Charles Stuart, Edward Nicholas, and George

Morley in exile; Matthew Nicholas and Gilbert Sheldon in London; and George Bate in the protectoral court. The first act of Restoration was an act of murder.

But these were not all of the possible conspirators, in and out of England, who might have assisted the principal insider, Dr. Bate. There was at least another ominous presence at the lord protector's death and a probable participant, Thomas Clarges. Born c. 1618, he became "a gentleman commoner" in Merton College, Oxford, and then "an apprentice to old Williams an apothecarie in St. Mary's parish Oxford." Prior to 1660 he was addressed as "Doctor," afterward "Sir Thomas." When he was "in the late King's Service at *Oxford*"—as he described his background—it may be assumed that he was familiar with Bate, Morley, Sheldon, and Edward Nicholas. His occupation as an apothecary was useful to a covert agent in the king's service. Through the influence of his brother-in-law, Gen. George Monck, Cromwell's commander in Scotland, Clarges went to London in the mid-1650s as an English member of Parliament for Aberdeen, agent for the army, and agent for the Edinburgh council. Monck in 1657 pressed Cromwell for Clarges's appointment as an admiralty commissioner.[89] Although in the protectoral household, he retained royalist sympathies. Clarges was clearly Monck's personal agent and provided him with private newsletters. In August 1658 he included information about Cromwell's illness.

What makes Clarges's presence so curious is that his brother-in-law, George Monck, from a royalist family in Devon, was important to the entire Restoration enterprise. As a youth Monck had begun a military career. Captured as a cavalier in 1644, he spent three years in the Tower, where he met a young widow who provided linen for wealthy prisoners, Anne Clarges Ratsford. They married in 1653. After release Monck saw opportunity in the protector's service, Cromwell beheld a capable officer, and in 1654 he appointed Monck commander in Scotland.[90] Royalists believed him susceptible to their blandishment and in the summer of 1658 made an approach, although the cautious Monck felt compelled to report it to Thurloe.[91] His brother, Nicholas Monck, undertook the royalist embassy in 1659 that led to the general's decision to march on London and prepared the way for restoration. Influenced by royalist relatives—especially his brother-in-law Thomas Clarges and brother Nicholas Monck—the general emerged in 1660 as a person, perhaps *the* person, crucial to restoration. The presence of Monck's medically trained brother-in-law, confidant, and personal agent in Whitehall Palace, standing next to Bate, raises questions about Monck's attitudes.

Clarges was a functionary at the center of affairs, and he reported information about Cromwell's health in three official letters to Lord Deputy of Ireland Henry Cromwell, two private newsletters to Monck, and an account of the Restoration added to Sir Richard Baker's *Chronicle of the Kings.* As an admiralty commissioner he routinely reported foreign news to Henry Cromwell and during August included references to the protector's health that were inaccurate. Clarges first mentioned the protector's condition in a letter to Henry on 10 August; he wrote from London that the protector at Hampton Court "is much amended; and will with his whole traine be this evening in Whitehall." This was so much nonsense. The reference to "much amended" implied recovery from a period of serious illness, but at the moment Clarges wrote, the protector was thought near death, as persons at Whitehall knew. He was neither amended nor able to accompany "his whole traine" to Elizabeth's burial at Westminster Abbey that evening. Clarges's misrepresentation is so astounding that it can only have been intentional. Two weeks later he again observed blandly in another letter to Henry that Cromwell's "recovery . . . is in a good measure advanced" and that he had traveled to Whitehall. He again did not say from what Cromwell was recovering. Malarial symptoms had appeared only three days earlier, thus Clarges could not have meant "recovery" from malaria that was "advanced." He must have meant something else. Finally, on 1 September he wrote that the illness "fils me with sad aprehensions" and that the disease "is a double tertian ague" (Bate referred to "bastard tertian" ague). The court's apprehensions were then caused by other symptoms, as he implied in his report to Monck dated the next day. In sum, these three letters to Henry Cromwell seriously misrepresented his father's health.[92]

At the same time Clarges's private newsletters to Monck reported events quite differently and more accurately. On the seventeenth—

the day Cromwell rode in the park and consulted with the doctors—Clarges wrote that Cromwell "is well recovered of a great distemper too much like that in Cannongate." This correctly reported that by the morning of 17 August he had nearly recovered from a serious illness, but the elliptical comment's immediate meaning is obscure. It must have meant something to Monck. Perhaps it alluded to Cromwell's dysentery in 1651, when his headquarters were at the Earl of Moray's house in the Canongate, Edinburgh. In 1658 no observer mentioned dysentery, so it is probable that this odd comment carried an ominous connotation. The traditional armorial motto "This is the path to heaven" appeared on all public buildings in the Canongate, from church to pillory, according to Sir Walter Scott.[93] At the street's nether end was Holyrood Palace, where in 1566 Charles Stuart's great-grandfather, Henry Lord Darnley, led the conspirators who abducted David Riccio from the chamber of his great-grandmother, Mary Queen of Scots, and murdered him in an adjoining stairwell. By 17 August Cromwell had indeed recovered from an attempt on his life. Clarges's 2 September newsletter to Monck was medically informative but curiously did not reiterate his previous day's claim to Henry Cromwell of ague. Contradicting that letter, he now referred to Cromwell's recent "good rest," the lessening of fits and sore throat, and hope for his recovery—"except some unexpected accident happen," the phrase that royalists used to refer to Cromwell's dying unnaturally. It is noteworthy that Clarges used it in writing to his brother-in-law Monck. He added that the protector's health was necessary "at this tyme that affaires are so unsettled." Affairs were not in fact unstable at that moment. The interlinear emphasis was less Cromwell's health than achieving political settlement, probably meaning Restoration.[94]

After the Restoration Clarges assisted in writing the "continuation" of *A Chronicle of the Kings of England,* which Sir Richard Baker, who died in 1645, had carried to the end of James I's reign. Clarges also arranged for Edward Phillips, the primary "continuator," to have access to Monck's private papers. The volume's title page stated that the book, dedicated to "the Prudent conduct, under God, of George [Monck] late Duke of Albemarle," contained information about "the most important and Secret *Transactions* of that Time," the Restora-

tion. It sets forth a thoroughly inaccurate narrative of Cromwell's illness and death. According to this version of events, Cromwell was
upset by Elizabeth's death and fell ill "of a Tertian Feavor, which at
first seem'd not to signifie much danger, but by degrees it grew upon
him" (not here the previously alleged double or bastard tertian ague).
It claimed "enthusiastick ravings" made the protector unaware "of his
own Danger." The chaplain Thomas Goodwin persuaded Cromwell
he would recover, and this amused the physicians, Clarges said.
Cromwell was taken to Whitehall "where with more convenience, than
at *Hampton-Court,* a respect might be had to his Health, and the publick
Affairs of the Nation." On 31 August, "Finding himself in Danger,"
the patient spoke privately to Thurloe and Goodwin about the succession. On 2 September, Thurloe and Goodwin sought his will regarding the succession, "perceiving his Distemper very much to increase,
and hourly gain upon him." Of the death, Clarges said, "contrary to
the real belief of many men, the ill-bodings of some, and the earnest
wish of others, he died not of a violent, but in his Bed a natural Death."[95]

Clarges's medical information—in the letters to Henry Cromwell,
Monck, and in the *Chronicle*—was as irregular as that of Bate. It must
be reiterated that prior to Elizabeth's death and not after, as these
sources insinuate, the protector fell seriously ill of gout and an undiagnosed but agonizing sickness. Clarges did not claim "ague" in his
correspondence until nearly a month later, in the 1 September letter to
the lord deputy of Ireland. No contemporary source mentioned "ravings." Clarges placed the idea of "Danger" at 18 August, when Bate
likewise noted sudden danger, a day after Cromwell swooned, received
a cordial, and made his private will. Clarges admitted medical mal-
feasance when he said the doctors were amused by the prayers of
Cromwell's ministers and therefore "less regardful of his Condition."
Cromwell was then taken to Whitehall, a site considered as malarial
as Hampton Court, until the convenient and presumed healthful St.
James's Palace could be prepared, but he was too ill to move another
time. Clarges's 1 September letter is a generally cited source for the
protector's dying of "a double tertian ague," yet only one day later he
wrote that Cromwell had slept well the *two* previous days and was
recovering. One of the letters is wrong. He referred to the illness as a

"Distemper" rather than ague. If the "Danger" were ague, it would certainly have been evident to a competent doctor the day prior to death. Clarges's concluding words protested too much. Like Bate, he disguised events and thus implicated himself.

After the protector's death Clarges remained at the center of things. The council of state's immediate concern was Monck's loyalty. Lord Deputy Henry Cromwell in Ireland was not a problem, but "Of *Scotland* they had some doubt," a reservation similar to that of Thomas Skinner, Monck's early biographer.[96] Dr. Clarges became their emissary to Monck despite misgivings about a royalist past. Richard Cromwell wished "to know how [Monck] stood affected to his Advancement." Thus, following Oliver's death, "*Richard* sent that evening to Mr. *Thomas Clarges*," because he was at court, and asked him to take letters to Monck. It is interesting that Clarges did not at this point in his contribution to Baker's *Chronicle* include his medical title, as he did elsewhere. Clarges accepted with alacrity this opportunity to speak with his brother-in-law. He traveled to Edinburgh and found army officers quiescent. His account did not reveal the subjects discussed during "many secret Conferences," but he and his brother-in-law would certainly have spoken in detail of Cromwell's death.[97] Thus, in September 1658, according to Clarges, who would have known, Monck was "weary of the uncertain condition, wherein he found both himself and the Nation, inthrall'd by the overruling Tyranny of the Souldiers." Clarges "began to perceive the General was in his Principles well fixed to restore his country to its Ancient Government, when-ever a fit occasion should present it self for the attempt."[98]

At last, in early May 1660, Parliament commissioned Clarges to convey the invitation for Charles Stuart to return. The apothecary took himself to Breda, arriving in the governor of Holland's coach-and-six, and presented Charles with a packet of letters. Monck's letter said he had sent "the only Person he trusted in the nearest Concernments and Consultations for his Restauration, as one to whom he desired his Majestie to give Credit to what he should say on that behalf."[99] Charles thereupon knighted Parliament's messenger, Monck's agent, and a man present in Whitehall Palace the day Cromwell died. This first royal favor was disproportionate for a parliamentary messenger but perhaps suitable for "the only Person" whom Monck trusted and who may have had a hand in the protector's death. When Monck "decided" for restoration has never seemed certain. He did not take irreversible action for over a year, but a week after the lord protector's death, Clarges recorded that the general was prepared to consider restoration on "a fit occasion." A generation after Clarges's death in 1695, the earl of Egmont recalled him as clearly having "so great a hand in bringing in King Charles the Second."[100]

Charles Stuart was beholden to many persons for restoration, and among his earliest rewards were two seriatim grants in July 1660. The first was "to Sir Thomas Clarges, of a messuage in the Green Mews and part of the Great Mews; rent 20*s.*" Clarges obtained choice real estate, to the irritation of other royalists who coveted it. The next item filed on the calendar was the grant "to Dr. George Bate, of the office of First Physician in Ordinary; fee, 100*l.* per year."[101] Bate's reward was also for unspecified service. By making these grants together, Charles implied that the recipients had undertaken their services together.

The situation seems almost obvious. Although any plan to murder Cromwell had to be disguised, it is nonetheless discernible in the record. Perhaps it has not been observed because it is an obvious "purloined letter" and the accomplishment of those who most clearly benefited. Charles Stuart's secretary, Edward Nicholas, advocated murder as a matter of policy, feared Parliament might soon make Cromwell king, and believed a person having "interest" with Cromwell and "infallible ways and means" could perform "so glorious a work." Charles offered reward for the murderer. The agent with interest and infallible means at the protectoral court was Bate, assisted faithfully by the apothecary Clarges; Sheldon, Morley, and Matthew Nicholas were intermediaries. Bate routinely used mercury-based "cordials" to treat gout, and he was in position to hand the protector remedies containing dangerous levels of antimony, mercury, and at the last, arsenic. During August the physician administered perhaps five poisonous cordials until, as Clarges wrote, "some unexpected accident" happened.

5

Infernal Saints

Charles Stuart regained his father's throne in May 1660, fulfilling "the king's cause" for which exiled royalists had long contrived. Charles encouraged punishing the high-court judges who had signed his father's death warrant, and in consequence the Convention Parliament settled miscellaneous political scores as the Houses of Commons and Lords casually negotiated lists of potential victims. Judges who had remained in England were summarily arrested, many tried, and several executed. A few weeks later, in January 1661, thirteen Fifth Monarchists were hanged after their small-scale rising in London failed to establish the government of saints, which would have ruled until Christ returned for the day of judgment. And in a final gesture, several days later the bodies of Henry Ireton, Oliver Cromwell, and two others were pursued into the grave and hanged on Tyburn's triple crossbeams, producing one of the Restoration's most memorable tableaus.

When Charles's supporters heard rumors in August 1658 that Cromwell was ill, they thought a restoration possible. Charles Stuart immediately drafted a declaration, with advice from Nicholas, and named the protector as the principal actor "in the murther of the King" and for nine years a usurper of "Royall Authority." He commanded Englishmen to restore him to power, and so that fear of punishment "not deterre any of them," he offered full, free, and gracious pardon to all subjects. The only exceptions were "the murtherers of the king our father of ever blessed memory." He attainted the dead protector as the very author of Stuart misfortune and retained the right to punish an unstated number of "murtherers." Several months later he described to one of his agents, John Mordaunt, a plan "to draw all persons whatsoever to serve me" by offering a general pardon, except for those who "actually sate in judgment for the taking away of the life of our said father," thus broadly defining the act of murder. In July 1659 he reiterated to his brother James that he would pardon "all men, except only those who sat actually upon the murder of our father, and voted for it." He authorized James to appoint a discreet agent to negotiate with any repentant judge who offered "a very extraordinary service" leading to restoration, and he promised not to prosecute and allow the person time "to convey away his estate . . . out of my dominions." He did not expect anyone to accept the opportunity—and none did.[1]

The Restoration did not occur as quickly as the royalists perhaps expected. Richard Cromwell assumed the protectorship with relative ease. The army and the republicans posed a threat to him and in May 1659 prompted his resignation. For a year thereafter, Parliament, supported by the army, ruled. In the summer of 1659 royalist conspirators, the Sealed Knot, attempted to coordinate a series of risings. Many plotters simply failed to carry out their parts, and Gen. John Lambert easily defeated Sir George Booth's thousand-man army. Parliament then lost its advantage because of bickering and indecision. Tension with the army increased until General Monck in Scotland took decisive action and reduced the number of regiments and officers, a policy he had recommended to Richard Cromwell. In early 1660 he marched to London and in February allowed the Long Parliament to reassemble. When republicans and army officers demanded a parliamentary remonstrance against the king and House of Lords, Monck ordered the officers to leave London and return to their regiments, and he gained the control that had eluded Richard. After Parliament adjourned, according to the standard interpretation, Monck saw royal restoration as a means to achieve stability. He then received an intermediary from Charles Stuart and replied asking "indemnity, arrears, confirmation of titles to former Church and Crown lands and a degree of religious toleration." Charles saw his opportunity, moved from Spanish Catholic Brussels to Dutch Protestant Breda, issued the new declaration, and offered Monck a political reward.[2]

Charles issued the second declaration in April 1660 and promised "a free and general Pardon . . . to all our subjects" who within forty days declared themselves loyal and obedient subjects—omitting only such persons "as shall hereafter be excepted by parliament."[3] He thus invited Parliament to visit retribution upon some persons, placing on others the burden of his vengeance. Widespread vengeance was impossible because during the 1650s politics and society had become an amalgam of persons with parliamentary and monarchical inclinations.[4] Instead, king and Parliament narrowed their reaction to a limited group—the high-court judges whom royalists branded as "regicides."

The royalists had already marked the judges. In November 1659 their ire fell on the court president, John Bradshaw, who had read the sentence against Charles I. After his burial in Westminster Abbey, "several jeering bookes and also ballads" hinted that he was fortunate to have died in his bed. One ballad assaulted "that infernal saint John Bradshaw" and predicted, with some accuracy: "Hell will not silent keep its chiefest crime, / The Grave will presently throw up thy slime."[5] A royalist broadside was distributed around London containing a mock epitaph:

> If any neere unto this grave deare apeare,
> Aske but the Prince of Darkness who lyes heare;
> Kinge-killing murderer, heele tell thee that
> H'hath made him now his deare associate.

By March 1660 published lists named seventy-five judges (fifty-nine signed the warrant) and thirty-three as witnesses against the king. Bradshaw headed the list because he pronounced sentence against Charles I. Cromwell was second, and Ireton and Thomas Pride were twenty-fifth and twenty-sixth, respectively.[6]

Pride's notoriety was the result of his leading the troopers who in 1648 purged the Commons, making possible the king's trial, and his signing the death warrant. He had not been politically active in the Commonwealth but became a victualing contractor to the navy and the high sheriff of Surrey, where in 1654 and 1656 he purchased Nonsuch Great Park and the adjoining Worcester House. As sheriff he led the soldiers who enforced the council of state's order suppressing the royal sport of bearbaiting in Southwark; his troopers shot seven bears, an action royalists held against him as much as—if not in fact more than—they did the purge and signing the king's death warrant.[7]

The Convention Parliament's House of Commons read a bill of general pardon, indemnity, and oblivion on 9 May 1660, two weeks prior to Charles's return. The bill appeared to conciliate the twenty-year crisis because it offered amnesty to persons "active in the warr."[8] But it accepted Charles's insistence on exempting the high-court judges from the amnesty. A recent historian has described the bill's underlying hypocrisy: it had "from the first an air of ceremonial artificiality in that its principal victims were not the leaders of the republic as such, but the men who had sat in the regicide court."[9]

Retribution against the judges became Parliament's interest in the months following the Restoration, and members in order discussed indemnity, attainder, and exhumation. The Commons read the indemnity bill the second time (thus opening debate) on 12 May, and William Prynne presented documentation from 1650, when the house had accepted the high court's journal into its records. Since "divers of the present members" were named in these records, the house pressed them to speak about their participation in the 1649 tribunal, "which they did with much detestation of that horrid fact," as Sir Edward Dering described the scene. Three claimed to have attended only one high-court session, another to have attended many but not the one in which the king's sentence was pronounced, and one to have signed the death warrant under Cromwell's duress. All begged "the mercy of the King and the house." The session was calm until the final respondent outraged many members. John Lenthall, son of the Cromwellian speaker, William Lenthall, argued that anyone who at any time took up arms against the king—not just the judges—was as guilty "as he that cut off his head." Collective guilt could have upset the bill's indemnity for collaborators conspicuously sitting in Parliament and on the bench. Furor ensued and the house forced Lenthall to kneel at the bar and accept recrimination. The speaker pronounced a reprimand but concluded with more conciliatory words: "The disposition of his Majesty is to Mercy . . . and it is the Disposition of the Body of this House to be Healers of Breaches." The Commons then began debating whom to exempt from pardon and which lives to put at risk. On Monday, 14 May, debate turned to the number of persons to exempt, that is to say condemn. Members argued for few exemptions, others for as many as a dozen. They agreed to exempt seven, although they did not consider which seven judges to condemn. The Commons ordered the sergeant to arrest as many of the judges as possible, with assistance of "all officers civill and military." It also ordered the arrest of persons who had performed the execution.[10]

Fear especially spread though republican circles because the judicial net had dropped over so many persons. Forty-four fled into exile, including Edmund Ludlow. On 14 May, Cromwell's funeral effigy, "which was made and shewn with so much pomp at Somerset House," was found in Westminster Abbey and hanged from a window in Whitehall.[11]

The following day, debate first referred to the four judges whose bodies Parliament later disinterred and defiled. After lengthy discussion the Commons resolved to attaint Cromwell, Ireton, Bradshaw, and Pride so as to seize their estates, as they could not pay for their alleged crimes with their lives. Debate indicated an interest in symbolic punishment, for there was thought that "their effigies will be tried."[12]

Charles landed at Dover on 25 May and arrived in London four days later. Bonfires marked the way and illuminated the city. In Westminster, Cromwell's effigy was placed on a post with the Commonwealth's arms, then set ablaze "that every one might take better notice of them." In Sherbourne, Dorset, when Charles was proclaimed, "the witty Wags of the Town" set up a parody of the high court of justice, including effigies of Bradshaw and Cromwell. The mock court condemned the men, the effigies were hanged, then "so hacked and hewed . . . that in a short time but little remained."[13]

A week after the return, Charles spoke to the House of Commons and recommended "speedy dispatch" of the indemnity bill. He thought the Commons had already deliberated the matter longer than necessary.[14] The Commons returned to the bill a week later and debated it during June. The Commons and Lords agreed to ask Charles for a proclamation against the judges, with special reference to those who had fled the country. The proclamation condemned the exiles without due process, saying they had "out of the Sense of their own Guilt, lately fled and obscured themselves." Treason trials were impossible in their absence, and the bill allowed two weeks for them to reappear. The herald-at-arms read the proclamation on 18 June, making known that the king would pardon all persons not exempted.

The Commons prepared a list of seven persons to be exempted. Gen. Thomas Harrison had been captured (he simply surrendered), but the other six were now on the Continent.[15] On 8 June they listed twenty persons to be penalized but not executed—including William Lenthall, John Desborow, Sir Arthur Haselrigg, John Lambert, and John Goodman. They considered listing John Milton, Latin secretary for Cromwell's council of state and defender of the king's trial. The poet Andrew Marvell, formerly in Cromwell's secretariat with Milton and now the member for Hull, probably saved his colleague from judgment, although Milton went into hiding for several weeks. Not until 11 July did the Commons pass the bill, which went to the Lords. On 18 July several of the captured men were brought to London and secured in the Tower.[16] Charles asked for action and addressed the upper house on 27 July, noting that he had urged the Commons to pass the bill "as a necessary foundation of that security we all pray for." He chided them for having been "too long about the work" and urged the Lords not to delay further. On 10 August the Lords passed a bill much altered from the Commons's version.[17]

A conference committee worked to reconcile the two versions of the bill, and some persons were not listed in the final act simply because the two houses could not agree on each other's victims. Personal connections were more important than records, as Milton's case implies, and in consequence many received indemnity. Sir Edward Dering's diary for 13 August records casual negotiations: "Collonell Hacker we consented to be put in for life, and Sir Gilbert Pickering and Thomas Lister we consented to absolve." The Commons listed sixteen as "incapable of future employment," disputed twelve whom the Lords had condemned, disbarred from civil and military office all who signed the death warrant. They discussed whether those who were dead were as guilty as those living, permitting seizure of their estates. There was no decision regarding the status of the deceased, although there was speculation that the House of Commons would soon bring in a bill "against *Cromwell, Bradshawe, Ireton,* and *Pryde.*"[18]

On 29 August the king attended both houses and gave assent to several bills, and the speaker introduced the session. In florid words he condemned the protectorate, saying that several months earlier England had been "a great Prison, where the worst of Men were our Governors, and their vilest Lusts the Laws by which they governed." Retribution therefore could be justified. When he turned to "An Act of free and general Pardon, Indemnity, and Oblivion," the drumbeat of his speech increased. The judges were not men but "Monsters, guilty of Blood, precious Blood, precious Royal Blood . . . Perverters of Religion; subverters of Government; false to God; disloyal to the best of Kings; and perfidious to their Country." He claimed it had been necessary to exempt some persons "that they might be made Sacrifices to appease God's Wrath, and satisfy Divine Justice."[19]

Charles gave assent to several bills, including the indemnity, and spoke in contrastingly subdued tones. He assented to Parliament's legislation, saying he had long sought passage of these bills as "the Foundation of much Security and Happiness to us all." His "Discretion and Conscience" extended pardon to persons defined in the act of indemnity, but he promised vigor when "Malice is notorious, and the public Peace exceedingly concerned." He claimed to value popular affection and know no better way to make himself "sure of your Affections than by being just and kind to you all."[20]

The Essex parson Ralph Josselin learned of the royal assent to the indemnity bill while dining with his village's mayor; he wrote in his diary, "I was glad I was so well imployed on a day when so memorable an act was past."[21]

The Convention Parliament heard further reference to the indemnity act when the king recessed the houses on 13 September. Charles thanked them for attending to the public good more than to his own and bade them go "to your Countries, and do me much more Service there." The lord chancellor addressed them with a vivid assertion. "You know Kings are, in some Sense, called Gods, and so they may in some Degree be able to look into Men's Hearts; and God hath given us a King who can look as far into Men's Hearts as any Prince alive. . . .

He hath given us a Noble and Princely Example, by opening and stretching his Arms to all who are worthy to be his Subjects, worthy to be thought Englishmen."[22] The Stuarts had not yet forgotten James VI and I's *True Law of Free Monarchies*—which declared that "Kings are called Gods by the prophetical King *David,* because they sit upon God his Throne in the earth, and have the count of their administration to give unto him"—nor learned from two decades of turmoil.[23]

After Parliament recessed, dispersed by royal command and unable to comment, the state began judicial proceedings against the judges. The high-court judges in custody—those without friends, money, or belief in the necessity of flight—were brought to trial. Weekly newssheets described these events with uncommon detail. A writer addressed readers, an unusual editorial gesture, saying, "now at last you'l have that long expected *Tryal.*" To be certain the defendants were unpitied, he referred to "those wretched men (forgive me for calling them Men)."[24] These trials indicate how royalists would have treated Ireton or Cromwell, had they been alive.

The October trials of those not given indemnity appear unfamiliar despite familiar legal trappings. As John Kenyon remarked of trials following the popish plot, which began in 1678 when Titus Oates charged that Jesuit conspirators were planning to assassinate the king and raise a rebellion, the state of seventeenth-century criminal law is "so baffling and unpleasant to a modern reader" as to require brief explanation. Monarchs always assumed treason difficult to detect and thus sought to convict anyone accused, which they generally accomplished because the courts were a part of royal administration and judges advocates of royal policy. A treason trial was, in Kenyon's description, "a morality play staged as a demonstration of government power, an affirmation of kingly authority, and a warning to the unwary."[25] The prosecutor in 1660, Solicitor General John Heneage Finch, sought to stage nothing less than "the extirpation of 'the good old cause'" of the collapsed Commonwealth, according to the editor of his chancery papers.[26] The monarchy used criminal procedures of the day for that purpose. Typical of criminal defendants, the judges of Charles I were imprisoned secretly, did not know the charges, were unable to prepare a defense or subpoena witnesses and evidence, and

received no notice of witnesses and evidence against them. At trial
they had no counsel and defended themselves as best they could. There
were no rules of evidence allowing them to confront witnesses, see
originals of documents, and object to hearsay.[27] The first judicial pro-
ceeding was against Gen. Thomas Harrison, and from arraignment to
execution it occupied merely five days.

On 9 October a grand inquest was conducted at Hick's Hall. The
presiding judge was Sir Orlando Bridgman, lord chief baron of the
high court of exchequer, and he presented an indictment to the grand
jury against thirty-two persons "for compassing, imagining, adjudg-
ing the king" as defined in the treason statute of 25 Edw. 3. The grand
jury "returned the Indictment Billa Vera," and the court adjourned
until the next day at the Old Bailey in the City. It was left to the
Mercurius Publicus writer to explain that the arraignment was political rather than criminal: "Sir *Orlando Bridgman* gave such a *Charge*
as (if nothing before had been said or written of that matter) is sufficient to teach all Subjects their whole Duty and Allegiance."[28]

At nine the next morning the prisoners, who had been held for
several months, were taken from the Tower to Newgate. "A troope of
horse and a company of musketeers" surrounded their coaches as they
crossed London. Peter Mundy watched the parade and remembered
the day because in the jostling crowd he lost a lute book "which I
much valued." From Newgate the prisoners were taken to the Old
Bailey. There would be no question of fair trial. Samuel Pepys noted
that the judiciary had "such a bench of noblemen as hath not been
ever seen in England." The accused appeared "dismayed, and will all
be condemned without question."[29] The clerk read the indictment and
the court accepted their pleas. Most defendants simply pled not guilty.
Harrison attempted to address the court, but Sir Orlando silenced him,
refusing to do other than accept his plea. Court adjourned.[30]

Proceedings began the next day, 11 October, at seven in the morning; Gen. Thomas Harrison's was the first trial, and it was typical of
the series. During the short trial "the hangman in his ugly dress, with
a halter in his hand" was present the entire time "to terrify and aston-
ish" the victim.[31] Jury selection required Harrison personally to accept or challenge each panelman because he was not entitled to an

attorney. Finch began the prosecution with the assertion that he did not need to prove each point in the indictment against each defendant "for he that is in at one, is guilty in law, of all the rest, as much as if he had struck the fatal stroke itself." Curiously, the solicitor general accepted a conception of collective guilt to which he had objected when John Lenthall raised it in the House of Commons. Six witnesses testified that Harrison was in the high court on 27 January 1649. Even though the prosecution had every advantage, king's counsel Finch still had to prompt answers:

> *Counsel.*   Did you see him on the 27th of January 1649, sitting there, which was the day of Sentence?
>
> *[Robert] Coytman.*   I cannot call that to memory. . . .
>
> *Counsel.*   Did you see the prisoner . . . sit on the bench as a ordinary spectator, or as one of the Judges?
>
> *Coytman.*   He was in the Court sitting among the rest of the Judges, as one of them.

The court was loath to allow Harrison to speak, although he did have that right. He reminded the court of the years of turmoil and that "divers of those that sit on the bench were formerly as active—" but here Sir Orlando stopped him and said "Pray, Mr. Harrison, do not thus reflect on the Court. This is not the business." Bridgman and others present, "the Court" reflected upon, were collaborators whose business now was not to revisit the Cromwellian past but to find Harrison guilty. Harrison claimed that as a judge he had acted under Parliament's authority, but Sir Orlando interrupted to assert that "this was not [in 1649] the House of Commons." The trial ended quickly and inevitably. Sir Orlando lectured the jury, "The Evidence is so clear and pregnant as nothing more. I think you need not go out." The panel took the hint, gathered at the bar, and agreed upon their verdict.[32]

In pronouncing Harrison's sentence from the treason statute, Sir Orlando intoned that Harrison would be: "hanged by the neck, and being alive shall be cut down, and your privy members to be cut off, your entrails to be taken out of your body, and, you living, the same are to be burnt before your eyes, and your head to be cut off, your body to be divided into four quarters, and head and quarters to be disposed of at the pleasure of the king's majesty, and the Lord have mercy upon your soul."[33] Mere death was insufficient under the statute—"being alive . . . you living"—and a contemporary narrator unfriendly to Harrison described this as an "awful and certainly barbarous sentence."[34] The court intended it to be executed in its literal brutality.

Condemned on 11 October, Harrison was two days later the first judge to be executed. At Newgate "he parted with his wife and friends with great joy and chearfulness." In midmorning he was tied to a hurdle and dragged along Fleet Street and the Strand to Charing Cross. Mobs jeered him all the way, but "his eyes and hands lifted up to heaven." The gallows stood on a platform surrounded by railings. Harrison forgave the hangman who placed the rope around his neck, hugged his servant, and climbed the ladder "with an undaunted countenance." He was positioned to face the Banqueting House, "where that precious innocent bloud of our late Sovraign . . . was spilt." Site was important to this ritual too. Before stepping from the ladder he made a long declaration of faith that "this will make me come the sooner into his glory" and ended with belief that "by my God I will go through this death, and he will make it easy to me." It was not to be so. According to one account, "He was not so much thrown off the Ladder by the Executioner, but went as readily off himself." The hangman stripped the clothes from Harrison's strangling and gasping form, cut down the "half hang'd" and naked body, tossed it alive onto a bench, and began butchering it open while the crowd jostled for better views as the hangman drew the entrails from the dying man. Harrison tried to rise up—perhaps a reflex to a knife ripping into his abdomen—and seemed to give the hangman "a box on the ear." But the executioner pushed him down, then castrated and eviscerated the sentient human form according to the statute's requirements. He sliced into the chest, ripped out the heart, and held the thing aloft while proclaiming, "Behold the heart of a traitor." Harrison was at long last dead. The executioner finished butchering the body into quarters and tossed the heart and intestines onto a fire. The bloody quarters were "throwne together like butchers meat brought from the shambles" and taken on the hurdle back to Newgate.[35]

When Harrison's heart was held high, Samuel Pepys, an eyewitness, recorded that "there was great shouts of joy." Having observed the execution of Charles I, he wanted "to see the first blood shed in revenge for the King." He went home and set up shelves in his study. Peter Mundy, who saw several of the executions "from a window" in Charing Cross, said of Harrison, "Hee died resolutely." Sir Edward Nicholas wrote smugly to a friend that Harrison, "one of the blackest of the traitors, was hanged, dying under a hardness of heart that created horror in all who saw him." Harrison's strength of character under such duress obviously disappointed the royal secretary, who noted of this and other executions that "the people show great satisfaction in what is done."[36]

And still they had not finished with what was left of General Harrison. Three days later his head was placed in a basket and set on the hurdle dragging John Cook to his Charing Cross execution. The heads of Harrison and Cook were then "fastened on two poles, and pitched on the north end of Westminster Hall." Whereupon Harrison's quarters were hanged "on the four gates of the City." Charles II, the merry monarch, had ordered this display of what remained of his victims.[37]

In the week following Harrison's death, there were seven more executions at Charing Cross, and even in the reeking streets of Stuart London, burning entrails and butchered carcasses raised a stench. Area residents found the situation so intolerable they sent the king a petition: "The stench of . . . burnt bowels had so putrified the air that there might be no more executions in that place." The final two executions were therefore conducted at Tyburn. All victims were subject to the same ritual sentence. Some may have been unconscious by the time they were cut down from the gallows for evisceration, but most probably were not, for executioners were adept at keeping victims alive as long as possible. Nicholas was elated to report that the crowds shouted "with joy on the death of the more hardened traitors." They shouted with particular joy during the execution of Hugh Peter; the newssheets reported that no person died "so unpytied, and (which is more) whose Execution was the delight of the people." The throng cheered when he climbed the ladder, when the executioner put the rope around his neck, and when his head was hacked off. A scribe sought to explain the meaning of it all: "There was such a shout as if the people of England had acquired a Victory."[38] On 20 October the indefatigable Pepys counted eight human quarters ("four upper and four lower") on Aldgate, seven on Bishopgate, four on Moorgate, and several on Cripplegate and Aldersgate. "Never the like was seene before at any tyme in the Citty of London," he wrote. He did think the display on the gates "a sad sight to see," agreeing with Mundy that it had been a singular time, for "what a bloody week this and the last have been."[39] A modern student of the Restoration has written of these executions, "The regicide itself had been a solemn and tragic ritual: these men died amidst the atmosphere of a bear-baiting."[40]

Retribution was in the air, and one need not wonder what torments the monarchy would have inflicted on the living Cromwell, Ireton, Bradshaw, and Pride. Royalists considered the four to be traitors—arch, vile, odious. They would have spared every mercy to have enlarged the suffering.

After these executions, the presiding judge at the trials, Sir Orlando Bridgman, was promoted on the bench. An undated royal warrant in October granted him the office of lord chief justice of the common pleas. On 23 October, the first day of the new judicial term, the lord chancellor and the judges "rode to *Westminster* in their wonted equipage." Riding with his lordship were Sir Robert Forster, lord chief justice of the king's bench, and Bridgman, "then Lord Chief Baron, now Lord Chief Justice of the Common Pleas."[41]

The Convention Parliament reconvened on 6 November, after a month's recess, as if "there had only been an Intermission of one Day."[42] The chronicler averted his gaze from October's executions and the flesh rotting on the City's gates, but Parliament still sought revenge. Later in the month "one Tench, the carpenter that made the scaffold [for Charles I's execution] was beheaded."[43] Other than such pathetic functionaries, few potential victims remained. Several judges had been indemnified, others were fugitive. The Convention turned to a bill attainting exiles, thereby allowing confiscation of their estates. The new bill attainted the four high-court judges presumed buried in Westminster Abbey.[44]

The day after reconvening, the Parliament gave first reading to

Finch's attainder bill, proposing to make 30 January a perpetual fast day and to attaint "Oliver Cromwell, and diverse others, Actors in the horrid Murder of the late King, which had already suffered, or were dead." Prynne wanted the bill to order execution of those exempted from execution but subject to other penalties. Another member moved that debts of the condemned be paid and estates revert to the crown. A third member moved that exceptions to the indemnity, short of execution, should be affirmed. At this stage the House of Commons was concerned with debts and estates. The attainder bill was amended over the next few weeks, and the house received petitions from heirs of high-court judges pleading special cases. Captain Silius Titus wanted all these cases left to royal mercy; the resolute Prynne wanted judges attainted "notwithstanding the Merits of their Children, and then left to the King's Mercy." A member moved a separate bill to attaint Cromwell, Ireton, Bradshaw, and Pride.[45]

For the preceding months the monarchy and the Convention had enacted indemnity and attainder, and on 4 December the Commons came at last to the exhumations. They were discussing yet another petition. The nephew of Thomas Chaloner, "one of the King's Judges," protested that his uncle had not been named in previous legislation and should not now be named. Captain Silius Titus replied with sarcasm: he would make provision for the judges' descendants if it could be shown the judges had made provision "for the King's Children after his Death." Another speaker wanted a clause permitting payment of "just Debts, Legacies, and Funeral Expences" from forfeited estates "of those four Persons . . . who have been attainted after their Deaths." Others urged provision for debt payments so that "honest Creditors" were not punished. Many now-ardent royalists had once been willing creditors to the protectorate. The iron-willed Prynne said there had been no such proviso "for the Gunpowder Traitors, nor any else that ever were Traitors before." Captain Titus spoke a second time, for a point that foreclosed further discussion and brought the House of Commons to one of the more bizarre and symbolic resolutions in its history. Referring to October's hangings as a precedent for what he was about to propose, he said that "execution did not leave traitors at their graves, but followed them beyond it: and since the heads and limbs of some were already put upon the gates, he hoped the Commons would order the carcasses of those devils, who were buried at Westminster, Cromwell, Bradshawe, Ireton, and Pride, might be torn out of their graves, dragged to Tyburn, there to hang for some time, and afterwards be buried under the gallows." The Commons unanimously agreed and prepared an order that Sergeant-at-Arms James Norfolk "see execution done upon the bodies." According to parliamentary custom, Titus then carried the order he had introduced to the Lords for concurrence.[46]

The proposal for exhumation had not occurred by chance, as subsequent House of Commons actions imply. Several days after passing the order, the Commons "took it into their Heads" to vote several sums to persons "who had done signal Services for the Royal Family." The second sum moved was a £2,000 payment to Captain Titus, which being seconded was amended and raised to £3,000.[47] Titus was not just a random but vengeful member of the Commons. He was groom of the king's bedchamber and had acted as intermediary among Charles, Sir Edward Hyde, and English Presbyterians prior to the Restoration. He possessed the king's confidence. Charles had written Mordaunt prior to Restoration that Titus was "trusted by me . . . very honest and entire to me." Without such agents as Titus, the conspiracy to restore Charles might not have succeeded. Charles later ordered the chamberlain of London to pay Titus's grant and authorized a further £500 pension. A royal warrant for Titus a year later referred to part of the larger grant as "for secret service."[48] One may infer that Titus proposed the exhumation and hanging with Charles's knowledge. Titus almost certainly discussed this fulfillment of "the king's cause" with the monarch, with whom the idea may have originated.

The Lords prepared their order on 10 December and added details and a confusing phrase to the original motion, which had ordered the carcasses "be . . . dragged to Tyburn." According to the new draft the bodies would now "be taken up, drawn upon a hurdle to Tyburn, and then hanged up *in their coffins* for some time and afterwards buried under the gallows."[49] Hanging them "in their coffins" would have been impossible, but the order was so printed in the journal. In the manuscript the odd-sounding phrase was inserted with no caret. It really belongs to the line just above rather than below and probably should have been printed as "drawn in their coffins upon a hurdle to Tyburn and then hanged up for some time."[50] The Lords' draft also contained a mysterious phrase, a "small addition" that the Commons accepted. After naming the four judges, the Lords placed a parenthetical note in the order: "That the Carcasses . . . (whether buried in Westminster-Abbey, or elsewhere) be with all expedition, taken up, and drawn upon a hurdle."[51] Their reference to "elsewhere" is at least curious because Pride had been buried in Surrey in 1658, and two years later there should have been no confusion over the body's location.[52] The small addition implied a suspicion that one of the three graves in Westminster Abbey was empty—a suspicion that would prove correct.

Pepys was a royalist who eagerly watched Harrison die but felt uneasy about exhuming the bodies. On the day the Commons voted, he wrote with reference to the lord protector that the proposed vengeance "doth trouble me that a man of so great courage as he was should have that dishonour, though otherwise he might deserve it enough." Sir Edward Nicholas, now secretary to a king, had no doubts; with glee he wrote Sir Henry de Vic that "The Commons have ordered the carcasses . . . to be taken up."[53]

Charles dissolved Parliament on Christmas eve, calling the act of indemnity and oblivion "the principal corner-stone . . . that creates kindness in us to each other; and confidence is our joint and common security." Again the king's moderate speech did not match events. In early January 1661 an attempted rising by a handful of Fifth Monarchy Men, led by Thomas Venner, excited London but collapsed quickly.[54] The government immediately staged more trials and on 19 January began more savage executions. By the twenty-fourth the latest heads had been stuck on London Bridge.[55]

The exhumations were two days later, and the Venetian ambassador had noted that they were to be punctual. The following February the privy council secretary, Nicholas, claimed to the earl of Winchelsea that the order, which he enclosed, had been "punctually executed on the 30th of January," when the bodies of "that execrable Traytor, and some of his archest accomplices" were publicly humiliated.[56] On the contrary, the order's execution was anything but punctual. Approved on 8 December, the act of attainder given royal assent on 29 December, exhumation did not occur until 26 January. Delay was necessary to give authorities time to consider whether any of the bodies were buried "elsewhere."

Sergeant-at-Arms James Norfolk led the exhumation party into Westminster Abbey on Saturday, 26 January 1661, opened the protector's vault at the east end of Henry VII's Chapel, and allegedly began "taking up the bodies." Stonemason John Lewis removed paving stones from the floor and dug into the vault. Lewis opened Bradshaw's grave two days later. Norfolk paid him fifteen shillings for the work. The Middlesex sheriff and the new dean of Westminster added civil and divine sanction to the sergeant's activity.[57]

Little is certain about Norfolk's discoveries and activities. The official *Mercurius Publicus* was devoid of detail: "This day in pursuance of an Order of Parliament, the Carcasses of those two horrid Regicides *Oliver Cromwel* and *Henry Ireton* were digged up out of their Graves, which (with those of *John Bradshaw* and *Thomas Pride*) are to be hang'd up at Tyburn, and buried under the Gallows."[58] Royalists such as Nicholas added no further information. Compared with the detailed if sometimes dubious reports for October's trials and executions, the January reports were terse. In fact the reluctance of the authorities was unusual. There were no fulsome descriptions of bringing the devils forth from their graves, carting them to Holborn, dragging them to Tyburn amid joyful and jeering crowds, hanging on the gallows, holding high the traitors' heads. For over three centuries narrators have as a result told a concise story—dug out, dragged to, buried under. It is generally important enough to mention, not large enough to question. James Heath ended his 1663 biography with a short paragraph that the bodies of Cromwell, Ireton, and Bradshaw were "digged out of their Graves, carried to the *Red Lyon* in *Holborn* . . . drawn in Sledges to *Tyburn,* where they were hanged." Thomas Skinner's 1685 continuation of Bate's *Elenchus* described in a sentence how Parliament ordered "their Bones and stinking Carcasses to be raised and buried under *Tyburn*" but incorrectly added that they were "dragg'd through the City." The story has passed virtually unaltered. Lady

Antonia Fraser elaborated it but misdated the exhumation to 29 January (Tuesday), surmised that the bodies lay one night at "an inn . . . guarded by soldiers," and described them as hanged "in full gaze of the public." But exhumation was on 26 January, the bodies lay two nights presumably guarded by persons unknown (probably not by conspicuously attired "soldiers"), and save that of Bradshaw, the corpses were neither identified nor revealed. Ronald Hutton's *Restoration* quickly mentions the event: "The crowd at Tyburn was entertained by the sight of three corpses suspended in varying stages of decomposition, while apprentices cut off their toes."[59]

One certainty is that Parliament ordered four bodies exhumed but Norfolk looked for only three. When Parliament referred to dead judges, it meant Cromwell, Ireton, Bradshaw, *and* Pride. Silius Titus named the four in his resolution, and no member of the Commons doubted their burial in the Abbey, but apparently members of the Lords had doubt, for they amended the order to exhume the four "whether buried in Westminster-Abbey, or elsewhere." Thomas Pride's corpse was absent because it had been buried "elsewhere." When Norfolk came to the Abbey six weeks later he had decided that it was inconvenient and unnecessary to look for Pride, who died on 23 October 1658 and was buried at Nonsuch, Surrey.[60] His illness, death, and burial were known in the capital, although occurring miles from London and during the interval between the death and the funeral of Cromwell. News published on the day he died said that "Col. Pride is conceived to be dead by this morning; he was very near it this morning."[61] A newsletter sent to Monck in Scotland reported a few days later that "Saturday last the Lord Pride dyed, whose death is heere much deplored."[62] Had he not died he would have been among the judges in 1660 whom the royalists baited like bears.

It is certain that Norfolk located and removed Bradshaw's corpse, buried in the Abbey fourteen months earlier. It is not clear when workmen opened the grave—not Saturday the 26th, because the official announcement under that date claimed only that those "two horrid Regicides *Oliver Cromwel* and *Henry Ireton* were digged up." Norfolk's first duty was to relieve the protector's vault of its contents, and he had no doubts about Bradshaw's location. Workmen opened that grave later—probably Monday—and found the corpse "was green and stank." They removed it sometime Tuesday.[63] On Wednesday there was comment about this corpse's odor, and witnesses at Tyburn identified Bradshaw's features when the body was unwrapped.

Two accounts describe Norfolk's discovery of Cromwell's corpse. The first was a handwritten paper "carefully preserved" by Robert Harley, earl of Oxford, and published in the *Harleian Miscellany* in the mid-1740s. The *Gentleman's Magazine* reprinted it in 1751 because a skeptical correspondent thought "there is great room to doubt, and that some further lights may be acquired by proposing it in your Magazine."[64] The reader was apparently disappointed in receiving light, for the magazine printed no further comments. According to the Harleian paper, Norfolk went by order of the House of Commons to Westminster Abbey.

> Whereupon the said serjeant went, and, in the middle Isle of *Henry the Seventh*'s Chapel, at the East end, upon Taking up the Pavement, in a Vault, was found his Corpse; in the Inside of whose Coffin, and upon the Breast of the Corpse, was laid a Copper-plate, finely gilt, inclosed in a thin Case of Lead, on the one Side where of, were engraved the Arms of *England,* impaled with the Arms of *Oliver;* and, on the Reverse, the following legenda, viz.
>
> *Oliverius Protector Reipublicæ Angliæ, Scotiæ, & Hiberniæ, Natus 25. April.* 1599, *Inauguratus* 16. *Dec.ris* 1653, *Mortuus* 3. *Sept.ris,* 1658. *Hic situs est.*

At the bottom and in another hand the paper indicated that Norfolk claimed the plate, thinking it gold, and bequeathed it to his son-in-law at Colchester.[65] In the 1780s a student of the Cromwellians, the Reverend Mark Noble, reiterated this account in his study of the family: Norfolk and his attendants "found in a vault, at the east end of the middle ai[s]le, a magnificent coffin, that contained the body of Oliver . . . upon whose breast was a copper plate, double gilt."[66]

The second account appeared years later among miscellany in an 1809 number of the *European Magazine*. A correspondent who signed himself as S.S.B. of Islington claimed to have information about the exhumation, in which he saw a cautionary tale for the emperor Napoleon, "the present grand disturber of the peace of nations." He had found a "memorandum . . . amongst the papers of a distant female relation . . . who died about thirty years ago, at an advanced age," which contained information.

> Sr James Norfolk, high sheriff of Middlesex, after King Charles ye Second came in, found out ye Body of Oliver Cromwell, which was hid in ye wall in Westminster-Abby; & when discover'd, was with great difficulty got at, ye Body being first wrapt in a sheet of lead, and afterwards put into a wooden Coffin, & cemented close; it was then put into a leaden Coffin, & another wooden one, and so on for about half a dozen, & cement poured between each to make it secure, that several pick-axes were broken before they cou'd gain their ends; but at length, after much labour & toil, they came to ye sheet of lead which inclos'd his body. To a chain about his neck hung a gold gordget with his name & other writing upon it; which being taken off, Sr James caus'd him immediately to be hung up upon ye gallous at Tyburn. The gold Gordget he kept himself; & told ye whole affair at Sr. John Wolstenholm's my great grandfather's table, Sr Philip Mathews my Grandfather, & his wife my grandmother being present, which latter told it to me, M. D. —Margaret Dawson.[67]

The magazine offered no comment.

These two records have not been accounted in modern writings. From the 1910s to the 1930s *Notes and Queries* printed items reviewing Cromwellian mortality, culminating in an acrimonious exchange between F.J. Varley and Esmond de Beer concerning Ireton's death. Neither the Harleian nor the Islington account received attention. Varley did note the Islington story in *Oliver Cromwell's Latter End* but cited an inaccurate reprint from 1830 to validate his assertion that Cromwell had been in different coffins.[68] More recently, Lady Antonia Fraser referred to a variety of material but not these stories.

The accounts contain information both by inclusion and by exclusion. Their provenance is untidy, but the Harleian account may derive from Norfolk, whereas the Islington account almost certainly does. They appear to have originated at the scene and to have been transmitted independently. They narrate the same event and contain differing but consistent details. Both assert that Norfolk found Cromwell's body and that a metal plate, or gorget, identified it. The Harleian account places the plate on the corpse's breast, describes it as gilded copper in a lead case, and quotes the engraving. The Islington account places the plate on a chain around the corpse's neck (hence on the breast), describes it as gold, and says it had his name and "other writing." This is the plate that the Society of Antiquaries exhibited in the 1730s.[69] At least one impression of the plate was taken at that time but not published until 1926. A memorandum on the same quarto sheet with the impression was dated 1737 and said the impression came from a gilded copper plate "found in a leaden Canister laying on the Breast of the Corpse." Further, Norfolk had "preserved" these items and bequeathed them to his daughter and son-in-law at Colchester.[70]

The accounts say that Norfolk found the gorget on the body, which indicates that he unwrapped the corpse. Such plates were often attached to the lead sheet, but Cromwell's was attached to the body. Dr. Bate had written that embalmers wrapped the body in "a fourfold Cerecloath." To find the gorget, therefore, Norfolk had cut through the heavy cerecloth and revealed the body. The wrappings, already damaged by putrefaction, would not have appeared fresh, a point that marked Cromwell's corpse.

The two accounts seem to place the corpse in the Abbey differently—"in a vault" and "hid in ye wall"—but in fact refer to the same location. The vault was under the easternmost end of the chapel's middle aisle; it abutted Henry VII's vault, located centrally under the middle aisle and just to the west. Within the protector's vault "massive walls, abutting immediately on the royal vault of Henry VII, are the only addition to the structure of the Abbey dating from the Commonwealth." Not only were there massive walls, but within the vault a smaller vault "which seems to have been expressly constructed with a view to isolation and secrecy."[71]

The architectural record is unclear, but this isolated area may have been altered about 1680 when the Ormond family buried two bodies there.[72] The evidence indicates that on the night of 10 November 1658 the protector's corpse was privately buried in this inner vault within the wall abutting upon the royal vault. From thence in 1661 workmen extracted nested containers "with great difficulty" from "ye wall" which was "in a vault."

The Islington account claims the body "was with great difficulty got at." According to Dr. Bate the corpse—wrapped in cerecloth and a lead sheet—was placed in a wooden coffin. At the site, according to this account, the coffin was sealed in a series of containers. This is possible. In 1658 Cromwell's corpse was brought to the Abbey and buried, and the burial party needed to seal it against the effects of further putrefaction. This was the probable reason, rather than security, the coffin was so difficult to get at.

Witnesses saw the body after Norfolk brought the coffin from the vault and opened the lead sheet and the cerecloth to find the gorget. The annalist Thomas Rugg recorded: "Oliver Cromwel's vault beeing broke open, the people crowed very much to see him, who gave sixepence a peece for to see him."[73] The crowing crowd would only have paid such a fee to see the actual corpse. A reasonable inference is that they saw the state coffin, open cerecloth, decomposed body, and identifying gorget.

There is no Abbey record for either burial or exhumation. Sometime after the Restoration an "over zealous loyalist" damaged the register.[74]

Drawing information from various sources permits three observations regarding Norfolk's activities on 26 January.

He excavated the lord protector's coffin. He found the one coffin that was carried from Whitehall to Somerset House with the corpse, displayed unopened with the effigy lying on top, removed secretly on 10 November, and buried privately in a wall within the protector's vault. Accounts of the funeral do not mention this coffin because it had been buried beforehand; they mention only the prominently displayed effigy. There are consistent references to the coffin in fall 1658 and January 1661. Dr. Bate said the embalmers put the lead-cased body in a wooden coffin. The Reverend Mr. Prestwich described it as "an elegant coffin of the choicest wood." Peter Mundy saw at Somerset House a "pretious" wooden coffin "ritchly garnished with iron worcke, all guilt." Sergeant Norfolk recovered a "magnificent" coffin. And at

Tyburn on 30 January a witness described Cromwell's coffin as "a very rich thinge, very full of guilded hinges and nayles."[75]

Norfolk thus excavated the corpse of Oliver Cromwell, lord protector of England, Scotland, and Ireland. The excavators would have been unwise, as Noble said, "to confess themselves baffled."[76] But they did not need to do so for they had located and disinterred the corpse according to Parliament's order. The references are consistent with the Abbey's ground plan, Dr. Bate's description of the embalming, the body's private burial, the identifying gorget, and Rugg's eyewitnesses.

Norfolk did not, however, excavate Ireton's coffin or corpse, because they were not in the vault. Narrators have assumed that Norfolk found Ireton, because the *Mercurius Publicus* and royalist chroniclers also assumed he did. If Ireton had been interred on 26 February 1652 in the protector's vault, Norfolk would easily and readily have found his remains in a coffin near Cromwell's, and sources would have clearly mentioned the discovery. Royalist authors simply assumed that Cromwell *and* Ireton were dug up, but sources closer to events do not confirm this. Neither the Harleian nor the Islington paper mentions a second corpse, though Norfolk had every reason to note fulfilling his orders. Rugg's curiosity seekers would have crowed just as much to see the lord deputy's remains as they did to see Cromwell's, and the annalist would have recorded the display. The crowing crowd saw only one corpse. In short, observers had no reason to say so much about Cromwell's corpse and nothing about Ireton's—unless it was not in the vault.

The absence of Ireton's body is a final demonstration that his corpse had been buried in Ireland—probably Limerick, possibly St. Mary's churchyard—and that the army shipped a symbolic coffin to London. No corpse was reported during Ireton's funeral, but an effigy was displayed at Somerset House and carried to Westminster, where John Owen delivered a sermon. No burial was reported. The charade passed unnoticed, except to a few observers such as General Ludlow, who knew about the secret burial, and Lucy Hutchinson, who suspected it.

This then was the vault's defect that Norfolk feared to find. Of the three corpses presumed to be in the Abbey, Ireton's had been buried "elsewhere." Norfolk dared not confess himself baffled because he had to fulfill Parliament's order. He had four days to produce a substitute "Ireton," and not to have done so would have raised questions that no one in 1661 was prepared to answer.

Coffins were taken from the Abbey on Monday night, 28 January, and hauled to the Red Lion, a coaching inn in Holborn. The Red Lion was not named until slightly later, but newssheets did report that the carts went from Westminster to Holborn. Thomas Rugg, however, recorded at the time that bodies were taken "from West[m]inster to the Red Lyon inn in Holborne."[77] Parliament had specified that the bodies "be taken up, drawn upon a hurdle to Tyburn," implying the hanging should have directly followed the exhumation. The route to the Red Lion was not noted, but through Whitehall and Long Acre would have offered unobserved access to the inn's paddock from the south.[78]

What happened at the Red Lion was never explained, and no writer has found the episode strange. Travelers leaving the City of London for the West crossed the River Fleet bridge at Newgate, went up "Oldboorne hill," and journeyed along the high street to St. Giles and Uxbridge. The road led from Newgate prison in the City to the execution ground at Tyburn, a place first mentioned in the reign of Henry IV, and Holborn Hill was known as "the heavy Hill to Tyburn." During the reign of the great Harry, houses had first been built westward in the country around the Great Turnstile above Lincoln's Inn Fields.[79] In the early seventeenth century "the high *Oldboorne streete,* from the North end of *New-streete* [Chancery Lane], stretcheth . . . (in building lately framed) up to S. Giles in the field." The buildings along High Holborn included "faire houses . . . and lodgings for Gentlemen, Innes for Travillers."[80] One of those inns was the Red Lion, a popular name for inns and alehouses. Several bore the name in the suburbs "without the walls" west of the River Fleet bridge.[81]

Accounts of the exhumation state that agents took carts from Westminster Abbey to the Red Lion *in Holborn,* and this designated the Red Lion between the Great and Little Turnstiles and on the Holborn high street's southern side. The site was in the county Middlesex—west of the Holborn Bar at Staple Inn, beyond London's westernmost ward, Faringdon Without, and beyond the Freedom of the City. The

inn occupied adjoining houses fronting the high street; they are recorded
in a 1586 property transfer. At that time a large garden extended to
Lincoln's Inn Fields. In the 1630s one William Whetstone illegally built
a line of five houses at the rear of this garden, known as Holborn Row
(now Whetstone Park). Open space remained between buildings facing
High Holborn and Holborn Row. Just east of the Red Lion in 1661 a
narrow garden extended from Holborn through to the fields.[82]

In the early seventeenth century, part of the open area behind the
Red Lion was developed into a paddock, a "*Yard* chiefly for *Coach
Horses* and *Stablings.*" It was known as Red Lion Yard. This paddock
provided convenient livery facilities for nearby residents and visitors
to London. It made the Red Lion "a Place of a pretty good *Trade.*" In
Hollar's orthographic map, the Red Lion Yard, coach house, and open
passages giving access to Lincoln's Inn Fields are visible.[83]

The Red Lion's location and the passage through the paddock are
described in an early-eighteenth-century doctor's advertisement. The
doctor, who evidently treated venereal diseases and lived in one of
Whetstone's houses, advertised that "those that desire privacy, they
may come through the Red Lyon Inn, in Holborn, between the two
Turnstiles, which is directly against my back door, where you will see
the sign of the Blue Ball hang over my door."[84] These buildings and
the furtive route through Red Lion Yard are visible on Hollar's map.
The Red Lion faced the Holborn high street, a thoroughfare filled
with carts, hackney coaches, and traffic. In 1661 the property had access to Lincoln Inn Fields, an area used for recreation, duels, and ar-
tillery practice. On its lonely paths occurred occasional robberies and
murders.[85] Facing the busy high street, backing onto Lincoln's Inn
Fields, near the City but in county Middlesex, and suited to secrecy,
the Red Lion was the unusual location to which Norfolk directed the
carts he escorted from Westminster.

The announcement for Norfolk's transfer was as concise as for
Saturday's exhumation. Monday night, "*Cromwell* and *Ireton,* in two
several Carts were drawn to *Holborn* from *Westminster.*"[86] Later information specified that the bodies were taken "to the *Red Lyon* in
Holborn, where they continued all Night."[87] The public did not witness the transfer, although some persons allegedly jeered at the cor-

tege. There was no public viewing of putative "bodies" or coffins while they continued at the Red Lion. There were no crowing crowds because there was secrecy. Bradshaw's corpse was taken from the Abbey to the Red Lion sometime late Tuesday.

The Red Lion's paddock was an excellent location in which to supply a body to represent Henry Ireton, between Saturday and Wednesday morning. In the paddock someone could also have substituted Cromwell's corpse with a body obtained from "resurrection men," who did a thriving but illegal business supplying corpses to anatomists. Lincoln's Inn Fields provided unobserved access to the paddock behind the Red Lion.

December's act of attainder appointed 30 January as a perpetual fast day, and Nicholas described it "as an Anniversary solemne fast and humiliation for the horrid murder of his late Majesty." John Evelyn was introspective on this "day of humiliation to deplore the sinns which so long had provoked God against this Afflicted Church & people." Pepys attended a service and heard a sermon on "the justice of God in punishing man for the sins of his ancestors." He took "a rare walk" across Moorfields because of the fine weather. Afterward he went to "my lady Batten's" and met his wife when the two women returned from Tyburn.[88]

The procession to Tyburn left the Red Lion before Wednesday's dawn. Lady Antonia Fraser has written that "the dawn start was to prevent the populace from pelting the hurdles with stones, brickbats and mud since the corpses were to be reserved for a more awful fate."[89] This is odd speculation—leaving aside the question of handy brickbats in a city built of wood, straw, and wattle—since the authorities did not explain their procedures. Criminals on their way to execution, and the condemned judges in particular, were tied to hurdles precisely so people could insult them and throw objects. Authorities who did not display tender mercy to condemned judges on their way to execution would certainly not have been tender to three dead ones. The dawn start probably had another purpose. If people crowded Holborn from the Great Turnstile to St. Giles, it is possible they might have endangered Norfolk's charade.

The winter weather was mild. "No cold at all," Pepys noted of that month, "and the rose-bushes are full of leaves, such a time of the year as was never known in this world before here."[90] The bodies were hauled in coffins tied onto hurdles—Bradshaw and Ireton were in simple coffins, Cromwell in the "very rich" one taken from Westminster Abbey. From the Red Lion to St. Giles, about one-third the way to Tyburn, the parade followed the Holborn high street, lined with recent construction but with fields north and south of the buildings. West of St. Giles it entered open country for the remaining one and one-half miles to Tyburn. A newssheet published the next day said that "the universal outcry of the people went along with them," but there is no indication that crowds lined the road as routinely happened when a famous criminal was taken to execution.[91] The stench from Bradshaw's corpse, which had overpowered workmen opening his grave, was noted: "The body turned to putrifaction, cast a most odious s[c]ent all the way it went."[92]

The procession arrived about ten o'clock, and there was a crowd. The Venetian ambassador reported that events occurred "before a great crowd amid the universal approval of the city and of all the people." Nicholas claimed this "signal spectacle of justice drew many thousands of people out of the city to behold it." John Evelyn did not attend but also thought "Thousands of People . . . spectators." When Mrs. Pepys and Lady Batten returned to London, where Samuel met them, they offered no memorable observations.[93]

Upon arrival, the carcasses "were pull'd out of their Coffines and hang'd at the several Angles of that Triple tree."[94] The permanent gallows was made of three upright posts connected by beams. This perhaps explains in part why Norfolk did not retrieve Pride's body, for three corpses fulfilled the requirement of the gallows. Despite the confused wording in Parliament's exhumation order, the bodies were not "hang'd in their coffins" but dragged to Tyburn in coffins from which they were removed, then hanged. Thomas Rugg's clear description of these events agrees with the newssheets: "The carcasses . . . [were] taken out of theire coffines and in theire shrouds hanged by their necks untill the goeing' downe of the sune, then cutt downe, theire heads cut of, and theire bodies buired in a grave made under the gallowes."[95]

What the crowd saw was a tableau of two heavily swathed bundles and a lightly wrapped one dangling from the gallows. Bradshaw's body was identified; the others were not. Samuel Sainthill, a merchant in the Spanish trade, recorded Bradshaw in a winding sheet, "the fingers of his right hand and his nose perished, having wet the sheet through." Peter Mundy also described Bradshaw as "in a winding sheete." Sainthill, who stood near the gallows, wrote, "the rest very perfect . . . I knew his face, when the hangman, after cutting his head off, held it up." Darkness had descended by the time the bodies were decapitated, which proceedings were conducted by torchlight. Apprentices cut off Bradshaw's fingers and toes for souvenirs.[96]

Ireton's alleged corpse was hanged in cerecloth rather than a winding sheet, and Mundy thought it "supposed to be embalmed."[97] But according to Sainthill this corpse was not fresh: "Ireton having been buried long, hung like a dried rat, yet corrupted about the fundament."[98] The body was not visible because it remained tightly wrapped. Identification of the genuine corpse would likely have been difficult, of course, if not impossible after a decade, but the point is that authorities did not reveal the corpse. The "corrupted . . . fundament" suggests, if anything, a criminal's corpse given over to an anatomist.

Cromwell's alleged corpse was wrapped in cerecloth, rather than in a winding sheet, and looked "like a mummy swathed up, with no visible legs or feet." This description is from a notation attached to a drawing in the margin of Sainthill's journal. Sainthill mentioned that Cromwell was "in a green-seare cloth, very fresh, embalmed." Mundy described Cromwell as wrapped "in searcloth, supposed to be embalmed."

But Bate had written in circulated copies of his *Elenchus Motuum* that the embalming failed, for he said the corpse "purged and wrought through all." The body could not in 1661 have been described, even cavalierly, as "very fresh."[99] Norfolk had also unwrapped the cerecloth to find the identifying gorget. It is probable, therefore, that the fresh body on display at Tyburn was not the corrupted one buried in and taken from the Abbey, implying that a substitute body had been placed in Cromwell's coffin while it was at the Red Lion Inn's paddock.

Then there was the matter of the heads. According to official accounts the bodies hung "until the Sun was set; after which they were taken down."[100] Parliament's order did not include decapitation. Who so ordered and when is not clear, although dismemberment was part of a "traitor's death." Nicholas reported that "their heads [were] ordered" to be severed and placed at Westminster Hall.[101] As mentioned, only after winter's early darkness did the ceremony conclude with the heads being hacked from the torsos. Because of the thick cerecloth the hangman needed eight chops to sever "Cromwell's" head and four for "Ireton's." The "loathsome" trunks were then "thrown in a deep hole under the Gallows."[102] John Evelyn was apparently not present but thought "under that fatal and ignominious Monument, in a deepe pit" was an appropriate resting place.[103] Within a short time, however, the common hangman set the heads "upon poles on the top of *Westminster Hall*"—Bradshaw at the center, "Cromwell" and "Ireton" on either side.[104] Mundy understood the symbolism: "Their heads were set on a pinacle at the west end of Westminster Hall, right over the High Court of Justice where the old King was sentenced to dy."[105] Since the Restoration's vengeance fell upon the judges, the president of the court was placed at the center. There the royalists left them, the visible skulls as "the Brand-marks of their Posterity, and the expiatory remains of their accursed crime."[106]

The explanation for what happened has never rested easily, but sufficient evidence accounts for the narrative's irregularities. The Tyburn display was Wednesday, 30 January, but Norfolk opened the protector's vault on Saturday, four days earlier than Parliament's order required. Tuesday ought to have been early enough. Rumors about Cromwell's burial and ambiguities about Ireton's funeral may have recurred. The locations of their bodies were not especially relevant until, ironically, the Parliament and the monarchy decided to pull "the carcasses of those devils" from their graves and hang them. It was necessary to know where they lay, in the Abbey or elsewhere. Not to produce the bodies would verify rumors, settle ambiguities, and allow the dead saints to embarrass the monarchy. Charles might well have minded the emperor Charles V's response to the Bishop of Arras, who suggested taking vengeance on Luther's corpse—"I war not with the dead, but with the living," he said.[107]

Norfolk excavated Bradshaw and Cromwell but not Ireton.

Bradshaw's corpse was "green and stank," and Norfolk did not remove it to the Red Lion Inn until Tuesday. Cromwell's body was excavated on Saturday, and Norfolk visibly disrupted the fourfold cerecloth to find the gorget around the body's neck. The corrupted corpse must have been so fragile that Norfolk wondered whether it could be hanged. Although Ireton's body was supposed to be in the same vault, Norfolk did not find it.

Two coffins were removed from Westminster to the Red Lion Inn in Holborn. There was no apparent reason to sequester exhumed corpses in a paddock for two nights and one day nor to store them on private property when the government had available such facilities as Newgate prison. Holborn was northeast of the Abbey, whereas Tyburn was northwest, and a direct parade Wednesday morning would have been expedient and according to parliamentary order. The parade from Holborn to Tyburn allowed fewer spectators than a parade from Newgate to Tyburn. These irregularities imply that after opening the vault Norfolk discovered something so "wrong" as to require a secret remedy prior to Wednesday, a remedy unthinkable in Westminster's sacred precincts but practical in the Red Lion's paddock.

On Wednesday observers noted Bradshaw's stinking carcass, Cromwell's magnificent state coffin, and Ireton's plain box. Norfolk excavated one body from the protector's vault, further indication that Ireton had been buried in Ireland. Had Ireton been buried in the Abbey, he would certainly have been in a magnificent state coffin, not in a plain box. At Tyburn, Bradshaw's body was in a winding sheet, which was opened, and observers recognized the face. Apprentices did cut off Bradshaw's fingers and toes but not those of the two unwrapped corpses. "Cromwell's" corpse was described as being very fresh and embalmed, but the body had purged so badly in 1658 as to require early burial; Norfolk cut open these soiled wrappings and revealed at least part of the body to find the gorget. It is probable, therefore, that the "Cromwell" displayed at Tyburn was not the body excavated from the Abbey.

After sunset the executioner hacked through heavy cerecloth to remove the heads, further indication that "Cromwell's body" was bogus. Removing the head from the corpse was difficult, but it ought to have been an easy matter, were the corpse the one from which Norfolk had removed the cerecloth at Westminster Abbey. The executioner required eight attempts to complete the task. Torchlight did not allow those spectators who remained to observe in detail what happened. Nonetheless, the heads were not presented to public view but left wrapped in cerecloth. Prior to the display at Westminster Hall, they were probably unwrapped and covered with pitch.

The Tyburn pantomime marked the victory of "the king's cause" over the infernal saints.

6

$\mathcal{H}ic$ $\mathcal{S}itus$ $\mathcal{E}st$

The weight of evidence indicates that two of the three bodies at Tyburn were bogus. There was an irreconcilable disparity between Cromwell's corrupted corpse buried in Westminster Abbey and the fresh one hanged at Tyburn. Henry Ireton had been buried in Ireland. Only John Bradshaw's body was genuine.

For the Tyburn "Cromwell" to have been bogus required persons with motive, opportunity, and method to have obtained possession of the genuine corpse and buried it elsewhere. Such substitution has usually been thought unlikely or even preposterous. Nonetheless, the circumstances bear examination. Oral traditions on this point began appearing in print during the latter eighteenth century. Prestwich published "*The Secret!*" of Cromwell's burial in 1787. A few years later, in 1799, Leman Rede wrote that "it was known" at the time that Cromwell's remains had been secretly buried after the exhumation.[1] In 1881 an observant writer in *The Gentleman's Magazine* suspected that something had occurred with Cromwell's corpse. He recounted that at the Red Lion Inn "some other corpse [was] substituted in its place by Cromwell's partisans" and concluded that "it is very probable."[2] Antiquarians Peter Cunningham and Henry Wheatley thought otherwise: "No contemporary or early writer, so far as we know, alludes to any such tradition, which has all the appearance of being a late invention."[3] Wilbur Cortez Abbott pronounced such traditions unworthy of historians' attention. "In spite of the enormous industry and investigation lavished upon the question by antiquarians," he wrote, "it is, historically, of little or no importance what became of his mortal remains."[4] More recently, Lady Antonia Fraser dismissed the story as a legend "more alluring than the truth."[5] That truth is presumed to be the version contained in the *Mercurius Publicus* and Sir Edward Nicholas's letters.

But there was more to the story than met the eye. It was briefly told without substantiating details—dug out, dragged to, buried under. Disparity between the body exhumed from the protector's vault and the one hanged in Cromwell's name indicates that substitution was possible, but were identifiable persons with motive, opportunity, and method able to carry out a secret burial? The question cannot be answered with certainty, of course, but a consistent pattern of circumstantial evidence supports the tradition that one or more individuals "obtained his remains . . . and . . . buried them secretly in a meadow to the north of Holborn."[6]

England's greatest poet at the time seems an unlikely plotter, but compelling circumstances of motive and opportunity point to John Milton as one of the persons who planned a substitution and secret burial. In January 1661 he lived quite near the Red Lion Inn and had a clear motive to arrange the protector's covert burial in close-by Red Lion Fields. He had served loyally as Cromwell's Latin secretary and was notorious among royalists for his defense of Charles's trial. In 1660 he went into hiding while Parliament debated the indemnity bill, reappearing only after it received royal assent and he came within the terms of pardon. Compared to the persons executed, Milton received lenient treatment because such friends as Andrew Marvell intervened for him. During October 1660, while the judges were being tried and executed, the London book market carried an attack on Milton by his old antagonist-in-print and Bishop George Morley's close friend, the then-deceased Salmasius. The unfinished book was in dense Latin and its influence is uncertain, but after its publication Sergeant Norfolk "officiously seised him" in November and placed him under arrest. Marvell raised the case in the Commons, for Norfolk had demanded a bribe totaling £150. Sir Heneage Finch, fresh from prosecuting the judges, demanded that Milton be hanged. The case was resolved in December when Milton was released and received a pardon.[7]

In the modern *Life Records of John Milton,* his activities for early

1661 are undocumented. It is a monumental work, but it does not list daily or weekly entries. At the time he would have been troubled by his recent experiences—this is biographer William Riley Parker's reasonable interpretation. Parker speculated unconvincingly, however, that Milton "tried to put politics out of his mind, so that he could resume the composition of his epic," *Paradise Lost.*[8] It may be that he ignored events outside his small Holborn house, but that was not in character. The poet could hardly have taken up the enormous project so soon after his imprisonment and brush with the gallows. Parliament ordered the exhumation of the four judges a week before his release from prison, and the news gave him reason to consider arranging Cromwell's civil burial. He had not favored the protector's single-person government, but he did admire Cromwell.[9] By January 1661 he must have thought a decent burial of Cromwell preferable to public defilement.

Milton's opportunity to arrange a secret burial comes from his living near the scene. He lived in Holborn on two occasions, but his biographers have not considered the houses important enough to locate, despite available information. The location of his house in early 1661 probably explains the relevance of the Red Lion Inn to the shadowy events there—Milton had a long-standing familiarity with the property and its neighborhood. One of his nephews, Edward Phillips, wrote that in the late 1640s he moved from "his great House in *Barbican,* and betook himself to a smaller in *High Holborn,* among those that open backward into *Lincolns-Inn* Fields."[10] This specific description places the house quite near the Red Lion Inn and on the same side of the road. He must have known of the paddock's access from Lincoln's Inn Fields, and he may often have walked through the paddock and into the high street. During the 1650s he lived in Westminster. Then in 1660 he received the pardon, emerged from hiding, and "took a House in *Holborn* near *Red Lyon Fields*"—this also according to his nephew.[11] He lived in this house only a few months before he unaccountably moved again. Parker speculated without having located the property that the "house in Holborn was for some reason unsatisfactory (perhaps it lacked a garden), and he soon moved to another . . . in the parish of St. Giles Cripplegate."[12]

On the morning of 30 January 1661 Milton's house was along the western edge of Red Lion Fields and a few yards from the commotion occurring on the high street to Tyburn. The antiquarian John Aubrey sought information about Milton's residences and scribbled among his memoranda, "He lived in several places, e.g. Holborn neer K[ing]'s gate."[13] The editor of *The Life Records of John Milton,* J. Milton French, erred in saying Aubrey's passage "carries no suggestion of date," then concluding that it perhaps referred as much to Milton's Holborn residence in the late 1640s as in 1661 and placing it in the records under both dates.[14] Actually, the memorandum does carry a suggestion of date, and reference to Hollar's 1658 map and the Fairthorne and Newcourt map surveyed a decade earlier resolves the matter.[15] The 1640s house was "in *High Holborn,* among those that open backward into *Lincolns-Inn Fields*"; it faced Holborn from the south side and was no more than a few yards from the Red Lion Inn. The 1660–61 house was "neer K's gate," not in the high street. Kingsgate was a short north-south street with a few houses along its western side, approximately on the line of modern Southampton Row (constructed in the early twentieth century as part of the Kingsway project). Therefore, it was west of Lincoln's Inn Fields and north of the busy Holborn high street; Red Lion Fields spread eastward. This location, which was "neer K's gate" and "near *Red Lyon Fields,*" cannot be confused with his earlier residence located among those houses "in *High Holborn*" that "open backward into *Lincolns-Inn* Fields."

Milton may well have lived in the house on the Fairthorne and Newcourt map that stands by itself "neer" Kingsgate. It is nearly surrounded by open land and has a tree-filled garden stretching to the north; Red Lion Fields is immediately to the east. The building had been incorporated into a small row of houses by 1658, but there was still the garden to the north and the open Red Lion Fields to the east. Whatever the reason Milton removed from Kingsgate after the exhumation of Cromwell's body, it was not because the house lacked a garden, for there was considerable open land around it. The property resembled others where he lived: he liked to take long walks and "he alwayes had a garden where he lived."[16] Proximity of this house to Red Lion Fields and Milton's detailed knowledge of the byways around the Red Lion Inn gave him opportunity to consider the burial of Cromwell's corpse. The blind poet could not participate, of course, but he could encourage others.

Among others possibly associated with Milton was his friend and fellow member of the protector's Latin secretariat, Andrew Marvell. Both had walked in the protector's funeral. Marvell represented his native town, Hull, in the Convention Parliament and had saved Milton from exemption, perhaps from the gallows, and secured his release from prison. His biographer, Pierre Legouis, believes he had no reason to fear for his own life, though he suggested that Finch may have directed his "hanging" comment at Marvell rather than Milton. Marvell's activities in January are also poorly documented, but he definitely remained in London after Parliament's dissolution.[17] On 17 January 1661 he addressed a short letter from Westminster to Hull's mayor. He had surprisingly little to say—noticeable because his other letters to the Hull corporation were loquacious. He enclosed a newssheet but little otherwise because, he wrote slyly, "there being litle at present to be publickly communicated." He did note that the Fifth Monarchists had been tried and would soon be executed and that he had forwarded the last Parliament's published acts by ship, "for I know no readyer way of conveyance." His next and longer letter was dated 7 February, when he did publicly communicate more chitchat. He said a grand jury had given the untried judges, who were in custody, copies of "the Prayer book printed for the last Fast for the kings death" on 30 January.[18] He did not refer to the spectacle of the Tyburn hangings a week earlier, an interesting omission. Later in the year he came to blows in the Commons with the royalist and future cabal leader Thomas Clifford. His biographer wondered, "Did this misadventure contribute to the decision he took soon after of going abroad?" He thereafter spent many months away from England.[19]

The noteworthy point about Marvell, however, is posthumous— his interment in 1678 at St. Giles in the Fields, a church and neighborhood just west of Red Lion Fields and Kingsgate with which he seems otherwise unconnected. Legouis quoted an unnoted source that placed the grave "in the South isle by the pulpit," but the location is uncertain. The Hull council authorized a monument in the church to honor

Marvell's "great meritts with the Corporation," although the parson allegedly did not allow its erection. In the 1730s the church was demolished and a new one built; none of the original grave markers apparently survived. The question is not so much the burial marker placed in the old church as a memorial window lost to the new one. The antiquarian Aubrey sought to locate Marvell's grave and adduced a startling piece of information "from the sexton that made his grave" that cannot be disregarded. According to the sexton, Marvell "lies interred under the pewes in the South side of St. Giles' church in-the-fields, under the window wherein is painted in glasse a red lyon (it was given by the inneholder of the Red Lion Inne in Holborne)."[20] Thus passed a poet whom contemporaries remembered, if at all, as a member of Parliament and a "Patriot," a word beginning to denote monarchy's critics.[21] Legouis did not refer to the red-lion window, but the red lion denoting his burial is as curious as the innholder's placing it in Marvell's memory.

Then there were Praisegod Barbon and, especially, his son Nicholas. The elder Barbon, "a leather-seller in Fleet Street," was a quaint and quirky seventeenth-century character born about 1596 whose name runs through the era's history of nonconformity and is attached to the 1653 Parliament of Saints, the Barebones Parliament. After Cromwell's death Barbon sought to maintain the Commonwealth and avert a Restoration. He and others "such as are lovers of the good old cause" petitioned Parliament in February 1660 to oppose reconciliation with the monarchy. They were, their petition said, "lovers of justice and righteousness and freedom in the worship of God, and are lovers of a Commonwealth and doe acompt it the best government."[22] Royalist pamphleteers assaulted him. He accepted pardon under the indemnity act but kept in touch with old friends. In November 1661 he was imprisoned and Sir Edward Nicholas personally directed the gathering of information about him, but eventually he was released. He was buried at St. Andrew's, Holborn, in 1679.

Nicholas Barbon was about twenty years of age in January 1661, he was in London, and he had imbibed a lifetime of antimonarchical sentiment. By July he was a student at Leiden, where English radicals congregated, and in October he received a medical degree at Utrecht; three years later he became an honorary fellow in the College of Physicians. Prior to his stay in the Netherlands he was probably familiar with some of London's doctors. It was not as a doctor that he made his mark but as an innovator of fire insurance and a developer of real estate following the 1666 disaster. His biography is a straightforward story of a seventeenth-century entrepreneur—except for another enigma inside a riddle. According to a diarist, "Dr. Barebone, the great builder, having sometime since bought the Red Lyon Fields . . . to build on . . . employed several workmen to goe on with the same." In the early 1680s the old radical's son, who had grown up in nearby Fleet Street, began to develop the real estate known as Red Lion Fields.[23]

Here was another connection, for there was to be a story that Cromwell had been secretly buried on the land that Barbon purchased. The open field was ready for development in the 1680s, as the metropolis recovered from the great fire and began to expand. Barbon's project for Red Lion Fields marked the beginning of a century and a half's westward growth in terraces, squares, and rows that eventually reached Paddington. The development of Red Lion Fields began in controversy. In July 1684 an imbroglio arose between Dr. Barbon's workmen and "the gentlemen of Gray's Inn," who resisted the spreading city that even prior to Tudor times no regulation had controlled.[24] The gentlemen may have slowed the development, but by the 1690s a square had been erected around a particular place in Red Lion Fields that Barbon and one Ebenezer Heathcote had marked as the center of Red Lion Square. The square was surrounded by streets and houses and supplied by alleys, not unlike Inigo Jones's plan for Covent Garden in this regard. Covent Garden, however, was planned as an open and busy urban piazza—the market developed later—whereas Red Lion Square was from the beginning designed as a rustic garden within the city, not as an urban piazza.

A London survey in 1708 described Red Lion Square as "a pleasant Square of good Buildings; it is in Form near a parallelagram. . . . Area is two Acres."[25] John Strype described it in the 1710s: "It hath graceful Buildings on all sides. . . . The middle of the Square is inclosed from the Streets . . . by a handsome high Palisado Pail; with Rows of Trees, Gravel Walks, and Grass Plats within. . . . Out of this Square are several Streets which lead to other Places. . . . *Fisher's street,* better built than inhabited, falls into *King's Gate street.*"[26] Residents sought parliamentary authority to beautify the square in the 1730s, saying it had become unsightly.[27] Yet Sutton Nicholls's 1731 drawing, taken from the upper floor of a house near the center of the southern side, shows a place as handsome as Strype described. The drawing also shows how close the square was to the edge of the metropolis, even in the fourth decade of the eighteenth century.[28] A few years later a writer said Red Lion was "a neat Square, consisting of well built uniform Houses, inhabited by Gentlemen, and has a pretty Garden in the middle of it."[29]

In the late 1740s a curious monument and substantial architectural elements appeared in the square without explanation. This addition may have been the result of residents' action during the prior decade. Some years later a resident said the monument had been erected "at the suggestion of Mr. Dillingham, an eminent apothecary in the neighborhood," and thus "the pillar got the name among the neighbors, of *Dillingham's Glyster-pipe.*"[30] The 1754 edition of Stow's *Survey* described these architectural additions as though they had been standing for some years—"a handsome Watch-House built at each Corner . . . and a fine Obelisk of Stone in the Center."[31] A survey published in 1761 described the square as handsome and noted that it was "adorned with a lofty obelisk placed upon a pedestal in the center." An accompanying map for binding into the volume marked the monument's location and may now be its only physical trace.[32] Other writers over the years confirmed these descriptions.[33] In a 1771 book criticizing the rustic design of urban squares, James Stuart wrote a melancholy prose reverie about the square similar to Thomas Gray's graveyard meditation but with an unsettling undertone of *vanitas.* In this one square of the several he discussed, Stuart became morbidly preoccupied with moldering beneath the sod, remembrances of death, and paths leading to the grave.

> I never go into it without thinking of my latter end. The rough sod
> that "heaves with many a mouldering heap," the dreary length of

its sides, with the four watch-houses like so many family vaults at
the corners, and the naked obelisk that springs from amid the rank
grass, like the sad monument of a disconsolate widow for the loss
of her first husband, all form together a *memento mori,* more
powerful to me than a death's head and cross marrow-bones; and
were but a parson's bull to be seen bellowing at the gate, the idea
of a country churchyard, in my mind, would be complete.[34]

The obelisk stood behind the high and locked pale at the
square's center, where axes drawn from the corner vault-like watch
houses crossed. It was variously but always funereally described
as "a plain obelisk," "the naked obelisk," "the sad monument," "a
clumsy obelisk." Carved at the base was an ambiguous, even mysterious, inscription:

> *Obtusum*
> *Obtusioris Ingenii*
> *Monumentum.*
> *Quid Me Respicis, Viator?*
> *Vade.*

This inscription might have been altogether unrecorded had not Thomas Pennant published it in 1790, taking note of Red Lion Square not
because there were any buildings of interest but "merely for the sake
of some lines on its clumsy obelisk."[35]

The monument engaged the viewer but discouraged his advance.
It asserted a premise that the inscription disguised. And what did it
mean? A report published in the same year as Pennant's book claimed
that Dillingham, said to have been responsible for the column, "had
sufficient evidence of the circumstances" regarding Cromwell's secret burial in Red Lion Fields and "was a warm admirer of the [good
old] cause."[36] The oral tradition that Leman Rede published in 1799
asserted that Cromwell's grave was in Red Lion Square and "the obelisk is thought by many to be a memorial erected to his manes by an
apothecary who was attached to Cromwell's principles, and had so
much influence in the building of the square, as to manage the marking of the ground."[37] In the 1840s, John Heneage Jesse published a
similar memory concerning the memorial: "Formerly there existed a

favorite tradition among the inhabitants of Red Lion Square and its vicinity, that the body of Oliver Cromwell was buried in the centre of their square, beneath an obelisk which stood there till within the last few years." Jesse first thought the story improbable, but he began to wonder if the protector's bones did indeed molder "beneath this spot." He speculated that Ireton and Bradshaw were also there.[38] Because he considered the tradition without reference to other information, he missed its point: Cromwell alone was buried in the square—not Cromwell, Ireton, and Bradshaw. The monument covered the bones of Cromwell, disguised their presence, discouraged disturbance. "Why do you stare at me, traveler? Be gone."

Such a monument ought to have stood for centuries in that pale-defended garden, but sometime in 1789 or early 1790 it vanished, and one reason may have been Sir John Prestwich's publication of *"The Secret!"* of Cromwell's burial. His 1787 *Respublica* was a detailed collection of protectoral ceremonies, ensigns, and armorial bearings, and in it the author claimed the secret came to him from "the only remaining honourable person whose ancestor alone knew it." The authority was probably his Cromwellian forebear, the Reverend John Prestwich, who had reliably recorded other information about the protector's funeral and first burial. *"The Secret!"* of Cromwell's burial was that "His remains were privately interred in a small paddock near Holborn; in that very spot over which the obelisk is placed in Red-Lion-Square, Holborn." This story did not mention the Red Lion Inn, but there was of course a paddock on its property.[39] The monument had certainly vanished by mid-1790. In July 1787 *The Gentleman's Magazine* quoted Prestwich's present-tense reference to where "the obelisk is placed," but in August 1790 the magazine reported that the monument "is now taken down, together with the stone watch-houses at the four corners of the inclosure, [and] perhaps some inquisitive inhabitant may be tempted to investigate the matter."[40]

Critics have attacked Prestwich because the secret was "not discussed in the book at any length."[41] When the book was published in May 1787, Prestwich apparently feared the possibility of a sedition charge, and he sought to avoid this by an obsequious dedication that said he had written "from the real Dictates of an Honest Heart, firmly attached to the Illustrious House of Hanover, and entirely devoted both to the Interest and to the Permanency of this our Commonwealth of Britain."[42] Alert readers might have noted, incidentally, that his publisher was "J. Nicholls, Red-Lion-Court-Passage, Fleet-Street."[43] The reviewer of *Respublica* in *The Gentleman's Magazine* indicated that there was a fine line between sedition and loyalty. He wrote that expression of loyalty to the Hanoverian dynasty was necessary "in this democratic age, when the independency of three estates on each other is so eagerly aimed at on the continent of America, and the annihilation of one of three as furiously contended for on that of Europe." Any reference to the good old cause—and particularly a memorial to the protector, however disguised—could be politically suspect in the uncertainty of the late 1780s. The writer labeled Prestwich's book "a very innocent muster-roll of banners, commissions, honours, and summonses to parliament, under the administration of the Protector" but reiterated the statement about secret burial in Red Lion Square, "where the obelisk is placed." The following year the magazine stated that it was time "to bring such curiosities out of obscurity" because the "rancorous zeal of ecclesiastics" was less than formerly.[44]

Another factor relating to the obelisk's disappearance may have been the proposal in the late 1780s to raise a monument to Milton in the parish church of St. Giles, Cripplegate. His gravestone had disappeared during minor repairs a few years after his burial.[45] Several patrons publicly discussed erecting a memorial but first wished to locate the grave, which previously had been "ascertained only by tradition," before they erected a monument. In late July 1790 workmen found a coffin beneath the pavement where the common councilmen's pew stood. Gravedigger Elizabeth Grant charged the curious sixpence to look into the excavation with a candle. On 4 and 5 August the coffin was displayed, and public controversy flared as to whether the corpse was Milton's.[46] The poet William Cowper thought disturbing the corpse for any reason an indecency:

> Ill fare the hands that heav'd the stones
> Where Milton's ashes lay,
> That trembled not to grasp his bones,
> And steal his dust away![47]

It is possible that discussion of Milton's grave, in addition to the publication of Prestwich's secret, caused anxiety among some and a desire to remove the obelisk from Red Lion Square—leaving behind the legend of Cromwell's ghost that nineteenth-century residents recited on foggy nights.

Last among the testimonies, personal and physical, were references to Ebenezer Heathcote, who assisted Nicholas Barbon in the laying out of Red Lion Square. Leman Rede's 1799 anecdote said that "the Protector's friends" had obtained the body and buried it "in a meadow to the north of Holborn." He identified the person who marked Barbon's ground and influenced the plan for Red Lion Square only as "an apothecary." Another tradition identified the apothecary as Ebenezer Heathcote, a resident of Holborn and a zealous republican married to "the daughter of one of Ireton's commissaries." According to this story he bribed the guards at the Red Lion Inn, obtained Cromwell's body, and buried it in Red Lion Square where the obelisk stood.[48] In 1661 the site was in the open Red Lion Fields north of the Red Lion Inn and its paddock. A nighttime burial in this "meadow" was possible. References to Heathcote's activities do not mention Ireton, whom the republican apothecary also had an obvious motive to bury secretly. The omission gives credence to the story: Heathcote did not retrieve Ireton's remains for burial because there was no Ireton to retrieve, only Cromwell.

In 1881 a writer observed of the Heathcote story, "This strange story, in itself less improbable than any of the others, unfortunately rests on no good authority."[49] A few years later a genealogical volume relating to families named Heathcote provided good authority. It referred to "Mary, daughter of Ebenezer Heathcote, of Kingsgate, Holborn, apothecary."[50] The reference made Ebenezer historical, gave him a residence and a family, and together with tradition made the story more probable than any of the others.

Heathcote's house in Kingsgate, moreover, returns the question to Milton, raising the possibility—perhaps demonstrating the likelihood—of a plan involving Milton and other "friends." There were few houses along Kingsgate, and it would be incredible if Cromwell's Latin secretary and the republican son-in-law of one of Ireton's commissaries did not know each other. Of the few houses represented on Hollar's map as in Kingsgate and across from Red Lion Fields, Heathcote arguably lived in one that was close to Milton's house "near Kingsgate."

Thus there were two poets, two Barbons, and one apothecary, all with motive and opportunity. Much evidence for Cromwell's exhumation and burial comes from sources that are unofficial, antiquarian, and disregarded—Rugg's diurnal, the Harleian paper, the Islington memorandum, inhabitants' memory, oral traditions, Prestwich's secret, Heathcote's story. Despite their disparate origins, all refer just to one body, Cromwell's, and agreement on this point indicates the stories originated independently among persons with direct knowledge. Fabricators along the line would certainly have assumed, erroneously, from public information that both Ireton and Cromwell had been exhumed and would have included both names in their tales of secrecy. Although any one of these sources seems incomplete by itself, collectively they make a consistent and credible narrative point.

An objection might be that these persons did not have a method for obtaining Cromwell's corpse, but Sergeant-at-Arms James Norfolk did. He appears in narratives, if at all, as a mere functionary who carried out Parliament's exhumation order. The probability of a bogus "Cromwell" at Tyburn casts immediate suspicion upon him. Only he could have made possible the removal of and substitution for Cromwell's body. He exhumed the corpse, opened the cerecloth, and knew Cromwell's corpse on 30 January to the exclusion of all other corpses. If the exhumed corpse were not hanged at Tyburn, as evidence indicates, Norfolk obviously had to know. He was in charge of the proceedings, and his assistants could not have allowed substitution without his knowledge and approval.

Far from being an innocent functionary, Norfolk had an overwhelming motive to permit the body's substitution—avarice. When the protectorate collapsed, Norfolk, like others, had to overcome his past and make his future way. In October 1660 the king accepted petitions concerning title to the Commons sergeantcy. Norfolk apparently had received a royal warrant for the post, but at least two other men contested his "trying to obtain the said office." Some house members may have opposed him as well—a petition charged that "one Norfolk engaged in the rebellion, and very offensive to the House."[51] He incurred debts contesting the sergeantcy as well as paying for the office. The sergeant's stipend was two shillings, threepence per day, and an incumbent required imagination in the best of times.[52] In an England where public office could be private property, the rules of *baksheesh* obtained.

The sergeant's venality was demonstrable. He arrested and imprisoned Milton with an old Commons order, even though the poet had been pardoned under the parliamentary indemnity act. He demanded extortionate bribes from Milton. This outrageous case came into the record only because Marvell raised it in the House of Commons, but Norfolk may have undertaken other extortions as well. Milton was released, but the manner of resolution is as unclear as extortion is clear. Marvell probably negotiated the release because as a member of the Commons he knew the sergeant to be, in a modern phrase, "a man who likes talking to a man that likes to talk."[53] During the exhumation on 26 January, Norfolk retained the gorget found around Cromwell's neck because he assumed it to be gold; another source said politely that he "preserved" it. In his public and official capacity he thus stole material evidence for his personal gain. When the gorget proved to be gilt copper, he could neither profit from nor produce it. To keep it from public view, he bequeathed it to his son-in-law. Furthermore, he even charged spectators a fee to look at the corpse he had exhumed on Parliament's order. And in 1661 Col. Thomas Hunt petitioned the king "for the benefit of a bail bond taken without orders by Sergeant Norfolk, for appearance of Col. Ludlow, one of the late King's murderers." Charles approved the petition and ordered Norfolk to deliver the bond to Hunt as "reward for his loyal sufferings."[54] Sir James, as he became, was a mercenary who seized his chances. When approached for Cromwell's corpse, he simply saw another chance.

The following is therefore possible. Milton, distraught over his recent experience but following affairs from prison and Kingsgate, reacted to the exhumation order with an emotion such as he described in Samson's questioning men's fate at the hands of a God who

Oft leav'st them to the hostile sword
Of heathen and profane, their carcases
To dogs and fowls a prey, or else captived:
Or to the unjust tribunals, under change of times,
And condemnation of the ingrateful multitude.[55]

Andrew Marvell acted on Milton's behalf and in Cromwell's memory
in those changed times. As a member of the Commons he was able to
speak easily with Norfolk, whom the house had made responsible for
the excavation. The sergeant opened the protector's vault four days
early, in case there was a problem. He exhumed the body of Cromwell
from Henry VII's Chapel and that of Bradshaw from another Abbey
location; he did not find the body of Ireton in the protector's vault,
where it was supposed to have been buried. Marvell arranged for
Norfolk to carry Cromwell's corpse to the Red Lion's paddock, a place
with which Milton was familiar. Placing the coffin in Holborn was
not a coincidence but a contrivance. Nicholas Barbon, soon to receive
a medical degree, arranged with a city resurrection man for corpses to
represent the missing Ireton and to substitute for Cromwell. Heathcote,
Milton's near neighbor, handled arrangements at the paddock. He was
in a position to deal with the guards, perhaps plainclothed members of
a regiment the monarchy had yet to disband. Barbon and Heathcote at
a later time carried the protector's corpse the short distance from the
paddock to Red Lion Fields and at night buried it in the "meadow."
Milton may even have attended the burial in that field so near his
house. In another context the faithful Marvell expressed a resonant
concern for his sightless friend: "Through that wide Field how he his
way should find / O're which lame Faith leads Understanding blind."[56]

Nicholas Barbon and Ebenezer Heathcote literally knew where
the body was buried, for they put it there. When Barbon later acquired
the field, he and Heathcote marked the ground and created a memorial square wherein the protector could lie undisturbed. This *rusticus
in urbus* square was Cromwell's cemetery, and ironically it helped set
a fashion for garden squares across the West End.

Keeping such a plan quiet seems unlikely, but it involved few
persons, none of whom had reason to divulge the story. Partisans would

not risk a second exhumation, Norfolk would not risk explaining his venality. Milton perhaps admonished his friends about the virtue of silence in terms similar to Samson's lamentation for his crime,

> Shameful garrulity. To have revealed
> Secrets of men, the secrets of a friend,
> How heinous had the fact been, how deserving
> Contempt, and scorn of all.[57]

The lack of contemporary evidence may be the natural result of "the fidelity with which the secret was preserved."[58] Some people eventually did know of Heathcote's participation, such as his fellow apothecary Dillingham, and the mournful obelisk locked within the pale inevitably prompted speculation when Prestwich published its secret. In those days only a few people referred to the secret quietly, while others dismissed it. The recent loss in North America and the revolution in France rendered the good old cause suspect. When public speculation occurred, the obelisk "vanished." The plot was successful in 1661 because it left few clues and many ambiguities.

The royalist version has been pervasive, but it is undocumented. Parliament's December order is sometimes cited as if it were a narrative account of January's events. The order was not precisely carried out, even by royalist accounting, and therefore does not record events. Exhumation occurred four days early, Pride's body was not exhumed, the business was not punctually done, Parliament did not mention the Red Lion, the bodies were not hanged in their coffins, beheading was not ordered. Official newssheets printed secondhand announcements for which there is no contemporary confirmation. Assertions that two "horrid Regicides" were exhumed on 26 January are elsewhere unsupported. Newssheets claimed that bodies were taken by cart "to Holborn," then to Tyburn where they were hanged and taken down after sunset. Compared to the detail for the October executions of the judges, these are sparse reports.

The royalist record includes Sir Edward Nicholas's letters, which are secondhand accounts. He wrote the earl of Orrey three days afterward and said that Cromwell, Ireton, and Bradshaw had been "dug out, exposed at Westminster Abbey, drawn to Tyburn and then hanged till sunset." The bodies were thrown in a pit, the heads placed at Westminster Hall, so he claimed. Newssheets said as much. For Sir Edward these events were public pantomimes in which symbol outweighed fact. The point was that the nation should see the hanging of degraded and failed rebels, as it witnessed the hanging of the Fifth Monarchists a week earlier. He wrote Orrey that 30 January had been "a solemn fast" and that the events were a "signal spectacle of justice, which drew many thousands of people out of the city to behold it."[59] He developed his metaphor in a letter to Sir Henry de Vic: "The archtraitor Cromwell, and two of his choicest instruments, Bradshaw and Ireton, finished the tragedy of their lives in a comic scene at Tyburn; a wonderful example of justice."[60] A week later he wrote that the bodies were hanged "in view of thousands, attracted by so marvelous an act of justice."[61]

The display continued with setting the heads on Westminster Hall, where in royalist opinion the three had committed treason by judging and condemning Charles I.

Interest in "Cromwell's head" has produced a considerable tradition. On an unspecified date during the 1680s a great wind allegedly blew down one of the three skulls from the Hall's roof but not the other two. The unidentified skull fell at an unnamed sentinel's feet. Sometime later his daughter sold it to a family in Cambridgeshire, and from there it passed to a dissolute actor named Samuel Russell. About 1780 the skull reappeared, displayed by a museum owner, James Cox, who afterward bought it. He sold it to three speculators for £230, and they also displayed it. From there it came into the possession of Josiah Wilkinson. It descended to Canon Wilkinson, and at the latter's death it passed to Cromwell's college at Cambridge, Sidney Sussex.[62]

In the 1930s Karl Pearson and G.M. Morant examined the skull and, deciding it was not a forgery, declared it came from a time around the Restoration and was similar in "frontal breadth and probable age" to Cromwell. The two authors found no documentation for the skull in the years after 1684, when they presumed it to have been blown down, and its reemergence a century later. Pearson and Morant assumed that the skull lost importance as the years passed because there was less emphasis on it as a warning against attacking divine right:

"William and Mary, we may remind the reader, were to be joint sovereigns *by vote of the people.*"[63] They made two observations. The head had been cut in half and the skullcap removed in a process that was, according to a contemporary handbook, "as you doe in Anatomie," and the head had been separated from the trunk after embalming. They found "nothing improbable" in the head being that of Cromwell. Although they believed this a "moral certainty," they nonetheless left the answer "to be reached by the reader."[64]

The authors were more interested in countering the idea of forgery than in describing circumstances surrounding the Tyburn display. They did consider whether the bodies were pulled from or hanged in their coffins, although sources are clear that authorities removed the corpses. They surmised in passing that if the coffins had been opened prior to the hanging, "Possibly some preparation of the bodies was made at the Red Lion in Holborn or in Westminster Abbey before the taking to Holborn with a view to the proceedings at Tyburn." They did not explain what preparation might have been required. (It would be most unlikely for preparation to have been undertaken in the Abbey's sacred precincts, although it is certain that Norfolk opened Cromwell's coffin, found the identifying gorget, and charged the curious a fee to look at Cromwell's body.) They were not curious why Norfolk excavated only one body from the protector's vault rather than two, nor why he sequestered two coffins for two nights on a private Holborn property. They wrote in a note that the "stay at the Red Lion has given rise to various wild tales, such as the rumour that the bodies were interchanged with others during those two nights." There was no explanation for the presence of Ireton's body at Tyburn, although there is no evidence that Norfolk excavated it from the protector's vault. Without attending to Sergeant Norfolk, the authors assumed it unlikely that royalists would have left the bodies "unguarded or with untrustworthy guards."[65]

Sequestering Cromwell's coffin at the Red Lion prior to the Tyburn display surely allowed the substitution of another corpse for his. Norfolk was hardly a trustworthy functionary, and he willingly participated in a profitable business that also allowed him to fulfill Parliament's order. He needed a body to represent Ireton, and thus he had reason to cooperate with Marvell, a member of the Commons, when approached about a substitution for Cromwell. The medically inclined Nicholas Barbon was in a position to arrange for two bodies with a redemption man or anatomist. A possible source for one or both of the bodies at Tyburn was the Fifth Monarchy executions ten days earlier; of thirteen victims, several were not quartered, and coincidentally, according to Mundy's diary, "Eleven heads were set on London Bridge."[66] The hangings occurred in congested streets, scenes of the victims' alleged treachery, and resurrection men had ample opportunity to acquire for an anatomist bodies that had not been quartered. The head had been split as "you doe in Anatomie," as the above authors mentioned. In this regard, it is important to note that Sainthill and Rugg say Norfolk allowed the Tyburn executioner to unwrap only Bradshaw's corpse, which was recognizable despite a poor state of preservation. He did not allow the executioner to remove the wrappings from "Cromwell" and "Ireton," who remained swathed like mummies. After sunset the bodies were decapitated—"Cromwell's" with special difficulty, although Norfolk had opened the wrappings of the exhumed body and obtained the gorget—and even in the darkness the heads were not identified.

The gentlemen of Sidney Sussex buried the head in 1960. A plaque at the chapel memorializes the event. The skull's location was not given, lest royalists or undergraduates purloin it.[67]

We can reasonably conclude that this object, which has presented itself as Cromwell's head over many years, was that of someone else. This leads to a final point about the lord protector, namely, the fact that in the decades after his death his family was silent about the display of his alleged head and, more interestingly, the alleged display of his body. They made no comment, expressed no dismay, undertook no retrieval of the skull placed atop Westminster Hall and the body buried under the gallows. The Stuart Restoration may have forced them into momentary silence, but Richard Cromwell lived until 1712, and as the years passed he could easily have taken measures to protect the putative remains of his father. Various persons reported stories about the protector's dying wish for burial, although there is no indication that any of them had been present. There was talk of burial in the Thames, at Naseby field, in the chapel at Windsor Castle. The stories may have been ruses to confuse the issue and protect "*The Secret!*" One must assume that the family did not seek the protector's remains because the body was buried in Red Lion Fields. Milton would have vouchsafed the burial, it seems, because he and the Bendish-Cromwell family were "in Great Intimacy" before and after the protector's death.[68] The family could be at peace because the protector's friends had secured a decent burial at Red Lion Fields. *Hic situs est.*

The Tyburn display and affixing the skull were successful because, in the end, Englishmen understood the deaths of Ireton and Cromwell as political emblems rather than personal events. Site, ceremony, and image—Tyburn, executioner, and gallows—conveyed to an illiterate populace the monarchy's warning against political experiment and usurpation, a warning so terrible that almost none dared question the tableau's substance. Whatever the future of the house of Stuart, monarchy and its dependent hierarchy would be secure. So, too, Englishmen understood events within the accepted religious beliefs. Church practice emphasized the body's physical preservation until judgment day and saw exhumation as an outward sign of disgrace. Adherents believed Parliament's order attainted the men for treason and dismemberment denied them resurrection "youthful and fair." Puritans, however, emphasized inward grace and the triumphant soul's elevation to salvation when the body died. Burial was a mere civil decency because the soul's grace was irrespective of the body. Cromwell's friends believed he had a covenant of grace, and exhumation did not theologically trouble them. But they prevented civil indecency to his remains by burying them in Red Lion Fields. Tyburn, a place of skulls, was far from the secret grave, yet it was

> Here pilgrims roam, that strayed so far to seek
> In Golgotha him dead, who lives in heaven.[69]

*A*ppendix

Contents

Letters to Henry Cromwell from John Thurloe, Charles Fleetwood, and Viscount Fauconberg

From *A Collection of the State Papers of John Thurloe, Esq.,* ed. Thomas Birch, vol. 7 (London, 1742).

John Thurloe to Henry Cromwell, 27 July 1658, Whitehall
(pp. 294–95)

His highnesse's constant residence at Hampton-court, and the sicknesse of my lady Elizabeth, which hath been, and is a great afflication to hym, hath hindered the consideration of those matters, which my former letters mentioned, that very little or nothinge hath been done therein for these 14 dayes. . . .

Charles Fleetwood to Henry Cromwell, 3 August 1958
(p. 309)

Deare Brother,

It hath pleased the lord, when all hopes wer even at an ende, and the doctors did beleive my lady Elizabeth's condicion was desperat and near expiring, it pleased the lord beyond all expectation, as a return of prayer, as we have cause to say, to give hir a composure of spirits by sleepe; and since friday last [30 July] she hath bine dayly upon the recovery, and so continues in a very hopefull way. His highnes hath bine for thes 4 or 5 dayes very indisposed and ill; but this night hath had a very good refreshment by sleepe, and is now much revived, his paynes and distemper abated, and is much amended. The Lord sanctefy thes various dispensations, and gather up our hearts by all more to himselfe, that we may have weaned affections from this poor empty world. Thes late providences hath much retarded our publicke resolutions, that it will be October ere the parliament can sitt. Things are under much silence, and I hope more union. Little from Flanders: the siege at Gravelin continues; the Spanyard have their hopes of supplyes from Germany. With my most humble service to all deare relations with you, I remaine

Your most affectionate brother and humble servant.

Viscount Fauconberg to Henry Cromwell, 14 August 1658, Hampton Court (p. 337)

My Lord

The sorrow wee all have had for that excellent sister of your lordshipp's the poor lady Elizabeth, and feare for his highnesse, now, blessed be God, in a hopefull way of recovery, has put a stand to all businesse, and rendered this place barren of any news. . . .

John Thurloe to Henry Cromwell, Whitehall, 17 August 1658 (p. 320–21)

May it please your Excellency,

I was necessitated to omitt the writeinge by the last post, being obliged to attend my lady Elizabeth's funeralls [10 August], shee beinge this day se'nnight at night interr'd at Westminster, wheither shee was carryed from Hampton-court. Your lordship is a very sensible judge, how great an affliction this was to both their highnesses, and how sadd a familye she left behinde her [6 August], which sadnesse was truly very much encreased by the sicknesse of his highnesse, who at the same tyme lay very ill of the gout, and other distempers, contracted by the longe sicknesse of my lady Elizabeth, which made great impressions upon hym; and since that, wheither it were the retireinge of the gout out of his foot into his body, or from some other cause, I am not able to say, he hath beene very dangerousely sicke, the violence whereof lasted 4 or 5 dayes; but, blessed be God, he is now reasonable well recovered, and this day he went abroad for an houre, and findes himselfe much refreshed by it, soe that this recovery of his highnes doth much allay the sorrow for my lady Elizabeth's death. Your excellencye will easiely imagine, what an alarume his highnes sicknesse gave us, beinge in the posture wee are now in. How farre the danger wee then apprehended will be teacheinge to us of the thinges, which wee hitherto could never learne, is very doubtfull: however, God hath given us a further space, and the Lord give us hearts to make a good use of it. Truly all our worke and buissines for these 14 dayes hath beene only to bemoane the sadd condition of the publique affaires, and to observe the great consternation all sober men were in at the report of his highnesse sicknesse, which in truth was exceedinge great; soe that I am able to give your excellencye noe account of any further progresse made in our buissines. All that will depend upon his highnes perfect recovery, which wee hope will be now within a few dayes. Wee have not much neither of forreine newes. The kinge of Sweeden hath yet beene upon noe action; but now somethinge of that kinde is expected from hym, he haveinge imbarqued hymselfe with 7000 horse and foot at a place called Kiel, and intends, as they say, for parte of the elector of Brandenburgh's countrye, or else to releive Thorne, which is still besiedged by the Poles and Austrians. Gravelinge remeynes yet beseiged. The surrender thereof is expected every day; and certeinely it cannot hold out many dayes, unlesse it be relieved, which it seems the Spanyard will endeavor to doe, and for that end is upon his march, and was come within 8 or 9 mile of it, and haveinge got by marshall Turenne, who is close upon his reare; soe that it is likelye to be a very difficult worke to get in any releife without a battle, and a victory too, mareshall Turene beinge able to fight the Spanyard, whilest marshall la Ferté meinteynes the seige.

Your Excellencye's
Most humble and faithfull servant.

Charles Fleetwood to Henry Cromwell, 17 August 1658 (p. 340)

Deare Brother,

The solemnising of the funeralls of the deare lady Elisabeth occationed my silence the last weeke. The Lord teach us by that sore stroake, since which his highnes hath bine very much indisposed, troubled with paynes in his bowells and backe, and could not sleepe; but the Lord hath bine pleased to give a return to the prayers of his poore people, and he is now both eased of his paynes, and his sleepe returned to him. This dispensation with the former allso hath bine very awakening in itselfe, if we may have hearts to learn therby. Our publicke affayres have bine much at a stande since his highnes illnes, which may easily be beleived, when we consider how great a concernment ther was therin. Oh! that we might in soime proportion have sutable effects from such a dispensation! It showld be much upon our hearts to be earnest with the Lord, that we might be as well instructed, as we have bine corrected. Heare is very litle newes stirring. . . . The Lord can turn all for good, which that we se in this, is the hopes of

Your most affectionate brother, and humble servant.

John Thurloe to Henry Cromwell, 24 August 1658 (pp. 354–55)

My Lord,

His highnesse continueinge ill hath given a stopp to all buissines: he was soe well upon friday [20 August], that wee hoped the worst of his sicknesse was over; but it pleased God, that upon saterday morneinge [21 August] he fell into a fitt of an ague, and by its course ever since, it appeares to be a tertian. The fitts were longe and somewhat sharpe; but yet the last was not soe badd as the former. This beinge the intervall day, he came from Hampton-court hither, all the doctors judgeinge this to be much the better place, besides the advantage, which the change of aire usually gives for the recovery out of agues. And although it be an ill tyme of the yeare to have an ague in, yet it being a tertian, and his highnesse beinge pretty well in the intervalls, the doctors doe not conceive there is any danger as to his life. However your excellency will easily ymagine, how much trouble wee are all under here; and though it shall please the Lord to recover him againe, yet certeinely considering the tyme that this visitation is in, and other circumstances relateing thereunto, it cannot but greatly affect us all towards God, and make us deepely sensible, how much our dependance is upon him, in whose hands is the life and breath of this his old servant; and if he should take him away from amongst us, how terrible a blow it would be to all the good people of the land; and that therefore wee should be carefull, how wee walke towards God, least we provoke him to depart from us, and bringe upon us this great evil. The people of God here pray much for his recovery, and I hope those in Ireland will doe the same; and to have his life spared and his health restored by prayer, is a great addition to the mercy. I will not trouble your excellency with any thinge now: I have noe heart to doe it, untill it please God to heare prayer in this matter; nor indeed is there any great matter of newes, but what is in print. I rest,

Your Excellencye's
Most obedient and humble servant.

His highnes is just now enteringe into his fitt; I beseech the Lord to be favourable to him in it.

Charles Fleetwood to Henry Cromwell, 24 August 1658 (p. 355)

Dear Brother,

I gave you in my last an account of his highnes hopefull recovery; but the lord was pleased upon thursday last to let his distemper return, and hade a very sore second fite upon saturday, whic is now turned into a tertian ague. This last fitt was yeasterday, but not so great as the former fitt, and did rest the last night very well, and is in a hopefull way. The physitians advise his highnes coming to London, which is done this day, and to remaine at Whitehall for some time. Jameseshowse is conceived much better ayre than Whitehall, and is preparing for his highnesse's reception; but if the Lord please to remove the presant distemper suddenly, it will be endeavored to get his highness into some fresh ayre, wheare he may have the liberty to use recreation. This dispensation hath indead that in it, which ought exceedingly to awaken us, and to be earnest with the Lord, that we may search for what he thus reproves. Ther is none but are deeply concerned in this, that have a true love to this blessed cause: for the further carying on of the same, the Lord will bring him forth with more vigour, life, and zeale. His highnes hath hade very great discoveryes of the Lord to him in his sicknes, and hath had some assurances of his being restored, and made further serviceable in this worke: this latter is secretly kept, and therefor I shall desire it may not goe further then your own breast; but I think ther is that in this experience, that may truly be worthy of your further knowledg. The counsell have reade your letter, and are at presant in no condicion to answer the contents thereof by any additionall supply, then what is already ordered; the letter is referred to a committee: what we can doe, you may be assured of: in perticuler wherein I can serve you, I hope you will beleive there is none more ready then

> Your most affectionate brother, and humble servant.

John Thurloe to Henry Cromwell, 27 August 1658,
"2 in the morninge" (p. 362)

My Lord,

Doctor Worth beinge upon his returne to Ireland, I was not willinge to omit that opportunitye to present to your excellency my most humble service; and to give you an account of his highnes present condition. His fitt upon tuesday night was somewhat more favorable then the former; and the good intervall, which he had after it, gave us good hopes, that his ague was very much upon the decreasinge; espetially the fitt, which he is now in, beginninge very favourablye, the cold part of it slippinge over without any observation. But truely the hot fitt hath beene very long and terrible; insoemuch, that the doctors feare he will scarce get through it. However, he is now fallen into a breathinge sweate, which we hope he will come well out of. I knowe, my lord, how much I shall trouble, greive, and afflict your lordship by this newes; but truly consideringe the station you are in, I durst not omitt to lett your excellency knowe, that his last fitt hath rendered his highnes condition very dangerous; and I doubt our feares are more then our hopes. How wee are all like to be left as to outward appearance, I need not mention. I write of it with great perturbation, yea and perplexity of mind; only wee have a sure refuge to flye to, who hath not yet failed us; and I trust he will appeare in this tyme of our need. To-morrow is set apart for prayer by divers ministers and Christians, on the behalfe of his highnes; and wee hope the Lord will heare us, and grant the petitions wee are to desire of him. I have not writt thus planely to any person but your excellency, and I thought it necessary to doe it towards you, that your excellency may be in the best posture in all events, and may have your heart exercised towards God, according to the importance of the buissines, which is the greatest that ever this nation saw. Doctor Worth's application for his owne particular was in an ill tyme, his highnes havinge beene sick ever since he first moved it; but I shall not omit to serve him, if the Lord affordes the opportunity. The kinge of Sweden hath againe invaded the Dane, and very probablye hath Copenhagen by this tyme.

Your Excellency's
Most obedient and humble servant.

John Thurloe to Henry Cromwell, 30 August 1658, "9 o'clock at night" (pp. 363–64)

May it please your Excellencye,

I gave you some account by Doctor Worth of his highness condition, as it then was; but least he should delay his journey, or miscarry in it, I thought it necessary to send this expresse, to the end your excellencye may fully understand how it is with his highnesse. This is the 13th day since his ague took him, haveinge beene sicke a fortnight before [since about 30 July] of a generall distemper of body. It continued a good while to be a tertian ague, and the burninge fitts very violent. Upon saterday [28 August] it fell to a double tertian, haveinge 2 fitts in 24 houres, one upon the heeles of another, which doe extreamely weaken hym, and endaunger his life. And trulye since saterday morninge he hath scarce beene perfectly out of his fitts. The doctors are yet hopefull, that he may struggle through it, though their hopes are mingled with much feare. But truly wee have cause to put our hope in the lord, and to expect mercy from hym in this case, he haveinge stirred up the saints to pray for hym in all places. Never was ther a greater stocke of prayers goinge for any man then is now goeing for hym; and truly there is a generall consternation upon the spirits of all men, good and bad, feareinge what may be the event of it, should it please God to take his highnesse at this tyme: and God havinge prepared the heart to pray, I trust he will enclyne his eare to heare. And that which is some ground of hope is, that the Lord, as in some former occasions, hath given to himselfe a perticuler assurance, that he shall yet live to serve hym, and to carry on the worke he hath put into his hands.

I doe not yet finde, that there are any great stirringes yet upon this occasion; though the cavaliers doe begin to listen after it, and hope their day is comeinge, or indeed come, if his highnes dye. And truly, my lord, wee have cause to feare, that it may goe very ill with us, if the Lord should take away his highnes in this conjuncture; not that I thinke Charles Stewart's interest is soe great, or his partie soe powerfull in themselves; but I fear our owne divisions, which may be great enough, if his highnesse should not settle and fix his successor before he dyes, which truely I beleeve he hath not yet done. He did by himselfe declare one in a paper before he was installed by the parliament, and sealed it up in the forme of a letter, directing it to me, but kept both the name of the person and the paper to himselfe. After he fell sicke at Hampton Court, he sent Mr. John Barrington to London for it, tellinge hym it lay upon his study table at Whitehall; but it was not to be found there, nor elsewhere, though it hath beene very narrowly looked for. And in this condition matters stand, his highnesse haveinge beene too ill to be troubled with a buissines of this importance. This day he hath had some discourse about it, but his illness disenabled hym to con- clude it fully; and if it should please the Lord not to give hym tyme to settle his succession before his death, the judgment would be the soarer, and our condition the more dangerous; but I trust he will have com- passion upon us, and not leave us as a prey to our enemies, or to one another. All persons here are very reserved as to what they will doe, in case his highness should not declare his successor before he dyes, not beinge willinge to enterteyne any discourse of it, either because it is a matter too greivous to be thought of, or because they would not dis- cover any oppinion, which might crosse his highnesse thoughts in his life tyme. And this, my lord, is the whole account I am able to give your lordship of this sadd buissines, which I am sure will occasion much trouble and sorrow to you; but I could not omit my duty, judgeinge it absolutely necessary, that your excellency should under- stand all that passes or falls out upon this subject, that you may the better knowe, how to direct your prayers and counsells, and stirre up others alsoe to pray for his highnesse and 3 nations in this day of distresse. And as any thinge further occurrs (which I beseech the Lord may be for good) I shall suddeinly dispatch it away to you, and be ready to answer such commands, as your excellency shall lay upon me, beinge,

Your Excellencye's
Most humble, faithfull, and obedient servant.

Viscount Fauconberg to Henry Cromwell [in code], 30 August 1658 (pp. 365–66)

My Lord,

'Tis with unexpresable greif I now give your lordshipp the sad account of H. H. condition, which all the physitians have for some dayes judgd dangerous, more then ever. Tho' his loss must needs carry weight ynough in itselfe, yet the consideration of the miserable posture hee leivs these nations in is stupendious. My lord, I hold it my duty to acquaint you how wee stand at present; and then leave the further proceed of things to God's direction, and your lordship's wisdome.

A successor there is none named, that I can learn. T. has seem'd to be resolved to press him in his intervals to such a nomination: but whether out of apprehensions to displease him,!if recovering, or others hereafter, if it should not succeed, hee has not yet done it, nor doe I beleive wil. . . .

Your servant, B.

Monday, August 30.

Z. is now beyond al possibility of recovery. I long to heare from A. what his intentions are; if I may know, Ile make the game here as faire as may be; and if I may have commission from A. I can make sure of lord Lockart and those with him. Tuesday, August 31.

John Thurloe to Henry Cromwell, Whitehall, 31 August 1658 (p. 366)

May it please your Excelency,

I did by doctor Worth upon friday [27 August], and by an expresse yesterday, certifie your excellencye of his highnesse condition; since which thinges with him remeyne much as they did, if he doth not declyne more and more. Wee are willinge to hope the best; but truly he is in great daunger, and he is soe weake for the present, that he is capable of doeinge nothinge respectinge to the publique, that, for aught I see, things are like to be at his H. death (in case that evill day should now come upon us) as my last mentioned. It will be to noe purpose to agravate to your lordship the ill condition of things, it beinge our duty to look up to God, and eye hym; and that, my lord, I trust your lordship will doe, and, in the midst of your owne thoughts, to encourage yourselfe in the Lord your God. I will not trouble your lordship further, but rest

Your Excelencye's
Most humble and most obedient servant.

Charles Fleetwood to Henry Cromwell, 31 August 1658 (p. 367)

Deare Brother,

The Lord's hand hath bine very sorely upon us in the continuance of his highness under a very great distemper, called an ague, but mostly his heate gave us the sadde aprehension of danger he was under; and truly litle hopes as to men was, but the Lord is pleased to give some litle reviving this evening. After few slumbering sleepes, his pulse better, his water good all this day, till now at night ther hath bine very great feares, what the wombe of to-morrow might have brought forth.

The hearts of good people have exceedingly bine drawn forth. . . . I am just com out of his chamber, wheare both plupitians and relations wer much revived at the refreshment, which hath now bine given. This we may say, that his return will be, if the Lord restore him, as life from the deade, and as great a return of prayer as hath bine in a case of this nature known a long time. The Lord give us hearts sutably to be affected to what this providence calls for; which that we may, is the desire of him, who is

Your most affectionat brother, and humble servant.

Letters to Henry Cromwell and Thurloe, from Dr. Thomas Clarges and Gen. George Monck

From Thurloe, *State Papers,* vol. 7.

General Monck to John Thurloe, 10 August 1658, Dalkeith (pp. 322–23)

. . . I am very glad to heare, that his highnesse is well recovered againe from the fitt of the collick; and that my lady Elizabeth is in a hopefull way of recoverie. Wee have gotten a shippe for sending the men to Dunkirke, and got provisions ready; and wee expect men, on monday or tuesday next, when (if the winde serve) they shall sett sayle, if it please God. . . .

Clarges to Henry Cromwell, 10 August 1658 (p. 323)

May it please your Excelency,

From Germany wee heare, that the king of Sweden is with five and twenty thousand men (as it is thought) redy to attempt something upon the duke of Brabenburgh. . . .

From the leager before Gravelin the letters import, that two of the lieutenant-generalls were shott from the toune by cannon-shott, about monday the 2d instant. . . .

His highness by the blessing of God is much amended; and will with his whole traine be this evening at Whitehall. I am afraid your excelency's motions in progresse may make these adresses somewhat troublesome to you; but it is rather an error of ignorance than presumption in me, that makes me (perhaps) over-act my duty, which till your excelency commande me to the contrary, I shall continue to doe, as may become,

May it please your Excelency,
Your excelency's most humble and most obleiged servant.

General Monck to John Thurloe, 17 August 1658, Dalkeith
(p. 339)

My Lord,

I am sorrie to heere his highness hath bin so ill lately; but I hope the worst of his sickness is past. My prayers shall be to God to preserve his health; for truely if he should chance to bee called away, before it pleased God he had settled the government, I doubt wee should bee in a very sad condition. For newse heere wee have none, onely our three hundred soldiers for Dunkirke are to bee shipt to-morrow; which is all at present from

Your Lordshipp's
Very humble servant.

Thomas Clarges to Henry Cromwell, 24 August 1658
(pp. 355–56)

May it please your Excelency,

Since the takeing of Greavelin, cardinall Mazarine is gone towards Paris; which makes many beleive, the French army will attempt litle more this campaigne, though others think they will not loose the occasion of persueing their prosperous fortune. Neuport or Ipre are the next places in the expectation to be beseidged; and the first of them has bin for some weeks streightned by marshall Thurene. The prince of Conde and Marcin have got together a good body of horse, and are upon some designe, which will be discovered by the next. The calling of a parliament has bin lately delayed by reason of his highnes sicknes; but his recovery, which is in a good measure advanced, will draw on considerations about it. His highnes is this day come from Hampton-court to Whitehall, and the soldiers are to remove from St. Jameses, which is to be prepared for his residence; because Whitehall's scituation is too neere the water. The late disturbance of the minesters in Scotland was only from the Presbitery of Jaddard, who scrupled at the toleration of religion held forth in the *petition and advice;* but things will be well quieted quickly there, where a servant of your excelency is vigilant and carefull in all occasions. I am,

May it please your Excelency,
Your Excelencie's
Most humble servant.

Thomas Clarges to Henry Cromwell, 1 September 1658 (p. 369)

May it please your Excelency,

The violent sicknes of his highnes fils me with sad aprehensions, that I have skearse sense enough to give your excelency an acount of any thing. His disease is a double tertian ague, which at this season, in a person of his age and constitution of body (being much distemper'd by his late grief and melancholly, besides his other infirmities) is a very violent companion.

Yesterday a fast was kept by many of the officers of the army at my lord Fleetwood's house, and some considerations were had amongst them afterwards (as I am informed) conerning the present conditon of his highnes, and the posture of our affaires; but the result I know not, but hope it was for the best. I shall ad nothing more, but my prayers to the Lord for his highnes recovery, and the happines of your excelencie's family, shall never be wanting in,

May it please your Excelency
Your excelencye's most humble servant.

Oliver Cromwell's Illness and Death, According to His Valet

From [Charles Harvey], *A Collection of Several Passages concerning his late Highnesse Oliver Cromwell, In the Time of His Sickness; wherein Is Related many of his Expressions upon his Death-Bed* (London, 1659), 1–22.

His Highness being at *Hampton Court,* sickned a little before the Lady *Elizabeth* died, whose decease was on *Friday* the sixth day of *August,*

1658. shee having lain long under great extremity of bodily pain, which with frequent and violent Convulsion-fits brought her to her end.

But as to His Highness, it was observed, that the sense of her outward misery in the pains shee endured, took deep impression upon him, who indeed ever was a most indulgent and tender Father. . . . It was enough to have deprest and sunk the stoutest and most undaunted courage in the world; And I have often wondered hee was able to hold out so long, But that hee was born up by a supernatural power, at a more than ordinary rate. . . .

And yet wee could not bee more desirous hee should abide, than hee was content and willing to bee gone, as hee exprest near his end, knowing that there were better Mansions, a better Kingdome and Inheritance, a better Crown, and a better Throne. . . .

In the next place, let us consider the exercise of his Faith, in a few experiences of many (wherein he was Rich) declared by himself, and which were not ordinary, But such as few (I think) of the choicest Saints have attained unto, one whereof was as followeth.

Being at *Edinborough* in *Scotland* [in 1651], it pleased the Lord to exercise him with sore sicknesse, a high and dangerous Feavor, whereby hee was brought so low, that his Physicians and others had little or no hopes in reason of his recovery; For one fit of his distemper having lasted about twelve hours, Immediately a second fit returned upon him without any intermission, for as long a time and likely to have continued in that extremity, until thereby hee had expired. But behold this was Gods opportunity to shew his Power, and to magnifie his Word, a Portion whereof by the hand of the Spirit of the Lord was then given in unto him, not onely to feed his Faith, and revive his heart, but also to rebuke his Disease, *which immediately left him,* to the astonishment of himself and others, it being little less than a miracle. . . .

And therefore to come nearer, a few daies after the death of the Lady *Elizabeth,* his Daughter, at *Hampton Court,* which toucht him nearly, being then [6 August] himself under bodily distempers, forerunners to his sicknesse, which was to death, and in his Bed-chamber, hee called for his Bible, and desired a person honourable and godly, then (with others) present, to read unto him. . . .

But a little nearer yet, after his return to *White-Hall,* his sicknesse increasing upon him, hee was observed to bee in a very spiritual frame of heart, and full of holy expressions, catched up by one or other fearing God that were present, as a hungry man doth meat. A little whereof it was my comfort to meet with, the very night before the Lord took him to his everlasting rest, which were to this purpose following, *viz.*

Truly God is good, indeed hee is, hee will not— there his speech failed him, but as I apprehend it, it was, *hee will not leave mee,* this saying that God was good, hee frequently used all along, and would speak it with much chearfulnesse and fervour of spirit in the midst of his pains.

Again, hee said, I would bee willing to live to bee further serviceable to God and his People, but my work is done, yet God will bee with his People.

He was very restlesse most part of the night, speaking often to himself. And there being something to drink offered him, hee was desired to take the same, and endeavour to sleep, unto which hee asnwered,

It is not my design to drink or to sleep, but my design is to make what haste I can to bee gone.

Afterwards towards morning, using divers holy expressions, implying much inward consolation and peace, among the rest hee spake some exceeding self-debasing words, annihilating and judging himself. And truly it was observed, that a publick spirit to Gods cause did breath in him (as in his life-time) so now to the very last, which will further appear by that Prayer hee put up to God two or three daies before his end, which was as followeth.

LORD, Although I am a miserable and wretched Creature, I am in Covenant with thee, through Grace, And I may, I will come to thee for thy people, thou hast made mee (though very unworthy) a mean Instrument to do them some good, and thee service; And many of them have set too high a value upon mee, though others wish, and would bee glad of my Death; But Lord, however thou dost dispose of mee, continue and go on to do good for them, Give them consistency of Judgement, one heart, and mutual love, and go on to deliver them, and with the work of Reformation, and make the Name of Christ glorious in the World; Teach those who look too much upon thy instruments, to depend more upon thy self; Pardon such as desire to trample upon the dust of a poor Worm, for they are they People too. And pardon the folly of this short Prayer, even for Jesus Christs sake, and give us a good night, if it be they pleasure.

Some variation there is of his Prayer, as to the account divers give of it, and something is here omitted; But this is certain, that these were his Requests, wherein his heart was so carried out for God and his People, yea for them who had added no little sorrow to his grief and afflictions that at this time hee seems to forget even his own Family, and nearest Relations.

And thus wee see in part something of the clearnesse and strength of his Faith in the Covenant of Grace. . . .

Oliver Cromwell's Illness, According to Richard Cromwell

From *The Parliamentary or Constitutional History of England, From the Earliest Times, to the Restoration of King Charles II* (London, 1763), 21:223–24 n.

Whitehall, August 28, 1658.
For my worthy Friend Captain John Dunche, *at* Peusey, *near* Abington, in Berkshire.

Sir,

I intended to have written to you by the first Return, but since his Highness has been so ill, that I have not had either Opportunity or Desire to set Pen to Paper; we have not been without very great Fears; for his Highness's Illness hath been such as hath put the Physicians to a Nonplus. Our Hopes are somewhat increased by this Fit of an Auge; and shall it please God to go on with his gentle Hand, and bring him temperately out of this Fit, and not renew it, at the Time his former Fit began, or visit us with a Quartan, we shall have some reviving Comfort, and cause to magnify his Goodness; it being a new Life to his Highness and the Affairs as they now stand, of this Nation, with the Protestant Interest of Christendom. I believe the Rumours of his dangerous Illness hath flown into all Parts of this Nation, and hath caused several Persons of ill Affections to prick up their Ears, which will cause Friends to be vigilant, for they will hope they have a Game to play: It is a Time that will discover all Colours, and much of the Disposition of the Nation may now be gathered. I heard that those who have been Enemies, others that have been no Friends, some or both, are startled; fearing their Possessions, and worse Conditions, not considering their Affection, in this Hazard his Highness is in. It must be the Goodness of God that shall save him, and his Knowledge of the State of *England* and Christendom; the Spirit of Prayer which is poured out for him, and the Faith which is acted on Behalf of him, gives us the best Comfort and Hopes: Mine and my Wife's Respects to your Father and Mother.

I rest yours,
R. Cromwell

Extracts from newsletters to General Monck from George Mabbott and Thomas Clarges

From *The Clarke Papers, Selections from the Papers of William Clarke,* ed. C.H. Firth (London, 1899), 3:161.

Aug. 14, 1658.—Tuesday last the Lady Claypoole was brought from Hampton to Westminster, and there interred in Henry the 7ths chappell. H. H. hath bin lately visited with a fit of sicknesse, so that about three dayes agoe wee had some doubts of his recovery, the greatnesse of his distemper of the goute and other distempers, with the sorrow for the death of his daughter, having deepe impression upon him; butt now hee is pretty well recovered, and upon the consideration of his mortallity will speedily resolve of something of settlement. [G.M.]

Aug. 17.—His Highnesse is well recovered of a great distemper too much like that in Cannongate. [T.C.]

Aug. 28.—Tuesday last his Highnesse returned from Hampton Court to Whitehall with a resolution speedily to nominate his successor, the temperate condition of his health ebbs and flows, his repose being obstructed with intervalls of restlesse paine. The Lord Richard Cromwell ('tis said) is appointed Generalissimo of all the forces of the nations. [G.M.]

Sept. 2.—His Highness hath had a very good rest the last night and the night before, and a sore throat he had hath left him, and the sharpness of his fitts are abated, so that their is good hopes of his recovery, except some unexpected accident happen. His health was never more necessary then at this tyme that affaires are so unsettled. [T.C.]

Oliver Cromwell's Illness and Death, According to Dr. George Bate

From George Bate, *Elenchus Motuum Nuperorum in Anglia: Or, A short Historical Account of The Rise and Progress of the Late Troubles in England . . . Made English* (London, 1685), sec. 2, pp. 233–36.

Let us now return home, and view at nearer distance the Preludes of *Cromwell's* approaching Death. Whilst he is delighted with *Triumphs* beyond Sea, he is hampered at home with difficulties and gnawing Cares. Besides the Death of his dearly beloved Daughter, the *Lady Cleypole,* who died of an inward Impostume in her Loins with great agony and pain, after she had in her Hysterical fits much disquieted him, by upbraiding him sometimes with one of his Crimes, and sometimes with another, according to the furious distractions of that Disease: The *Republicans* created him continual troubles and vexation; especially seeing his Son-in-law *Fleetwood* and his Wife [*Bridget Cromwell Ireton Fleetwood*] seemd to favour these Men, excuse, and intercede for them; nay, he refrained coming to his Father-in-laws House, though he lived hard by, and ought to have comforted His dying Sister amidst the mourning and bewailings of her Relations; and though *Cromwell* (as he told it to some) had made him his Heir in his last Will and Testament. Besides, *Desborough,* who had married his Sister, *Pickering* also, and *Sidenham,* whom he had made Privy Counsellors, and secret meetings with *Lambert,* and other leading Men of the *Republican* Party, whom they openly magnified, and extolled.

But all his Distemper was not in his Mind alone; for shortly after he was taken with a Slow Fever, that at length degenerated into a Bastard Tertian Ague. For a Weeks time the Disease so continued without any dangerous symptoms, (as appearing sometimes one, and sometimes another kind of distemper) that every other Day he walked abroad: but after Dinner his five Physicians coming to wait upon him, one of them having felt his pulse, said, that it intermitted, at which suddenly startled, he looked pale, fell into a Cold Sweat, almost fainted away, and orders himself to be carried to Bed, where being refreshed with Cordials, he made his Will, but onely about his Privat and Domestick Affairs. Next Morning early, when one of his Physicians came to visit him, he asked him, *why he looked so sad?* And when he made Answer, *That so it becomes any one, who had the weighty care of his Life and Health upon him; Ye Physicians,* said he, *think I shall die:* Then the Company being removed, holding his Wife by the Hand, to this purpose he spoke to him, *I tell you, I shall not die this hour; I am sure on't.* And because he observed him to look more attentively upon him at these words, *Don't think* (said he) *that I am mad; I speak the Words of Truth, upon surer grounds than Galen or your Hippocrates furnish you with. God Almighty himself has given that Answer, not to my Prayers alone, but also to the Prayers of those who entertain a stricter commerce, and greater intimacy with him. Go on chearfully, banishing all sadness from your looks, and deal with me as you would do with a Serving-man. Ye may have skill in the Nature of things, yet Nature can do more than all Physicians put together; and God is far more above Nature.* But being ordered to take his rest, because he had not slept the greatest part of the Night, as the Physician was coming out of the chamber, he accidentally met another who had been a long time very familiar with him; to whom, *I am afraid,* says he, *our Patient will be light-headed.* Then said he, *You are certainly a Stranger in this House: Don't you know what was done last Night? The Chaplains, and all who are dear to God, being dispersed into several parts of the Palace, have prayed to God for his Health, and all have brought this Answer,* He shall recover. Nay, to this degree of madness they came, that a Publick Fast being for his sake kept at *Hampton Court,* they did not so much pray to God for his Health, as thank him for the undoubted pledges of his Recovery, and repeated the same at *Whitehall.*

These Oracles of the *Saints* were the cause that the Physicians spake not a word of his danger. In the mean time *Cromwell* leaving *Hampton Court,* where hitherto he had lain sick, is brought to *London;* and the Physitians meet in a Consultation in the Camber of the aforementioned Doctor, who at that time was troubled with a grievous *Head-ach,* and an *Imposthume* in his Ear. But next Morning early another Physician coming, who had watched all Night with the Patient, and telling the rest how ill he had been in the last fit, they all conclude that he could hardly out-live another. This Sentence of the *Physicians* awaking the Privy Council, at an appointed time they come to advise him, that he would name his Successor. But when in a drowsy fit he anwered out of purpose, they again ask him, if he did not name *Richard* his eldest Son for his Successour, to which he answered, *Yes.* Then being asked where his Will was which heretofore he had made concerning the Heirs of the *Kingdom,* he sent to look for it in his Closet, and other places, but in vain; for he had either burnt it himself, or some body else had stole it. And so *Richard* being nominated his Heir, the Day following, being the third of *September,* he yielded up the Ghost about three of the Clock in the Afternoon; not, (as it was commonly reported) carried away by the *Devil* at Mid-night, but in clear Day-light, and the same Day that he had twice defeated the *Scots.* His Body being opened; in the *Animal* parts, the Vessels of the Brain seemed to be overcharged; in the Vitals the Lungs a little inflamed; but in the *Natural,* the source of the distemper appeared; the *Spleen,* though sound to the Eye, being within filled with matter like to the Lees of Oyl. Nor was that Incongruous to the Disease that for a long time he had been subject unto, seeing for at least thirty years he had at times heavily complained of Hypochondriacal indispositions. Though his Bowels were taken out, and his Body filled with Spices, wrapped in a fourfold Cerecloath, but put first into a Coffin of Lead, and then into a Wooden one, yet it purged and wrought through all, so that there was a necessity of interring it before the Solemnities of the Funerals.

Oliver Cromwell's Illness and Death, and the Restoration, According to Dr. Thomas Clarges and Edward Phillips

From Sir Richard Baker, *A Chronicle of the Kings of England . . . Wherein is added, The Reign of King Charles the First, and The first Thirteen years of his Sacred Majesty King Charles the Second . . . and likewise the most Remarkable Occurrences relating to his Majesties most Happy and Wonderful Restauration,* 6th ed. (London, 1674), 652–731.

The sixth of *August, Elizabeth* the Protectors second Daughter died at *Hampton-Court* of an Aposteme in some of the inward parts, which afflicted him very much, because he loved her above all his Children; and that sorrow was increased by the strength of her Sickness, and the grievous torments she endur'd. . . . The Grief which the Protector had contracted for her death, was very much augmented by his Trouble, to discern, that the Discontents sprung up amongst many of the Inferiour Officers of the Army, were fomented by *Fleetwood* and *Desborow . . .* in a Confederacy against the present Government, in favour of a Commonwealth. And a while after he fell sick himself of a Tertian Feaver, which at first seem'd not to signifie much danger, but by degrees it grew upon him: Yet his Imagination was so far transported with enthusiastick ravings, that insensible to his own Danger, he affirm'd, That GOD had reserved him to greater Attempts, than ever yet had been performed by him; and that he was assured he should not dye of this Sickness. In which Extasie, he was much heightned by *Goodwine* one of his Chaplains, who openly declared, *GOD had heard the Prayers of his Servants for him, and given him his Life;* and therefore he perswaded some of his Friends, to keep a kind of private Thanksgiving beforehand for his undoubted recovery. This Confidence amused his Physicians so much, that they were less regardful of his Condition. But nevertheless, it was advised he should be brought to *White-*

Hall, where with more conveniency than at *Hampton-Court,* a respect might be had to his Health, and the publick Affairs of the Nation, where he had not been many days, e're it visibly appeared he had but a few more to live. . . .

Upon *Tuesday* the 31th of *August,* finding himself in danger, he commanded his Servants, and all other persons, except Mr. *Thurloe,* and Dr. *Thomas Goodwyne,* out of the Room, and declared to them, *That in regard he found his Sickness and Weakness increasing, he was resolved to declare his Successor, according to the power given him by the late* Peition and Advice; *And therefore he desired them to take notice, that he Named and Declared his Son to succeed him accordingly.* They asked him, which Son? He Replied, *My Son* Richard, *my eldest Son.* . . .

Upon *Friday* (the third of *September,* the same Memorable Day of the Year, that in 1650, he overcame the *Scots* at *Dunbar,* and the Year following at *Worcester*) at three of the Clock in the afternoon he departed this Life.

Thus after so many hazards in the Field, so many ambushes said to have been laid against him at home, notwithstanding the Multitude of enemies, that, from all Parties and Interests whom his violent pursuit of Greatness had exasperated, conspired against his safety; contrary to the real belief of many men, the ill-bodings of some, and the earnest wish of others, he died not of a violent, but in his Bed a natural Death. The day of his death was ushered in by a Night as tempestuous as had been seen in this Age, as if the Elements had been in Combustion at the flight of a Spirit, which had made so great a Concussion in the Affairs of the World. . . .

Richard Cromwel was at *White-Hall, Charing-Cross,* and several other publick places in *London,* proclaimed Protector . . . about four of the Clock in the Afternoon. . . .

Thus far matters succeeded well; his Brother *Henry Cromwel* was Chief Governour of *Ireland,* and a Gentleman was sent to acquaint him with the present posture of Affairs. Of *Scotland* they had some doubt; but to endeavour to rectifie all things there, *Richard* sent that evening to Mr. *Thomas Clarges* (Brother-in-law to General Monck) to prevail with him, to go immediately into *Scotland,* with his Letters to *Monck,* to know how he stood affected to his Advancement: This *Clarges* was pitched upon as one who had great Interest in the General. . . . And although at first his having been in the late Kings Service at *Oxford,* made them *at White-Hall* unwilling to imploy him: yet he was esteemed of a moderate Behaviour, and had so demeaned himself in the pretended Parliament in the Year 1656, by his actings against the Kingship of *Cromwel,* that they would not then disoblige him, lest it should seem to be for that Reason. . . . *Clarges* willingly accepted of this occasion to go to General *Monck,* to be able to inform himself particularly of his inclinations: For although he had a Relation to him by Marriage, the Generals so far distant Residence, gave him little opportunity of other Converse with him than by Letters. . . . In Scotland . . . the General himself and he had many secret Conferences, and the General then declared himself weary of the uncertain condition, wherein he found both himself and the Nation inthrall'd by the overruling Tyranny of the Soulderies (who made themselves a divided Interest from the rest of the people). . . . From this Conference which was managed by both, with much reservedness; *Clarges* began to perceive the General was in his Principles well fixed to restore his country to its Ancient Government, when-ever a fit occasion should present it self for the attempt. . . .

The Guns from the Tower were all shot off, and all the Streets that Evening were fill'd with Bone-fires, and the Air with the Sound of Ringing of Bells; and all seem'd too little, to celebrate the content and exultation of the People, at that Dayes Solemnity.

Commissary *Clarges* made such speed in his journey to his Majesty, That on *Tuesday* the 8th of *May,* in the Morning, which was the Day after the happy making of his *Proclamation,* he arrived at *Bergen-ap-Zome* in *Holland,* half a Dayes Journey from *Breda;* There the Governour gave him a very Honourable Reception, and accommodated him with his Coach and six Horses to Breda; and a League before he came to the Town, the Lord *Gerrard* met him with two Coaches and Six Horses, and accompanied him to his Majesty, who received him with most Gracious Expressions of Satisfaction, as well that he was the first authorized Messenger, that came to him with the News of the intire Submission of his Kingdoms and Army to his Obedience: As for his Relation to that most Renowned General, from whose prudent Conduct and Courage principally, all that Happiness was derived to his Majesty, and his People.

He presented to his Majesty, a *Letter* from the General in Answer to his Majesties, sent before to him; and in it was inclosed the *Address* of the Army. . . .

This Letter was dictated by his Excellencie [General Monck] in the presence of many Officers of the Army, but he writ another short Letter with his own hand: Wherein he acquainted his Majestie, *That he chose to send* Mr. Clarges *to him, because he was the only Person he trusted in the nearest Concernments and Consultations for his Restauration, as one to whom he desired his Majestie to give Credit to what he should say on that behalf.*

After the reading of these Letters, and the Address inclosed in the former of them, His Majestie Knighted him, and by many kind expressions demonstrated his sence of his Merit and Service to him; and after he had been about an hour with his Majestie, he had his permission to attend his Royal Highness the Duke of *York* and the Duke of *Gloucester.* . . .

Samuel Sainthill's Diary

From Samuel Butler, *Hudibras,* ed. Treadway Russel Nash (London,, 1793), 2: 379–80.

The following is a transcript from a M.S. diary of Mr. Edward [*sic*] Sainthill, a Spanish merchant of those times, and preserved by his descendants—"The 30th of January, being that day twelve years from the death of the king, the odious carcases of Oliver Cromwell, Major General Ireton, and Bradshaw, were drawn in sledges to Tyburn, where they were hanged by the neck, from morning till four in the afternoon. Cromwell in a green-seare cloth, very fresh, embalmed; Ireton having been buried long, hung like a dried rat, yet corrupted about the fundament. Bradshaw, in his winding-sheet, the fingers of his right hand and his nose perished, having wet the sheet through; the rest very perfect, insomuch, that I knew his face, when the hangman, after cutting his head off, held it up: of his toes, I had five or six in my hand, which the prentices had cut off. Their bodies were thrown into an hole under the gallows, in their seare-cloth and sheet. Cromwell had eight cuts, Ireton four, being seare-cloths, and their heads were set up on the south-end of Westminster Hall." In a marginal note, is a drawing of Tyburn (by the same hand) with the bodies hanging, and the grave underneath. Cromwell is represented like a mummy swathed up, with no visible legs or feet.

Secret Burial

From Leman Thomas Rede, *Anecdotes and Biography* (London, 1799), 97.

The parliament which received Charles II. passed a resolution, by which the body of Cromwell was "ordered to be drawn on a hurdle to Tyburn, and there hung from ten o'clock till sun-set, and then buried under the gallows." The Protector's friends, however, it was known, obtained his remains soon after, and, according to traditionary reports, buried them secretly in a meadow to the north of Holborn. The precise spot is said to be at this time the centre of Red-Lion Square, and the obelisk is thought by many to be a memorial erected to his manes, by an apothecary who was attached to Cromwell's principles, and had so much influence in the building of the square, as to manage the marking out the ground; and further contrived to pay this tribute to his favorite's ashes.

Notes

The following abbreviations of frequently cited works are used in the notes:

CCSP   *Calendar of the Clarendon State Papers Preserved in the Bodleian Library.*

CSPD   *Calendar of State Papers, Domestic Series.*

CSPI   *Calendar of State Papers Relating to Ireland.*

CSPV   *Calendar of State Papers, Venetian.*

DNB   *Dictionary of National Biography.*

HMC   Historical Manuscripts Commission.

TSP   John Thurloe, *A Collection of State Papers,* vol. 7.

Introduction

1. Carlyle, *Letters and Speeches of Cromwell,* 3:213–14.

2. Firth, *Cromwell and the Rule of Puritans,* 1901 ed., 441; John Buchan, *Oliver Cromwell,* 533.

3. Varley, *Cromwell's Latter End,* 19.

4. Abbott, *Writings and Speeches of Cromwell,* 4:866.

5. Christopher Hill, *God's Englishman,* 190–91.

6. Fraser, *Cromwell,* 670–72.

7. Hutton, *Restoration,* 18.

8. Abbott, *Writings and Speeches of Cromwell,* 4:872.

9. Jones, "Booth's Rising," 417.

10. Everitt, *Community of Kent,* 302.

11. Hughes, *Politics, Society and Civil War,* 291–99, 302.

12. Coleby, *Central Government,* 64–67, which also quotes H.M. Reese, "The Military Presence in England, 1649–1660," Ph.D. diss., Oxford Univ., 1981.

13. Everitt, *Community of Kent,* 300.

14. Anthony Fletcher, "Oliver Cromwell and the Localities," in Jones, Newitt, and Roberts, eds., *Politics and People,* 187–203; David Underdown, "Settlement in the Counties, 1653–1658," in Aylmer, *Interregnum,* 178–82; Austin Woolrych, "Last Quests for a Settlement, 1657–1660," in Aylmer, *Interregnum,* 184–86.

15. Keeton, *Jeffreys and the Stuart Cause,* 69.

16. *Historical Account of Tryals and Attainders,* 170–71.

17. Yale, *Lord Nottingham's Chancery Cases,* 1:xvii.

18. Hutton, *Restoration,* 138–39; Seaward, *Cavalier Parliament,* 103–4; Jones, introduction to Jones et al., *Restored Monarchy,* 17.

19. Aylmer, introduction to Aylmer, *Interregnum,* 19.

20. Weir, *The Princes in the Tower,* xiii; see also Nicholl, *The Reckoning,* 3–5.

21. Preface to the first edition [1682], in Whitelock, *Memorials,* 1:vi–vii.

1. Outward Signs

1. For a poetic metaphor based on flowers, see Francis Quarles, "Hos Ergo Versiculos," in Fowler, *Seventeenth Century Verse,* 295.

2. The term *Anglican* is an anachronistic description for the Church of England between the Reformation and the nineteenth century, although scholars have freely used it. Edmund Burke perhaps first used the word *Anglicans* in 1797; *Anglicanism* did not appear in print for another half century (Sesek, *Images of English Puritanism,* 3).

3. John Donne, "Devotions: Nunc lento sonitu dicunt, Moeieris," in Donne, *Selected Prose,* 101; John Hall, "On an Hour-glass," in Saintsbury, *Minor Poets,* 2:218.

4. Thomas, *Religion and the Decline of Magic,* 603.

5. Le Goff, *Purgatoire,* passim; Stannard, *Puritan Way of Death,* 96–108; Solt, *Saints in Arms,* 25–27; Geddes, *Welcome Joy,* 104; Watters, *"With Bodilie Eyes,"* 15.

6. Scarisbrick, *Reformation and English People,* 36–37.

7. Meyer, *Elizabeth I,* 60–61.

8. Haugaard, *Elizabeth and the English Reformation,* 106.

9. Scarisbrick, *Reformation and English People,* 186.

10. Collinson, *English Puritanism,* 15–16; Collinson, *Godly People,* 10.

11. Collinson, *English Puritanism,* 10.

12. Yule, *Puritans in Politics,* 17–18; Hunt, *Puritan Moment,* x; Zaret, *Heavenly Contract,* 19.

13. Knott, *Sword of the Spirit,* 2.

14. Robert Herrick, "The Eucharist," in Herrick, *Poetical Works,* 371.

15. Edward Benlowes, "Theophila's Love-Sacrifice," in Saintsbury, *Minor Poets,* 1:368.

16. Henry Vaughan, "Man in Glory," in Vaughan, *Works,* 194.

17. William Strode, "Epitaph on the Monument of Sir William Strode," in Fowler, *Seventeenth Century Verse,* 357.

18. Solt, *Church and State,* 143–46.

19. Robert Herrick, "Neutrality loathsome," in Herrick, *Poetical Works,* 343.

20. Weever, *Ancient Funeral Monuments,* 17–18.

21. Wood, *Life and Times,* 2:66.

22. William Austin, "Sepulchrum Domus mea est," in Austin, *Poems,* 23.

23. Vaughan, "The day of Judgment," in Vaughan, *Works,* 530.

24. Robert Herrick, "A Dirge upon the Death of the Right Valiant Lord, Bernard Stuart," in Herrick, *Poetical Works,* 89.

25. Robert Herrick, "To Death," in ibid., 343.

26. William Austin, "Sepulchum Domus mea est," in Austin, *Poems,* 25.

27. Robert Herrick, "His Winding-sheet," in Herrick, *Poetical Works,* 188–89.

28. Thomas, *Religion and the Decline of Magic,* 604.

29. [Harvey], *Collection of Several Passages,* 7.

30. John Hall, "To the precious memory of Master William Fenner," in Saintsbury, *Minor Poets,* 2:204.

31. Bayly, *Practice of Piety,* 47, 59.

32. John Milton, "On Time," in Milton, *Poems,* 165.

33. Bolton, *Mr. Boltons Last,* 82–83.

34. John Hall, "Upon Mr. Robert Wiseman," in Saintsbury, *Minor Poets,* 2:207.

35. Geddes, *Welcome Joy,* 22–26.

36. Bolton, *Mr. Boltons Last,* 82–83.

37. John Hall, "Upon Mr. Robert Wiseman," in Saintsbury, *Minor Poets,* 2:207.

38. *Directory for Publique Worship,* 49.

39. Watters, "*With Bodilie Eyes,*" 16.

40. Stannard, *Puritan Way of Death,* 103; Owen, *Labouring Saints,* 23–24.

41. *Mercurius Politicus,* 24 Nov. 1659 (weekly newssheets are cited to the end of the week covered).

42. *Directory for Publique Worship,* 49.

43. *Mercurius Politicus,* 12 Aug. 1658.

44. John Hall, "On an Hour-glass," in Saintsbury, *Minor Poets,* 2:219.

45. Hugh Trevor-Roper, "The Culture of the Baroque Courts," in Trevor-Roper, *Renaissance Essays,* 223–38.

46. Strong, *Van Dyck,* passim.

47. Quoted in Strong, *Art and Power,* 153–70.

48. P.W. Thomas, "Two Cultures? Court and Country under Charles I," in Russell, *Origins of the English Civil War,* 181.

49. Solt, *Church and State,* 185–86.

50. Robin Clifton, "Fear of Popery," in Russell, *Origins of the English Civil War,* 144–67; *The Arminian Nunnery* (1641), quoted in Solt, *Church and State,* 164; Jim Sharpe, "Scandalous and Malignant Priests in Essex: the Impact of Grassroots Puritanism," in Jones, Newitt, and Roberts, *Politics and People,* 253–73; Hibbard, *Charles I,* 22, 169, and passim; Kevin Sharpe, *Personal Rule of Charles I,* 284–92.

51. Sherwood, *Court of Oliver Cromwell.*

52. *Kingdomes Faithfull Scout,* 2 Feb. 1649.

53. Wedgwood, *King's War,* 49–55.

54. Quoted in Ramsey, *Henry Ireton,* 150.

55. "Charles I, from an old engraving," in Firth, *Cromwell and the Rule of Puritans,* 238.

56. "Thou art slave to Fate, Chance, kings and desperate men, / And dost with poyson, warre, and sicknesse dwell" (John Donne, "Divine Poems, Sonnet X," in Donne, *Poems,* 1912 ed., 1:326).

57. Quoted in Smith, *Treason in Tudor England,* 164, 277–78 n. 1, 281 n. 76; Potter, *Fatal Gallows Tree,* 21–23; Elton, *Tudor Constitution,* 59–61.

58. Solt, *Church and State,* 152.

59. Abbott, *Writings and Speeches of Cromwell,* 1:750–51; Ramsey, *Henry Ireton,* 149–50.

60. *Moderate Intelligencer,* 1 Feb. 1649; *Kingdomes Faithfull Scout,* 2 Feb. 1649.

61. Henry, *Diaries and Letters,* 12.

62. Pierre Antoine Motteux, "A Song," in Fowler, *Seventeenth Century Verse,* 781; see also John Evelyn, *Fumifugium, or the Inconveniencie of the Aer and Smoak of London* (1661), in Evelyn, *Writings,* 127–56.

2. Ireton: Death and Destiny

1. James died at Theobolds, and on 4 April 1625 a procession carried

his body to Somerset House (then called Denmark House), where it lay in state; a poorly organized procession on 7 May carried it for burial in Henry VII's Chapel (Willson, *King James VI and I,* 447).

2. "What Became of Cromwell?" 561.

3. Frederick John Varley and Esmond S. de Beer debated the question of plague or fever in letters to *Notes and Queries* (vol. 176 [Jan.–June 1939]) but did not resolve the issue. A sampling of modern historians indicates the problem. Maurice Ashley thought "Ireton died of fever in the Irish bogs" (*The Greatness of Oliver Cromwell,* 261). Jasper Ridley claimed to the contrary—"There was plague in the town [Limerick], and Ireton caught it and died" (*Roundheads,* 76)—although in a later chapter on Edmund Ludlow he said, "Ireton died from the plague or some other form of fever" (245). Robert W. Ramsey stated in a biography of Cromwell's young son Henry that Ireton "died of the plague" (*Henry Cromwell,* 15), but in his book on Ireton he quoted a contemporary that he caught "cold" (*Henry Ireton,* 197). Antonia Fraser said Ireton "died of plague" (*Cromwell,* 397), and Christopher Hill made no reference to cause (*God's Englishman,* 144).

4. *Perfect Account,* 10 Dec. 1651.

5. Ashley, *Cromwell's Generals,* 65–78; Ramsey, *Henry Ireton,* 1–5; Ridley, *Roundheads,* 74–77.

6. Cooke, *Monarchy No Creature.*

7. Quoted in Ashley, *Charles I and Cromwell,* 109.

8. Austin Woolrych, "Putney Revisited," in Jones, Newitt, and Roberts, *Politics and People,* 103–16.

9. Ramsey, *Henry Ireton,* 101–51.

10. Esson, *Curse of Cromwell,* 89–101; *Paine-Full Messenger,* 25 Aug. 1649.

11. Esson, *Curse of Cromwell,* 102–55; Gentiles, *New Model Army.*

12. John Canon Begley, *The Diocese of Limerick,* 301–3; Esson, *Curse of Cromwell,* 149; *Montgomery Manuscripts,* 194; Cooke, *Monarchy No Creature.*

13. "Aphorismical Discovery," 3:19; John Jones to Morgan Lloyd, 9 Aug. 1651, Dublin, in Mayer, "Inedited Letters," 184; [Ireton], *Letter from the Lord Deputy,* 3–6.

14. [Ireton], *Letter from the Lord Deputy,* 5–6; Col. Sankey to Col. Pretty, 28 Oct. 1651, in *Severall Proceedings,* 13 Nov. 1651.

15. "Aphorismical Discovery," 3:19–20.

16. Simms, "O'Neill's Defence of Limerick," 21–29; Esson, *Curse of Cromwell,* 143–52; *Journals of the House of Commons,* 7:45.

17. *Perfect Diurnall,* 24 Nov. 1651.

18. Esson, *Curse of Cromwell,* 152.

19. "Hibernia Dominicana," quoted in Lenihan, *Limerick,* 180 n.

20. [Ireton], *Letter from the Lord Deputy,* 8

21. *Montgomery Manuscripts,* 193 n; Simms, "O'Neill's Defence of Limerick," 29.

22. Ireton to Cromwell, 3 Nov. 1651; *Mercurius Politicus,* 4 Dec. 1651; [Ireton], *Letter from the Lord Deputy,* 9; Irish Commissioners to the Speaker, 6 Nov. 1651, Dublin, in Ludlow, *Memoirs,* 1:494.

23. Bagwell, *Ireland under the Stuarts,* 2:277; Ludlow, *Memoirs,* 1:290-91.

24. Ludlow, *Memoirs,* 1:292–93

25. *Mercurius Politicus,* 11 Dec. 1651; Cooke, *Monarchy No Creature.*

26. Ludlow, *Memoirs,* 1:293.

27. *Mercurius Politicus,* 11 Dec. 1651.

28. Ludlow, *Memoirs,* 1:293-94.

29. MacLysaght, *Irish Life,* 1939 ed., 216.

30. Commissioners to the Council of State, 1 Dec. 1651, in Dunlop, *Ireland under the Commonwealth,* 1:92.

31. Barry, "Report from the Hon. Local Secretary for Limerick," 386–89; Fanshawe, *Memoirs,* 405 n. The "Hibernia Dominicana" claims that O'Brien was hanged in the market place (quoted in Lenihan, *Limerick,* 180 n).

32. *Mercurius Politicus,* 25 Dec. 1651; *French Intelligencer,* 9 Dec. 1651; *Weekly Intelligencer,* 9 Dec. 1651.

33. "Hibernia Dominicana," in Lenihan, *Limerick,* 180 n.

34. "Aphorismical Discovery," 3:21.

35. *CSPD, 1651,* passim; George Bate, *Elenchi Motuum,* 1:53; Heath, *Brief Chronicle,* 568; Fraser, *Chronicles of the Frasers,* 393, which is loosely based on Heath's *Brief Chronicle;* Warwick, *Memoirs of Charles the First,* 394; Hyde, *Rebellion and Civil Wars in England,* 5:290.

36. A.B. Worden, introduction to Ludlow, *Voyce from the Watch Tower,* 1–17.

37. *CSPD, 1660–61,* 519.

38. Ferrar, *City of Limerick,* 34; Noble, *English Regicides,* 1:370; Masson, *Milton,* 4:356–57; Murphy, *Cromwell in Ireland,* 384; Cusack, *History of Ireland,* 507; de Beer, "The Death of Henry Ireton," 390.

39. Slack, *Impact of Plague,* 7–17. Pneumonic plague is spread by a victim's coughing and sneezing and does not appear to have characterized post–1500 epidemics.

40. Ibid., 66, 243.

41. *Perfect Diurnall,* 8 Sept. 1651.

42. Irish Commissioners to the Lord Deputy, 3 Sept. 1651, Dublin, in Dunlop, *Ireland under the Commonwealth,* 1:39; Irish Commissioners to the Council of State, 22 Oct. 1651, in ibid., 1:49.

43. Whitelock, *Memorials,* 3:369–70.

44. Boate, *Irelands Naturall History,* 178; MacArthur, "English Malaria," 78; *Mercurius Politicus,* 2 Oct. 1651; *Diary,* 6 Oct. 1651; *Journals of the House of Commons,* 7:45, 80; Paul Slack, "Mortality Crises and Epidemic Diseases in England, 1485–1616," in Webster, *Health, Medicine and Mortality,* 31.

45. [Ireton], *Letter from the Lord Deputy,* 7.

46. Boate, *Irelands Naturall History,* 185–86.

47. Creighton, *History of Epidemics,* 1:566.

48. Beveridge, *Influenza,* 11–29.

49. Whitelock, *Memorials,* 2:371.

50. *Perfect Passages,* 12 Dec. 1651.

51. *Weekly Intelligencer,* 16 Dec. 1651.

52. *Perfect Account,* 10 Dec. 1651.

53. Josselin, *Diary,* 265.

54. *CSPV, 1647–52,* 209; Commissioners to Cromwell, 2 Dec. 1651, Dublin, in Dunlop, *Ireland under the Commonwealth,* 1:94; de Beer to the Editor, *Notes and Queries* 176 (Jan.–June 1939): 390; Gilbert, ed. *Contemporary History of Affairs in Ireland,* 3:301; Evelyn, *Diary,* 52; John Evelyn, *An Apologie for the Royal Party* (1659), in Evelyn, *Writings,* 99; Dr. Kirton to Sir R. Verney, 27 Jan. 1652, Florence, in HMC, *Seventh Report,* 458.

55. MacArthur, "English Malaria," 77.

56. Fox, *Insects and Diseases of Man,* 315–18.

57. *French Intelligencer,* 16 Dec. 1651.

58. *Severall Proceedings,* 11 Dec. 1651.

59. Owen, *Labouring Saints,* ii.

60. Irish Commissioners to the Speaker, 2 Dec. 1651, Dublin, in Ludlow, *Memoirs,* 1:496.

61. Warwick, *Memoirs of Charles the First,* 394; "Hibernia Dominicana," in Lenihan, *Limerick,* 180 n; "Aphorismical Discovery," 3:21.

62. Owen, *Labouring Saints,* ii; Ramsey, *Henry Cromwell,* 15. Col. Cromwell did write a letter about Ireton's death that was read to Parliament, but no copy survives (*Journals of the House of Commons,* 7:49).

63. *Mercurius Politicus,* 11 Dec. 1651; Irish Commissioners to the Council of State, 1 Dec. 1651, Dublin, in Ludlow, *Memoirs,* 1:495.

64. Abbott, *Writings and Speeches of Cromwell,* 2:234.

65. Brown, *Baptists and Fifth Monarchy Men,* 136–41.

66. *CSPD, 1651–52,* 276, 587.

67. Varley, *Cromwell's Latter End,* 62–63.

68. Royal College of Physicians, *Certain Necessary Directions;* Wood, *Life and Times,* 3:189.

69. Varley, *Cromwell's Latter End,* 63.

70. "Aphorismical Discovery," 3:22; Stannard, *Puritan Way of Death,* 102–3; John Hall, "Upon Mr. Robert Wiseman," in Saintsbury, *Minor Poets,* 2:207.

71. Guibert, *Charitable Physitian,* 143–46.

72. Wood, *Life and Times,* 1:483.

73. Varley, *Cromwell's Latter End,* 62–63. Varley concluded that plague "undoubtedly" killed Ireton and that he "must have been buried at Limerick."

74. *Severall Proceedings,* 11 Dec. 1651.

75. *Mercurius Politicus,* 11 Dec. 1651.

76. *Weekly Intelligencer,* 16 Dec. 1651.

77. *Severall Proceedings,* 11 Dec. 1651.

78. Cooke, *Monarchy No Creature.*

79. *French Intelligencer,* 9 Dec. 1651; *Weekly Intelligencer,* 9 Dec. 1651.

80. Hutchinson, *Memoirs,* 204; Whitelock, *Memorials,* 3:371.

81. *CSPD, 1651–52,* 52.

82. *Journals of the House of Commons,* 7:49; Ludlow, *Memoirs,* 1:295.

83. *Mercurius Politicus,* 29 Jan. 1652.

84. *Weekly Intelligencer,* 16 Dec. 1651; *Perfect Passages,* 12 Dec. 1651.

85. *Perfect Diurnall,* 15 Dec. 1651.

86. *Journals of the House of Commons,* 7:49; *Severall Proceedings,* 11 Dec. 1651; [Fisher], *Veni, Vidi, Vici.*

87. Ramsey, *Henry Ireton,* 20; *Journals of the House of Commons,* 7:49, 52.

88. Whitelock, *Memorials,* 3:371

89. Cromwell to Mrs. Elizabeth Cromwell, 15 Dec. 1651, in Abbott, *Writings and Speeches of Cromwell,* 2:508.

90. Josselin, *Diary,* 267.

91. Whitelock, *Memorials,* 3:372–74; Wheatley, *London Past and Present,* 2:336; Hutchinson, *Memoirs,* 203. Whether or not the meeting occurred on 10 December (the date under which Whitelock reported it), Cromwell's comment indicated his mind at the time of Ireton's death.

92. Zagorin, *History of Political Thought,* 146–49.

93. Noble, *Memoirs of the Protectorate-House,* 2:167–68.

94. *Mercurius Politicus,* 6 Nov. 1651, 4 Dec. 1651; Blair Worden, "Clas-

sical Republicanism and the Puritan Revolution," in Lloyd-Jones, Pearl, and Worden, *History and Imagination,* 192.

95. *CSPD, 1651–52,* 56, 66, 546.

96. Quoted in Wedgwood, *King's War,* 597.

97. *CSPI, 1647–60,* 385–86; *Directory for Publique Worship,* 49.

98. *Perfect Account,* 17 Dec. 1651.

99. *Mercurius Politicus,* 25 Dec. 1651; *Weekly Intelligencer,* 30 Dec. 1651.

100. *Mercurius Politicus,* 25 Dec. 1651; Whitelock, *Memorials,* 379; *CSPV, 1647–52,* 212; *Weekly Intelligencer,* 30 Dec. 1651.

101. *CSPD, 1651–52,* 66.

102. *Severall Proceedings,* 1 Jan. 1651; *Mercurius Politicus,* 25 Dec. 1651.

103. *Perfect Account,* 31 Dec. 1651.

104. Heath, *Brief Chronicle,* 568.

105. *Perfect Account,* 28 Jan. 1652.

106. *Weekly Intelligencer,* 3 Feb. 1652.

107. [Fisher], *Veni, Vidi, Vici.*

108. Hutchinson, *Memoirs,* 203.

109. Ludlow, *Memoirs,* 1:295.

110. A.B. Worden, introduction to Ludlow, *Voyce from the Watch Tower,* 1–5, 272. Ludlow had firsthand knowledge for this statement but not for the remainder of the sentence that alleges burial of Charles Stuart's friend in Ireton's place.

111. Wood, *Life and Times,* 1:478–83.

112. *True Manner,* 4–8; Heath, *Brief Chronicle,* 568; Varley, *Cromwell's Latter End,* 29–30.

113. *CSPV, 1647–52,* 215; Hutchinson, *Memoirs,* 203.

114. *CSPV, 1647–52,* 215; *Mercurius Bellonius,* 14 Feb. 1652; *Perfect Passages,* 2 Jan. 1652; Evelyn, *Diary,* 3:57–58.

115. "Calendar of the Muniments of Westminster Abbey," in HMC, *Fourth Report,* 180.

116. Wood, *Athenae Oxonienses,* vol. 2, col. 149.

117. Owen, *Labouring Saints,* passim.

118. *CSPD, 1654,* 5, 27, 35, 445. The tomb disappeared shortly after the Restoration.

119. Quoted in Stearns, *Strenuous Puritan,* 366–67.

120. Ludlow, *Memoirs,* 1:295; John Hall, "Upon Mr. Robert Wiseman," in Saintsbury, *Minor Poets,* 2:207.

121. Bate, *Lives, Actions and Executions,* 50

122. John Poortmans to Robert Blackbone, 19 June 1653, in *CSPD, 1652–53*, 425.

123. *Faithful Scout,* 13 Feb. 1652; Bolton, *Mr. Boltons Last,* 82.

3. Cromwell: *Ivit ad Plures*

1. Kenyon, *Stuart Constitution,* 300–302, 308–13.

2. Noble, *Memoirs of the Protectorate-House,* 1:228.

3. Andrew Marvell, "Poem upon the Death of O.C.," in Marvell, *Poems and Letters,* 1:125.

4. Trevor-Roper, "The Paracelsian Movement," in Trevor-Roper, *Renaissance Essays,* 156–58, 178–80.

5. Oliver Cromwell to the Lord President of the Council, 3 June 1651, in Abbott, *Writings and Speeches of Cromwell,* 2:421.

6. Fleetwood to Henry Cromwell, [July 1658], in *TSP,* 295. Flemish and Dutch paintings, popular among English collectors, depicted doctors as comic theatrical figures dressed in anachronistic *comedia del'arte* costumes. Jan Steen's seventeenth-century paintings of quacks examining pregnant prostitutes contrast significantly, for example, with nineteenth-century attitudes toward doctors represented in Samuel Luke Fildes's sentimental anecdote "The Doctor" or Thomas Eakins's heroic icon "The Gross Clinic."

7. Colonel Herbert Prise to Prince Rupert, 1 April 1646, in HMC, *Ninth Report,* 2:438.

8. Unsigned letter, 21 March 1651, London, in HMC, *Ormond Manuscripts,* n.s., 1:166.

9. *Perfect Diurnall,* 31 March 1651.

10. Cooper, "Historical Notes," 339–70.

11. *Severall Proceedings,* 20 Feb. 1651, reported the illness as "the country disease." MacArthur identified this phrase with dysentery ("English Malaria," 78).

12. *Severall Proceedings,* 15 May 1651.

13. *Perfect Diurnall,* 2 June 1651; [Harvey], *Collection of Several Passages,* 8–9.

14. The Dutch ambassadors to the greffier Ruysch, 11–21 Nov. 1653, in *TSP,* 1:584.

15. Bate, *Elenchus Motuum,* 2:199. Bate's use of the word "Liquor" is misleading, for it refers merely to a broth of some sort.

16. The Dutch ambassadors to the states general, 16 Oct. 1654, new style, in *TSP,* 2:652.

17. "Extracts from Newsletters," 25 Aug. 1658, in Clarke, *Papers,* 3:56; W. Nieuport to the states general, 17 Sept. 1655, new style, in *TSP,* 4:19; Peachey, "Thomas Trapham," 48.

18. Cromwell to his wife, 4 Sept. 1650, in Abbott, *Writings and Speeches of Cromwell,* 2:329.

19. "Extracts from the Newsletters, 1656," 22 Jan. 1656, in Clarke, *Papers,* 3:63.

20. *CSPV, 1657–59,* 104. Firth claimed that his signature was "shaky and feeble" in mid-1657 (*Cromwell and the Rule of the Puritans,* 440).

21. Thurloe to H. Cromwell, 27 July 1658, in *TSP,* 294.

22. *CSPV, 1657–59,* 226; *Publick Intelligencer,* 2 Aug. 1658.

23. Fleetwood to H. Cromwell, 3 Aug. 1658, in *TSP,* 309.

24. Monck to Thurloe, 10 Aug. 1658, Dalkeith, in *TSP,* 323. Monck responded to a letter from Thurloe, dated about 4 August; letters traveled from London to Edinburgh in about five or six days (see Monck to Thurloe, 15 Sept. 1658, Dalkeith, *TSP,* 386).

25. [Harvey], *Collection of Several Passages,* 1, 10.

26. Thurloe to H. Cromwell, 17 Aug. 1658, in *TSP,* 320.

27. *CSPV, 1657–59,* 236; Thurloe to H. Cromwell, 17 Aug. 1658, in *TSP,* 320; Fleetwood to H. Cromwell, 17 Aug. 1658, in *TSP,* 340.

28. "Extracts from Newsletters," 14 Aug. 1658, in Clarke, *Papers,* 3:161; Whitelock, *Memorials,* 4:334; Whitelock, *Diary,* 495.

29. *Publick Intelligencer,* 16 Aug. 1658; Thurloe to H. Cromwell, 17 Aug. 1658, in *TSP,* 320.

30. "Extracts from Newsletters," 14 Aug. 1658, in Clarke, *Papers,* 3:161. The report was written by George Mabbott, another of Monck's correspondents at Whitehall.

31. Fleetwood to H. Cromwell, 17 Aug. 1658, in *TSP,* 390; Thurloe to H. Cromwell, 17 August 1658, in *TSP,* 320.

32. "Extracts from Newsletters," 17 Aug. 1658, in Clarke, *Papers,* 3:161.

33. Fox, *Journal,* 308. Some editions of the *Journal* do not include this passage.

34. Bate, *Elenchus Motuum,* 2:235; Baker, *Chronicle,* 652. Edward Phillips, John Milton's nephew, continued the *Chronicle* with the assistance of Sir Thomas Clarges.

35. Bate, *Elenchus Motuum,* 2:234.

36. Fox, *Journal,* 308.

37. Fleetwood to H. Cromwell, 24 Aug. 1658, in *TSP,* 355; Thurloe to H. Cromwell, 24 Aug. 1658, in *TSP,* 354–55.

38. *CSPV, 1657–59,* 238.

39. Richard Cromwell to H. Cromwell, 24 Aug. 1658, quoted in Butler, *Richard Cromwell,* 76.

40. Thurloe to H. Cromwell, 24 Aug. 1658, in *TSP,* 354–55.

41. Fraser, *Cromwell,* 672; Whitelock, *Memorials,* 4:335; Whitelock, *Diary,* 496.

42. Thurloe to H. Cromwell, 27 Aug. 1658, *TSP,* 362.

43. *CSPV, 1657–59,* 238; *Publick Intelligencer,* 30 Aug. 1658.

44. Richard Cromwell to John Dunche, 28 Aug. 1658, in *Parliamentary History,* 21:223–24 n.

45. "Extracts from Newsletters," 28 Aug. 1658, in Clarke, *Papers,* 3:161.

46. Thurloe to H. Cromwell, 30 Aug. 1658, in *TSP,* 363–64.

47. *CSPV, 1657–59,* 240.

48. "Extracts from Newsletters," 2 Sept. 1658, in Clarke, *Papers,* 3:161; Thomas Clarges to H. Cromwell, 1 Sept. 1658, in *TSP,* 369; Fauconberg to H. Cromwell, 30-31 Aug. 1658, in *TSP,* 365.

49. Fauconberg to H. Cromwell, 30–31 Aug. 1658, in *TSP,* 365–66; Thurloe to H. Cromwell, 30 Aug. 1658, in *TSP,* 364; Bate, *Elenchus Motuum,* 2:236. Bate identified Barrington as a "valet."

50. [Heath], *Flagellum,* 1.

51. Marvell, "Poem upon the Death of O.C.," in Marvell, *Poems and Letters,* 1:125.

52. Wood, *Life and Times,* 1:258; Ludlow, *Memoirs,* 2:43. Ludlow mentioned wind but nothing of "mighty oaks crashing in his path" (Fraser, *Cromwell,* 674). Had such debris blocked the road, he could not have gotten as far as Epping, let alone continuing to London the next morning.

53. Edmund Waller, "Upon the late storm, and of the death of his Highness ensuing the same," Waller, *Poems,* 2:34–35.

54. Wood, *Life and Times,* 1:259.

55. *CSPV, 1657–59,* 240.

56. Fauconberg to H. Cromwell, 31 Aug. 1658, in *TSP,* 366.

57. Fleetwood to H. Cromwell, 31 Aug. 1658, in *TSP,* 367.

58. Ludlow, *Memoirs,* 2:43.

59. *CSPV, 1657–59,* 240; Fleetwood to H. Cromwell, 31 Aug. 1658, in *TSP,* 367.

60. [Harvey], *Collection of Several Passages,* 12–13. Harvey did not record the entire prayer, for he says "something is here omitted." One wonders if the omission related to Cromwell's comment about some persons being glad of his death. Fraser claimed that "it is to Harvey that we owe the tradition of his last moving prayer" (*Cromwell,* 676), but this was probably

not Cromwell's "last" prayer, because it was given two or three days before his death.

61. *CSPV, 1657–59,* 240; Clarke, *Papers,* 3:161.

62. [Harvey], *Collection of Several Passages,* 11–12, 5–7; *CSPV, 1657–59,* 241.

63. *Publick Intelligencer,* 6 Sept. 1658.

64. *Parliamentary History,* 21:240.

65. Thurloe to H. Cromwell, 4 Sept. 1658, in *TSP,* 372; Marvell, "Poem upon the Death of O.C.," in Marvell, *Poems and Letters,* 1:126; newsletter, 16 Sept. 1658, in HMC, *Fifth Report,* 143; Bate, *Elenchus Motuum,* 2:236; Josselin, *Diary,* 430; *CSPV, 1657–59,* 242.

66. Thurloe to H. Cromwell, 4 Sept. 1658, in *TSP,* 372. Ronald Hutton concluded, "By evening [of 3 September] it was accepted that he had named Richard as his successor. Whether he ever did so is unprovable" (*Restoration,* 21). For a discussion of the ambiguities of the transition, see Austin Woolrych, "Milton & Cromwell: 'A Short but Scandalous Night of Interruption,'" in Lieb and Shawcross, *Achievements of the Left Hand,* 185–218.

67. M. de Bordeaux to Cardinal Mazarin, 11 Sept. 1658, in Guizot, *Histoire de la République,* 2:645.

68. Thurloe to H. Cromwell, 7 Sept. 1658, in *TSP,* 374.

69. Speech of the protector to the officers of the army, in *TSP,* 447–49.

70. "Extracts from Newsletters," 6 Nov. 1658, in Clarke, *Papers,* 3:167.

71. Fauconberg to H. Cromwell, 14 Sept. 1658, in *TSP,* 386.

72. *CSPD, 1658–59,* 129; *Publick Intelligencer,* 6 Sept. 1658.

73. Marvell, "Poem upon the Death of O.C.," in Marvell, *Poems and Letters,* 1:129.

74. Cowley, "A Discourse by Way of Vision, concerning the Government of Oliver Cromwell," in Cowley, *Works,* 2:624.

75. *CSPD, 1658–59,* 139.

76. *Mercurius Politicus,* 23 Sept. 1658; *CSPV, 1657–59,* 248.

77. *Publick Intelligencer,* 27 Sept. 1658.

78. Varley, *Cromwell's Latter End,* 33–34.

79. Newsletter, 16 Sept. 1658, in HMC, *Fifth Report,* 144.

80. "Rev. John Prestwich Ms.," in Prestwich, *Respublica,* 175 n; Prestwich, *Respublica,* 188–89.

81. *CSPV, 1657–59,* 246; newsletter, 16 Sept. 1658, in HMC, *Fifth Report,* 144.

82. *Publick Intelligencer,* 11 Oct. 1658.

83. W. Smith to John Langley, 9 Oct. 1658, in HMC, *Fifth Report,* 173.

84. *Publick Intelligencer,* 18 Oct. 1658.

85. *True Manner,* 4–8; Noble, *Memoirs of the Protectorate-House,* 1:360–61.

86. "Rev. John Prestwich Ms.," in Prestwich, *Respublica,* 174–75.

87. Rachell Newport to Sir R. Leveson, 26 Oct. 1658, in HMC, *Fifth Report,* 146.

88. Mundy, *Travels,* 5:103.

89. *Mercurius Politicus,* 18 Nov. 1658; *True Manner,* 11–12.

90. "Rev. John Prestwich, Ms.," in Prestwich, *Respublica,* 175.

91. Verney, *Memoirs,* 3:422.

92. Bate, *Elenchus Motuum,* 2:237.

93. "Rev. John Prestwich Ms.," in Prestwich, *Respublica,* 172–73. The Reverend Prestwich assumed that putrefaction was the reason for the 20 September removal from Whitehall Palace, but putrefaction occurred by early November while the body was inside the magnificent-but-closed coffin displayed at Somerset House.

94. Stow, *Survey of London and Westminster,* 2:584; *Gentleman's Magazine* 53 (1783): 846.

95. *CSPD, 1658–59,* 152, 175, 184.

96. M. de Bordeaux to Cardinal Mazarin, 8 Nov. 1658, in Guizot, *Richard Cromwell,* 1:253–54.

97. Varley, *Cromwell's Latter End,* 32–33; Verney, *Memoirs,* 3:422, where the editor indicated in a marginal note that the letter was written about 11 November.

98. M. de Bordeaux to M. de Brienne, 17 Nov. 1658, in Guizot, *Richard Cromwell,* 1:260.

99. "Extracts from the Newsletters," 13 Nov. 1658, in Clarke, *Papers,* 3:167–68.

100. Dering, "Diary," 55.

101. *CSPV, 1657–59,* 268; Sir H. Moore to Edward Hyde, 12 Nov. 1658, in *CCSP,* 108.

102. *CSPD, 1658–59,* 184; Thurloe to H. Cromwell, 16 Nov. 1658, in *TSP,* 515.

103. *Mercurius Politicus,* 18 Nov. 1658.

104. "Rev. John Prestwich Ms.," in Prestwich, *Respublica,* 175; *CSPD, 1658–59,* 187.

105. *True Manner,* 12.

106. "Rev. John Prestwich Ms.," in Prestwich, *Respublica,* 175–76.

107. M. de Bordeaux to M. de Brienne, 29 Nov. 1658, in Guizot, *Richard Cromwell,* 1:268.

108. Evelyn, *Diary,* 3:224.

109. Cowley, "A Discourse by way of vision," in Cowley, *Works*, 2:624–25.

110. Dering, "Diary," 55.

111. "Rev. John Prestwich Ms.," in Prestwich, *Respublica*, 175–78.

112. Prestwich, "John Prestwich MS.," in *Diary of Thomas Burton*, 2:528 n.

113. *Mercurius Politicus*, 18 and 25 Nov. 1658; M. de Bordeaux to M. de Brienne, 29 Nov. 1658, in Guizot, *Richard Cromwell*, 1:269–70.

114. Thurloe to H. Cromwell, 23 Nov. 1658, in *TSP*, 528.

115. Noble, *Memoirs of the Protectorate-House*, 1:370; for a summary of alternative theories concerning burial sites, see "What Became of Cromwell?" 555–58.

116. Marvell, "Poem upon the Death of O.C.," in Marvell, *Poems and Letters*, 1:130.

117. John Dryden, "Heroique Stanzas," in Dryden, *Poems*, 1:12.

118. Cowley, "A Discourse by Way of Vision," in Cowley, *Works*, 2:625.

119. Owen, *Laboring Saints*, 21.

4. An Unexpected Good Accident

1. For views of Cromwell in the years following 1660, see Roger Howell Jr., "'That Imp of Satan': The Restoration Image of Cromwell," in Richardson, *Images of Cromwell*, 33–47.

2. *Publick Intelligencer*, 6 Sept. 1658.

3. Carlyle, *Letters and Speeches of Cromwell*, 3:213.

4. MacArthur, "English Malaria," 78.

5. Cartwright and Biddis, *Disease and History*, 141–42; MacArthur, "English Malaria," 78.

6. Willis, *London Practice*, 539–45.

7. Ibid., 545.

8. Dr. Thomas Sydenham, "Febres Intermittentes," in Dewhurst, *Dr. Thomas Sydenham*, 131–39.

9. MacArthur, "English Malaria," 76.

10. Fleetwood to H. Cromwell, 31 Aùg. 1658, in *TSP*, 367; Whitelock, *Memorials*, 4:335; Whitelock, *Diary*, 496.

11. *CSPV, 1657–59*, 242; *Publick Intelligencer*, 6 Sept. 1658.

12. *Publick Intelligencer*, 6 Sept. 1658.

13. For example, Fraser cited this as "the post-mortem" (*Cromwell*, 672).

14. Bate, *Elenchus Motuum*, 2:236.

15. Robbins, *Pathologic Basis of Disease*, 452–53, 771.

16. *Parliamentary History*, 21:240.

17. Fraser wrote that "the wretched stone . . . ultimately caused his death" (*Cromwell,* 671–72); Pascal, *Pensées,* 158.

18. Bate, *Elenchus Motuum,* 2:199; *CSPV, 1657–59,* 237–38.

19. Fleetwood to H. Cromwell, 31 Aug. 1658, in *TSP,* 367.

20. Whitelock, *Memorials,* 4:335; Whitelock, *Diary,* 496; Prestwich, "John Prestwich MS.," in *Diary of Thomas Burton,* 2:516.

21. Varley, *Cromwell's Latter End,* 19–20.

22. Petitfils, *L'affaire des poisons,* 17–18; Glaister, *Power of Poison,* 79–80, 87.

23. Paracelsus, *Selected Writings,* 169–70.

24. Gordon, *Medieval and Renaissance Medicine,* 662–64.

25. Dewhurst, *John Locke,* 227–28.

26. Mead, *Mechanical Account of Poisons,* pref., 104. The first book in English to study the effect of poison on a living body appeared in 1829 (Glaister, *Power of Poison,* 22).

27. Berman, *Toxic Metals,* 19; Haddad et al., *Poisoning and Drug Overdose,* 790; Klaassen, *Casarett and Doull's Toxicology,* 726.

28. Quoted in Berman, *Toxic Metals,* 150.

29. Mead, *Mechanical Account of Poisons,* 104; William Ramesey, *De Venenis,* 23–30.

30. Quoted in Goldwater, *Mercury,* 166.

31. Haddad et al., *Poisoning and Drug Overdose,* 790; Hardman et al., *Pharmacological Basis of Therapeutics,* 1657, 1660.

32. Hardman et al., *Pharmacological Basis of Therapeutics,* 1657–61; Klaassen, *Casarett and Doull's Toxicology,* 697, 711.

33. Glaister, *Power of Poison,* 78–79.

34. Hardman et al., *Pharmacological Basis of Therapeutics,* 1660–61.

35. Isselbacher et al., *Harrison's Principles,* 2462.

36. Glaister, *Power of Poison,* 33.

37. Hardman et al., *Pharmacological Basis of Therapeutics,* 1661; Klaassen, *Casarrett and Doull's Toxicology,* 697; Berman, *Toxic Metals,* 27.

38. There has been speculation that Cromwell did have malaria and died accidentally as the result of an incorrect treatment with Peruvian bark. This is improbable, if for no other reason than on 28 August, a few days before his death, doctors admitted to Richard Cromwell they were "in a Nonplus," unable after four weeks to identify the illness to the patient's son and successor.

39. Sir Edward Nicholas to Edward Hyde, Bruges, 10 Sept. 1657, in Nicholas, *Papers,* 4:13.

40. "Sir Orlando Bridgman," *DNB.*

41. Nicholas to Hyde, 10 Sept. 1657, in Nicholas, *Papers,* 4:13.

42. Underdown, *Royalist Conspiracy,* passim.

43. *CSPV, 1657–59,* 20.

44. Ibid., 168.

45. Ibid., 188.

46. Nicholas to Sir Henry Bennet, Bruges, 19–29 March 1657–58, in Nicholas, *Papers,* 4:34; for a plot in 1658 see Thurloe to Monck, April 20, 1658, in Clarke, *Papers,* 3:147–48.

47. Hyde to D. O'Neal, c. 12 April 1658; Hyde to Mordaunt, 12 April 1658, both in *CCSP,* 39–40.

48. *CSPV, 1657–59,* 201.

49. Nicholas to Hyde, 10 Sept. 1657, in Nicholas, *Papers,* 4:13.

50. *CSPV, 1657–59,* 201.

51. Bate, *Elenchus Motuum,* 2:198. These techniques amused Bate, but they are similar to those used by modern security services.

52. Joseph Jane to John Nicholas, 28 June 1658, Bruges, in Nicholas, *Papers,* 4:55.

53. Warwick, *Memoirs of Charles the First,* 427.

54. Sir George Warner, preface to Nicholas, *Papers,* 4:xii.

55. Sir Alexander Hume to Nicholas, 9 Dec. 1655, in Nicholas, *Papers,* 3:192.

56. Ibid., 3:264 n.

57. Hume to Nicholas, 14 Sept. 1658, in ibid., 4:69.

58. Nicholas to Thomas Ross, 1 Feb., n.s., 1655–56, in ibid., 3:264–65. Warner deciphered the code names. See also Thomas Ross to Nicholas, 7–17 Feb. 1655–56, Paris, *CSPD, 1655–56,* 166.

59. Charles to the Duke of York, 9–19 July 1659, in Bryant, *Letters of Charles II,* 73.

60. Nicholas to Hyde, 10 Sept. 1657, Bruges, in Nicholas, *Papers,* 4:13.

61. Hyde to Nicholas, 13 Sept. 1657, in Clarendon, *State Papers,* 3:365.

62. Hyde to John Nicholas, 18 Aug. 1658, Breda, in *CCSP,* 4:63.

63. Nicholas to Hyde, 1, 4, 6, 8 Sept. 1658, in *CCSP,* 4:69, 72, 74–75, 76.

64. Wood, *Athenae Oxonienses,* vol. 2, col. 424.

65. Marshall, *Intelligence and Espionage,* 130.

66. "George Bate," *DNB.*

67. Cromwell to Major-General Crawford, 10 March 1644, in Abbott, *Writings and Speeches of Cromwell,* 1:278.

68. "George Bate," *DNB.*

69. Peachy, "Thomas Trapham," 48.

70. Bate, *Elenchus Motuum,* passim.

71. Salmon, *Pharmacopoeia Bateana,* preface.

72. Ibid., 506–10.

73. Francis Newport to Sir Richard Leveson, 26 Jan. 1660, London, HMC, *Fifth Report,* 150; Edward Gower to Leveson, 2 May 1661, London, ibid., 202.

74. Bate, "Medical Diary 1654–1660."

75. *DNB;* Spalding, *Contemporaries of Bulstrode Whitelock,* 400, 284, 289.

76. *CSPD, 1660–61,* 138.

77. Ibid., 230.

78. Wood, *Life and Times,* 2:69.

79. Wood, "Diaries 7," fols. 19v–20r; Wood, *Life and Times,* 1:475 (Wood's ellipsis).

80. Wood, *Athenae Oxonienses,* vol. 2, col. 424.

81. Aubrey, *"Brief Lives,"* 1:95.

82.Edward Gower to Sir Richard Leveson, 2 May 1661, London, HMC, *Fifth Report,* 202.

83. Rugg, *Diurnal,* 123; *Parliamentary Intelligencer,* 29 Oct. 1660.

84. Marshall, *Intelligence and Espionage,* 146.

85. *Mercurius Publicus,* 8 Nov. 1660.

86. *Parliamentary Intelligencer,* 29 Oct. 1660.

87. Wood, *Athenae Oxonienses,* vol. 2, col. 769.

88. Ibid., vol. 2, cols. 1153–54; Bate, *Elenchus Motuum,* preface.

89. Wood, *Life and Times,* 2:215–16; Marshall, *Intelligence and Espionage,* 130; M.W. Helms and Leonard Taylor, "Thomas Clarges," in Henning, ed., *History of Parliament,* 2:75–80.

90. Ashley, *General Monck,* 42–96.

91. Monck to Thurloe, 3 July 1658, in *TSP,* 237.

92. Clarges to H. Cromwell, 10, 24 Aug., 1 Sept. 1658, in *TSP,* 323, 355–56, 369.

93. Scott, *Chronicles of the Canongate,* 1:1.

94. "Extracts from Newsletters," in Clarke, *Papers,* 3:161. Firth published four extracts—dated 14, 17, 28 August and 2 September. He credited them to Clarges, who actually wrote only those for 17 August and 2 September. George Mabbot, another of Monck's Whitehall correspondents, wrote the other two. Mabbot's newsletters contained accurate medical information, as cited in chapter 3.

95. Wood, *Athenae Oxonienses,* vol. 2, col. 72; Baker, *Chronicle,* title page, 652-53.

96. According to Thomas Skinner's curious comment, "It was certainly a great Oversight in *Cromwel* to continue so great a Command, as the Gov-

ernment of *Scotland,* in the Hands of General *Monk,* of whom he could have no great Security from his Principles" (*Life of General Monk,* 79).

97. Clarges was the unnamed person, one infers from another of Monck's biographers, Thomas Gumble, "in whom he much trusted" because "to others . . . he would not intrust his Opinion or Resolution" (*Monck,* 104).

98. Baker, *Chronicle,* 654.

99. Ibid., 731.

100. HMC, *Egmont Diary,* 1:113.

101. *CSPD, 1660–61,* 138.

5. Infernal Saints

1. Declaration of Charles II, in Nicholas, *Papers,* 4:72–73; Charles to John Mordaunt, 11 March 1659, in HMC, *Tenth Report,* 6:189; Charles to the Duke of York, 19 July 1659, in Bryant, *Letters of Charles II,* 72–73.

2. Hutton, *Restoration,* 1–123.

3. Bryant, *Letters of Charles II,* 84–85.

4. Hutton, *Restoration,* 107.

5. *Guild-Hall Elegie.*

6. Rugg, *Diurnal,* 12–13, 56–58.

7. For example see the satire *The last Speech and dying Words of Thomas (lord, alias colonel) Pride; being touched in Conscience for his inhuman Murder of the Bears in the Beargarden* (London, 1680, reprinted in *Harleian Miscellany,* 3:132–37).

8. Rugg, *Diurnal,* 93.

9. Hutton, *Restoration,* 132.

10. Dering, *Diaries and Papers,* 40–43; *Parliamentary History,* 22:286–88.

11. Dering, *Diaries and Papers,* 41–43; *Parliamentary History,* 22:286–90; *CSPV, 1659–61,* 148; *Exact Account,* 15 June 1660.

12. *Parliamentary History,* 22:289; Parker, *Milton,* 1:568; *CSPV, 1659–61,* 148.

13. *Mercurius Publicus,* 24 and 31 May 1660.

14. *Parliamentary History,* 22:344; Speech to the House of Lords, 27 July 1660, in Bryant, *Letters of Charles II,* 100.

15. *Parliamentary History,* 22:338–43; Rugg, *Diurnal,* 93.

16. Parker, *Milton,* 570; Dering, *Diaries and Papers,* 45; Rugg, *Dirunal,* 93.

17. *Parliamentary History,* 22:405; Bryant, *Letters of Charles II,* 100–101.

18. Hutton, *Restoration,* 133; Dering, *Diaries and Papers,* 48; *Parliamentary History,* 22:447.

19. *Parliamentary History,* 22:458.

20. Ibid., 460.

21. Josselin, *Diary,* 468.

22. *Parliamentary History,* 22:487–88. Of this noble prince with out-stretched arms, the earl of Rochester would write a famous poem, from which the best-known and least bawdy lines are: "Restless he rolls about from whore to whore, / A merry monarch, scandalous and poor." Rochester's was not the only poetic tribute to the royal privities, and it is in contrast with the lord chancellor's divine-right expression (John Wilmot, the Earl of Rochester, "[A Satire on Charles II]," in Fowler, *Seventeenth Century* Verse, 760–61).

23. Quoted in Solt, *Church and State,* 132.

24. *Mercurius Publicus,* 11 Oct. 1660; Hutton, *Restoration,* 134.

25. Kenyon, *Popish Plot,* 115–16.

26. Yale, *Lord Nottingham's Chancery Cases,* 1:xvii.

27. Stephen, *Criminal Law of England,* 1:273–304, 225–26; Keeton, *Jeffreys and the Stuart Cause,* 210–22; Sharpe, *Crime in Early Modern England,* 37.

28. Howell, *State Trials,* vol. 5, cols. 985-95; *Mercurius Publicus,* 11 Oct. 1660.

29. Mundy, *Travels,* 5:123; Pepys, *Diary of Pepys,* 1:263.

30. *State Trials,* vol. 5, cols. 995–1008.

31. Ludlow, *Voyce from the Watch Tower,* 214.

32. *State Trials,* vol. 5, cols. 1007–34.

33. Ibid., col. 1034.

34. *Trials of Charles the First and Some of the Regicides,* 329.

35. *Mercurius Publicus,* 18 Oct. 1660; *State Trials,* vol. 5, col. 1237; Mundy, *Travels,* 5:125; Bate, *Lives, Actions, and Executions,* 21; Rugg, *Diurnal,* 116.

36. Pepys, *Diary of Pepys,* 1:265; Mundy, *Travels,* 5:125; Nicholas to Sir Henry Bennet, 15 Oct. 1660, in *CSPD, 1660–61,* 312–13.

37. Nicholas to Sir Henry Bennet, 18 Oct. 1660, in *CSPD, 1660–61,* 316.

38. William Smith to John Langley, 20 Oct. 1660, in HMC, *Fifth Report,* 174; *Mercurius Publicus,* 18 Oct. 1660.

39. Mundy, *Travels,* 5:125–27; Pepys, *Diary of Pepys,* 1:115.

40. *State Trials,* vol. 5, cols. 1141–42; Hutton, *Restoration,* 134.

41. *CSPD, 1660–61,* 323; *Parliamentary Intelligencer,* 29 Oct. 1660.

42. *Parliamentary History,* 23:1.

43. Rugg, *Diurnal,* 128.

44. Hutton, *Restoration,* 134.

45. *Parliamentary History,* 23:6–7, 16.

46. Ibid., 37–39.

47. Ibid., 58.

48. Charles Stuart to Lord Mordaunt, 17–27 March 1660, in Bryant, *Letters of Charles II*, 82; *CSPD, 1661–62*, 12, 150, 172, 304, 308, 345, 443.

49. "Calendar of House of Lords Manuscripts," in HMC, *Seventh Report*, 123 (emphasis added).

50. Pierpoint, "Carcasses," 227. For a photographic reproduction of the order, see Taylor, "Proceedings of Parliament," 45.

51. *Parliamentary History*, 23:44–45.

52. "Thomas Pride," *DNB*.

53. Pepys, *Diary of Pepys*, 1:309; *CSPI, 1660–61*, 406.

54. *Parliamentary History*, 23:89; Pepys, *Diary of Pepys*, 1:7–11; Rogers, *Fifth Monarchy Men*, 110–22.

55. *Kingdomes-Intelligencer*, 28 Jan. 1661; Mundy, *Travels*, 5:130.

56. *CSPV, 1659–61*, 226; Nicholas to Winchelsea, in HMC, *Finch*, 1:101–2.

57. Noble, *Memoirs of the Protectorate-House*, 1:373.

58. *Mercurius Publicus*, 31 Jan. 1661.

59. [Heath], *Flagellum*, 196; Bate, *Elenchus Motuum*, 3:57; Fraser, *Cromwell*, 692–93; Hutton, *Restoration*, 134. "Apprentices" cut off only Bradshaw's fingers and toes because the other two corpses were not unwrapped.

60. "Thomas Pride," *DNB; Victoria History*, 3:268, 4:134.

61. Richard Temple to Sir R. Leveson, 23 Oct. 1658, in HMC, *Fifth Report*, 172.

62. "Extracts from Newsletters," Oct. 26, 1658, in Clarke, *Papers*, 3:167.

63. [Kennett], *Register and Chronicle*, 367.

64. *Gentleman's Magazine* 21 (1751): 5.

65. *Harleian Miscellany*, 2:270.

66. Noble, *Memoirs of the Protectorate-House*, 1:372.

67. S.S.B. to the Editor, 17–18; Stanley, *Historical Memorials*, 190. Norfolk was the House of Commons's sergeant-at-arms.

68. Varley, *Cromwell's Latter End*, 52–53.

69. S. to Editor. "In November 1733 Mr. West brought a note 'wrote many years since' on the plate found in Cromwell's coffin" (Evans, *Society of Antiquaries*, 66 n.).

70. E.E. Newton to Editor.

71. Chester, *Registers*, 521 n.

72. Stanley, *Historical Memorials*, 632 n.

73. Rugg, *Diurnal*, 143.

74. Chester, *Registers*, x.

75. Bate, *Elenchus Motuum,* 2:236; Mundy, *Travels,* 5:103; "Rev. John Prestwich Ms.," in Prestwich, *Respublica,* 172; Rugg, *Diurnal,* 145.

76. Noble, *Memoirs of the Protectorate-House,* 1:372.

77. Rugg, *Diurnal,* 145.

78. "Deserting the spacious street of Long Acre . . . [in 1646 Cromwell] acquired a house in near-by Drury Lane. The precise site is unknown, but it was certainly close to the famous Red Lion Inn of Holborn which played much part in the annals of the time" (Fraser, *Cromwell,* 179).

79. London County Council, *St. Giles-in-the-Fields,* pt. 2, pp. 3–4. See also Wheatley, *London, Past and Present,* 220. The last public hanging was in 1783, after which executions were conducted inside Newgate prison.

80. Stow, *Survey of London,* 486–87.

81. For example: "People that are Melancholy and distracted [with venereal disease], are kept and preserved from danger by Matthew Whitehorn, living in Bishops-gate street, London, without the gate, near the Red Lion Inn over against the Sun, in the house where the French Ministers have lived for years" (*French Intelligencer,* 9 Dec. 1651).

82. London County Council, *St. Giles-in-the-Fields,* pt. 2, pp. 3–9.

83. Strype, *Survey of the Cities,* vol. 2, book 4, 84; London County Council, *St. Giles-in-the-Fields,* pt. 1, pl. 3.

84. Thornbury, *Old and New London,* 4:545.

85. Brett-James, *Growth of Stuart London,* 329–30.

86. *Mercurius Publicus,* 31 Jan. 1661.

87. [Kennett], *Register and Chronicle,* 367.

88. Nicholas to Earl of Winchelsea, 14 March 1661, in HMC, *Finch,* 1:102; Evelyn, *Diary,* 3:269; Pepys, *Diary of Pepys,* 2:26–27.

89. Fraser, *Cromwell,* 692–93.

90. Pepys, *Diary of Pepys,* 2:26–27.

91. *Mercurius Publicus,* 31 Jan. 1661.

92. Mundy, *Travels,* 5:130.

93. *CSPV, 1659–61,* 226; Nicholas to the Earl of Orrey, 2 Feb. 1661, in *CSPI, 1660–62,* 205; Evelyn, *Diary,* 3:269; Pepys, *Diary of Pepys,* 2:26–27.

94. *Mercurius Publicus,* 31 Jan. 1661.

95. Rugg, *Diurnal,* 145.

96. Sainthill diary (see Appendix); Mundy, *Travels,* 5:130.

97. Mundy, *Travels,* 5:130.

98. Sainthill diary (see Appendix).

99. Ibid.; Mundy, *Travels,* 5:130; Bate, *Elenchus Motuum,* 2:236.

100. *Mercurius Publicus,* 31 Jan. 1661.

101. Nicholas to the Earl of Orrey, 2 Feb. 1661, *CSPI, 1660–62,* 205.

102. *Mercurius Publicus,* 31 Jan. 1661.

103. Evelyn, *Diary,* 3:269.

104. *Mercurius Publicus,* 7 Feb. 1661.

105. Mundy, *Travels,* 5:131.

106. Heath, *Brief Chronicle,* 787.

107. Hare, *Great Emperor,* 215.

6. *Hic Situs Est*

1. Prestwich, *Respublica,* 149; Rede, *Anecdotes and Biography,* 97.

2. "What Became of Cromwell?" 560.

3. Wheatley, *London, Past and Present,* 3:154.

4. Abbott, *Writings and Speeches of Cromwell,* 4:876.

5. Fraser, *Cromwell,* 694.

6. Rede, *Anecdotes and Biography,* 97.

7. Parker, *Milton,* 573–76; [Skiller,] "Life of Mr. John Milton," in Darbishire, *Early Lives,* 32; French, *Life Records of John Milton,* 4:349.

8. Parker, *Milton,* 577.

9. Woolrych, "Milton & Cromwell," 198–99; Shawcross, *John Milton,* 240.

10. E. Phillips, "Life of Milton," in Darbishire, *Early Lives,* 68.

11. Ibid., 75.

12. Parker, *Milton,* 577; E. Phillips, "Life of Milton," 68.

13. Masson, *Milton,* 6:215; Aubrey, "Minutes of the Life," in Darbishire, *Early Lives,* 4; Aubrey, "*Brief Lives,*" 2:66.

14. French, *Life Records of John Milton,* 4:335.

15. London County Council, *St. Giles-in-the-Fields,* pt. 2, pl. 3 ("Neighbourhood of St. Giles-in-the-Fields, *circ.* 1658" [Hollar]), and pl. 4 ("Neighbourhood of St. Giles-in-the-Fields, 1658" [Fairthorne and Newcourt]); the latter is a schematic map surveyed in 1643–47 and published in 1658 (Barker and Jackson, *London,* 158).

16. Aubrey, "*Brief Lives,*" 2:68.

17. Legouis, *Andrew Marvell,* 118–28.

18. Marvell, *Poems and Letters,* 2:18.

19. Legouis, *Andrew Marvell,* 129.

20. Aubrey, "*Brief Lives,*" 2:54.

21. Legouis, *Andrew Marvell,* 224–25; Wheatley, *London, Past and Present,* 2:112.

22. Rugg, *Diurnal,* 39.

23. Narcissus Lutterell's diary, quoted in H. Phillips, *Mid-Georgian London,* 206.

24. Brett-James, *Growth of Stuart London,* 324–30.

25. [Hatton], *New View of London,* 1:68.

26. Strype, *Survey of the Cities,* vol. 1, book 3, 254.

27. Wheatley, *London, Past and Present,* 3:155.

28. H. Phillips, *Mid-Georgian London,* fig. 283.

29. *History and Present State of the British Islands,* 2:163.

30. *Gentleman's Magazine* 60 (Aug. 1790): 702.

31. Stow, *Survey of London and Westminster,* vol. 1, book 3, 731.

32. *London and its Environs,* 5:250, and attached map entitled "New and Correct Plan."

33. Noorthouck, *New History of London,* 745; Harrison, *New and Universal History,* 538.

34. [Stuart], *Critical Observations,* 13–14.

35. Pennant, *Of London,* 165.

36. *Gentleman's Magazine* 60 (Aug. 1790): 702.

37. Rede, *Anecdotes and Biography,* 97.

38. Jesse, *London and Its Celebrities,* 2:34.

39. Prestwich, *Respublica,* vii, 149. The nineteenth-century antiquarian John Timbs, for example, erroneously claimed that Prestwich "does not give his authority for this statement; it may be a blunder, caused by the bodies of Cromwell, Ireton, and Bradshaw being carried from Westminster Abbey to the *Red Lion Inn*" (*Curiosities of London* [London, 1866], 751). However, Prestwich did give authority and did not confuse the carrying of three bodies to Holborn with the secret burial of one of them.

40. *Gentleman's Magazine* 57 (July 1787): 518; 60 (Aug. 1790): 702.

41. Pearson and Morant, "Wilkinson Head," 311.

42. Prestwich, *Respublica,* iii–iv.

43. *Whitehall Evening-Post,* 3–5 May 1787.

44. *Gentleman's Magazine* 57 (July 1787): 518; 58 (April 1788): 295.

45. Aubrey, *"Brief Lives,"* 66–67.

46. Neve, *Disinterment of Milton's Coffin; St. James's Chronicle: Or, British Post,* 5–7 Aug. 1790, 2–4 Sept. 1790. I wish to thank one of the readers for the press for drawing my attention to Neve's pamphlet.

47. Cowper, "Stanzas on . . . Milton," in Cowper, *Poetical Works,* 399.

48. "What Became of Cromwell?" 560.

49. Ibid.

50. Heathcote, *Some of the Families,* 177 n.

51. Petitions of Richard Bishop, Michael Crake, and Lt.-Col. Thomas Hunt, in *CSPD, 1660–61,* 347.

52. *CSPD, 1663–64,* 261.

53. Dashiell Hammett, *The Maltese Falcon* (1929; reprint, San Francisco, 1984), 130.

54. *CSPD, 1661–62,* 180–81, 265.

55. John Milton, "Samson Agonistes," in Milton, *Poems,* 369. Lady Antonia Fraser quoted part of these lines to show the theme of Cromwell's fate as "worthy of Milton" but did not consider the poet's possible involvement with events. The date of "Samson" is open to speculation. Parker placed composition c. 1645–53, but there is argument for composition after 1661 (ibid., 330–32), which makes such quotations especially intriguing. Christopher Hill disagrees that the phrases need apply to the exhumed corpses, saying "the same accusation [could be made] against the regicides and army leaders after they had been 'delivered bound' into Royalist hands" (*Milton and the English Revolution,* 436).

56. Marvell, "On Mr. Milton's Paradise Lost," in *Poems and Letters,* 1:138.

57. "Samson Agonistes," in Milton, *Poems,* 363.

58. "What Became of Cromwell?" 560.

59. Nicholas to the Earl of Orrey, 2 Feb. 1661, in *CSPI, 1660–61,* 205.

60. Nicholas to Sir Henry de Vic, 1 Feb. 1661, in *CSPD, 1660–61,* 500.

61. Nicholas to Sir William Curtis, 8 Feb. 1661, in ibid., 506.

62. Fraser, *Cromwell,* 697–98.

63. Pearson and Morant, "Wilkinson Head," 327 (emphasis in the original), 376.

64. Ibid., 271–78, 374.

65. Ibid., 310, 311 n.

66. Mundy, *Travels,* 5:129–30, 129 n.

67. Fraser, *Cromwell,* 698.

68. French, *Life Records of John Milton,* 4:391.

69. Milton, "Paradise Lost," in Milton, *Poems,* 589.

*B*ibliography

Newssheets, all in Thomason Collection, British Library, London

The Diary
An Exact Account
The Faithful Scout
The French Intelligencer
Great Britains Paine-Full Messenger
The Kingdomes Faithfull Scout
The Kingdomes-Intelligencer
Mercurius Bellonius
Mercurius Politicus
Mercurius Publicus
The Moderate Intelligencer
The Parliamentary Intelligencer
A Perfect Account of the Daily Intelligence
A Perfect Diurnall
Perfect Passages
The Publick Intelligencer
Severall Proceedings in Parliament
The Weekly Intelligencer
The Weekly Post

Eighteenth-Century Periodicals

Gentleman's Magazine
St. James Chronicle: Or, British Post
Whitehall Evening-Post

Documents

Bate, Dr. George. "Medical Diary 1654–1660." MS 893. Library of the Royal
College of Physicians of London, London.
Wood, Anthony. "Diaries 7." Bodleian Library, Oxford.

Books and Articles

Abbott, Wilbur Cortez. *The Writings and Speeches of Oliver Cromwell.* 4
vols. Cambridge, Mass., 1937–47.
"Aphorismical Discovery of Treasonable Faction." In John T. Gilbert, ed. *A
Contemporary History of Affairs in Ireland from 1641 to 1652.* 3 vols.
Dublin, 1880.
Aries, Philippe. *The Hour of Our Death.* New York, 1981.
Ashley, Maurice. *Charles I and Cromwell.* London, 1987.
———. *Cromwell's Generals.* London, 1954.
———. *General Monck.* Totowa, N.J., 1977.
———. *The Greatness of Oliver Cromwell.* New York, 1958.
Aubrey, John. *"Brief Lives," chiefly of Contemporaries.* Ed. Andrew Clark. 2
vols. Oxford, 1898.
———. "Minutes of the Life of Mr. John Milton." In Darbishire, *The Early
Lives of Milton.*
Austin, William. *The Poems of William Austin.* Ed. Anne Ridler. Oxford, 1983.
Aylmer, G.E., ed. *The Interregnum: The Quest for Settlement, 1647–1660.*
London, 1972.
———. *Rebellion or Revolution?* Oxford, 1986.
Bagwell, Richard. *Ireland under the Stuarts.* 3 vols. London, 1909.
Baker, Sir Richard. *A Chronicle of the Kings of England.* 6th ed. London, 1674.
Barker, Felix, and Peter Jackson. *London: 2000 Years of a City and Its People.*
New York, 1974.
Barry, James G. "Report from the Hon. Local Secretary for Limerick." *Journal of the Royal Society of Antiquaries of Ireland* 24 (1894): 386–89.
Bate, George (M.D.). *Elenchus Motuum Nuperorum in Anglia: Or A Short
Historical Account of the Rise and Progress of the Late Troubles in England . . . Made English.* London, 1685.
Bate, George (royalist). *The Lives, Actions, and Executions of the Prime Actors, and Principall Contrivers of that Horrid Murder of our Late Pious
and Sacred Sovereigne.* London, 1661.
Bayly, Lewes. *The Practice of Piety, Directing a Christian How to Walk that
He May Please God.* London, 1648.

Begley, John Canon. *The Diocese of Limerick in the Sixteenth and Seventeenth Centuries.* Dublin, 1927.

Belke, Thomas. *A Scripture Enquiry of Help.* London, 1642.

Berman, Eleanor. *Toxic Metals and Their Analysis.* London, 1980.

Beveridge, W.I.B. *Influenza: The Last Great Plague.* London, 1977.

Boate, Gerard. *Irelands Naturall History.* London, 1652.

Bolton, Robert. *Mr. Boltons Last and Learned Worke of the Foure Last Things.* London, 1632.

Bradley, E.T. *Annals of Westminster Abbey.* London, 1898.

Brett-James, Norman G. *The Growth of Stuart London.* London, 1935.

Brown, Louise Fargo. *The Political Activities of the Baptists and Fifth Monarchy Men.* Washington, D.C., 1912.

Bryant, Arthur, ed. *The Letters, Speeches and Declarations of King Charles II.* London, 1935.

Buchan, John. *Oliver Cromwell.* London, 1934.

Butler, John A. *A Biography of Richard Cromwell, 1626–1672, The Second Protector.* Lewiston, N.Y., 1994.

Butler, Samuel. *Hudibras.* Ed. Treadway Russel Nash. 2 vols. London, 1793.

Calendar of the Clarendon State Papers Preserved in the Bodleian Library. Ed. F.J. Routlege. 4 vols. Oxford, 1932.

Calendar of State Papers, Domestic Series, 1649–1660. Ed. Mary Anne Everett Green. 13 vols. London, 1875–86.

Calendar of State Papers, Domestic Series, of the Reign of Charles II. Ed. Mary Anne Everett Green, Francis Henry Blackburne Daniell, and Francis Laurence Bickley. 28 vols. London, 1860–1939.

Calendar of State Papers Relating to Ireland, 1625–1670. Ed. Robert Pentland Mahaffy, Francis Henry Blackburne Daniell, and Francis Laurence Bickley. 8 vols. London, 1900–1910.

Calendar of State Papers, Venetian, 1202–1675. Ed. Rawdon Brown and Allen B. Hinds. 38 vols. London, 1864–1940.

Carlyle, Thomas. *The Letters and Speeches of Oliver Cromwell.* 3 vols. New York, 1904.

Carpenter, Edward, ed. *A House of Kings: The Official History of Westminster Abbey.* New York, 1966.

Cartwright, Frederick, and Michael D. Biddis. *Disease and History.* New York, 1972.

Chester, J.L., ed., *Registers of the Collegiate Church or Abbey of St. Peter.* London, 1876.

Clarke, William. *The Clarke Papers, Selections from the Papers of William Clarke.* Ed. C.H. Firth. 4 vols. London, 1891–1901.

Clifton, Robin. "Fear of Popery." In Russell, *Origins of the English Civil War.*

Cock, F. William, to Editor. *Notes and Queries* 146 (Jan.–June 1924): 292–93.

Coleby, Andrew M. *Central Government and the Localities: Hampshire 1649–1689.* Cambridge, 1987.

Collinson, Patrick. *English Puritanism.* London, 1983.

———. *Godly People: Essays on English Protestantism and Puritanism.* London, 1983.

Cooke, John. *Monarchy No Creature of Gods Making.* Waterford, Ireland, 1652.

Cooper, W. White. "Historical Notes Concerning Certain Illnesses, the Death, and Disinterment of Oliver Cromwell." *Dublin Quarterly Journal of Medical Science* 5 (1848): 339–70.

Cowley, Abraham. *The Works of Mr. Abraham Cowley.* 2 vols. 11th ed. London, 1710.

Cowper, William. *The Poetical Works of William Cowper.* Ed. H.S. Milford. London, 1950.

Creighton, Charles. *A History of Epidemics in Britain.* 2 vols. Cambridge, 1881–84.

Cunningham, George H. *London: Being a Comprehensive Survey.* London, 1927.

Curtis, Henry, to Editor. *Notes and Queries* 146 (Jan.–June 1924): 272.

Cusack, M.F. *Illustrated History of Ireland.* 5th ed. London, 1871.

Darbishire, Helen. *The Early Lives of Milton.* London, 1932.

De Beer, Esmond S. "The Death of Henry Ireton." *Notes and Queries* 176 (Jan.-June 1939): 390.

De Beer, Esmond S., to Editor. *Notes and Queries* 176 (Jan.–June 1939): 390–91; 177 (July–Dec. 1939): 30–31.

Dering, Sir Edward. *The Diaries and Papers of Sir Edward Dering, Second Baronet, 1644 to 1684.* Ed. Maurice F. Bond. London, 1976.

———. "Diary of Sir Edward Dering, 17–23 November 1658." Photocopy in Sotheby and Co., *Catalogue of English Manuscripts . . . 26 June 1974.* London, 1974.

Dewhurst, Kenneth. *Dr. Thomas Sydenham (1624–1689): His Life and Original Writings.* Berkeley, Calif., 1966.

———. *John Locke (1632–1704), Physician and Philosopher, a Medical Biography.* London, 1963.

A Directory for the Publique Worship of God throughout the Three Kingdoms. London, 1652.

Donne, John. *The Poems of John Donne.* Ed. Herbert J.C. Grierson. 2 vols. 1912. Reprint, Oxford, 1966.

————. *Selected Prose.* Ed. Evelyn Simpson, Helen Gardner, and Timothy Healy. Oxford, 1967.

Dryden, John. *The Poems of John Dryden.* Ed. James Kinsley. 4 vols. Oxford, 1958.

Dugdale, William. *The Life, Diary, and Correspondence of Sir William Dugdale, Knight.* Ed. William Hamper. London, 1827.

Dunlop, Robert, ed. *Ireland under the Commonwealth, Being a Selection of Documents.* 2 vols. Manchester, Eng., 1913.

Esson, D.M.R. *The Curse of Cromwell: A History of the Ironside Conquest of Ireland, 1649–53.* London, 1971.

Evans, Joan. *A History of the Society of Antiquaries.* Oxford, 1956.

Evelyn, John. *The Diary of John Evelyn.* Ed. Esmond S. de Beer. 6 vols. Oxford, 1955.

————. *The Writings of John Evelyn.* Ed. Guy de la Bédeyè. Woodbridge, Eng., 1995.

Everitt, Alan. *The Community of Kent and the Great Rebellion, 1640–60.* Leicester, 1966.

Fanshawe, Ann. *The Memoirs of Ann Lady Fanshawe.* Ed. Sir Richard Fanshawe. London, 1907.

Ferrar, John. *An History of the City of Limerick.* Limerick, c. 1767.

Firth, C.H. *Oliver Cromwell and the Rule of the Puritans in England.* London, 1901. Reprint, London, 1938.

[Fisher, Payne]. *Veni, Vidi, Vici: The Triumphs of the Most Excellent and Industrious Oliver Cromwell . . . Whereto Is Added an Elegy upon the Death of the Late Lord Deputy of Ireland.* Trans. [Thomas Manley]. London, 1652.

Fletcher, Anthony. "Oliver Cromwell and the Localities." In J.R. Jones et al., eds., *Politics and People in Revolutionary England.* Oxford, 1986.

Fowler, Alastair, ed. *The New Oxford Book of Seventeenth Century Verse.* Oxford, 1992.

Fox, Carroll. *Insects and Diseases of Man.* Philadelphia, 1925.

Fox, George. *A Journal or Historical Account.* Philadelphia, n.d.

Fraser, Antonia. *Cromwell, The Lord Protector.* New York, 1973.

Fraser, James. *Chronicles of the Frasers.* Edinburgh, 1905.

French, J. Milton. *The Life Records of John Milton.* 5 vols. Rutgers, N.J., 1949–58.

Gardiner, Samuel Rawson. *The First Two Stuarts and the Puritan Revolution, 1603–1660.* New York, 1893.

Gaunt, Peter. *The Cromwellian Gazetteer.* Gloucester, 1987.

Geddes, Gordon E. *Welcome Joy: Death in Puritan New England.* Ann Arbor, Mich., 1981.

Gentiles, Ian. *The New Model Army in England, Ireland, and Scotland, 1645–1653.* Oxford, 1992.

Gibson, A. Craig. "Original Correspondence of the Lord President Bradshaw; With Other Documents Illustrating His Personal History." *Transactions of the Historic Society of Lancashire and Cheshire,* n.s., 2 (1861–62): 40–74.

Gilbert, John T., ed. *A Contemporary History of Affairs in Ireland from 1641 to 1652.* 3 vols. Dublin, 1880.

Glaister, John. *The Power of Poison.* New York, [1955].

Goldwater, Leonard J. *Mercury: A History of Quicksilver.* Baltimore, 1972.

Gordon, Benjamin Lee. *Medieval and Renaissance Medicine.* New York, 1909.

Guibert, Philibert. *The Charitable Physitian.* London, 1639.

A Guild-Hall Elegie, Upon the Funerals of that Infernal Saint John Bradshaw, President of the High Court of Justice. [London, 1659].

Guizot, François Pierre Guillaume. *Histoire de la République d'Angleterre et de Cromwell, 1649–1658.* 2 vols. Paris, 1855.

———. *History of Richard Cromwell and the Restoration of Charles II.* 2 vols. London, 1856.

Gumble, Thomas. *The Life of General Monck, Duke of Albemarle.* London, 1671.

Haddad, Lester M., Michael W. Shannon, and James F. Winchester, eds. *Clinical Management of Poisoning and Drug Overdose.* 3d ed. Philadelphia, 1998.

Halkett, Anne Lady. *The Autobiography of Anne Lady Halkett.* Ed. John Gough Nicholas. London, 1875.

Hardman, Joel G., and Lee E. Limbird. *Goodman's and Gilman's The Pharmacological Basis of Therapeutics.* 9th ed. New York, 1996.

Hare, Christopher [Marian Andrews]. *A Great Emperor: Charles V, 1519–1558.* London, 1917.

Harleian Miscellany. 8 vols. London, 1744–46.

Harrison, Walter. *A New and Universal History, Description and Survey of the Cities of London and Westminster.* London, [1775].

[Harvey, Charles]. *A Collection of Several Passages Concerning His Late Highnesse Oliver Cromwell, In the Time of His Sickness . . . Written by One That was Then Groom of His Bed-Chamber.* London, 1659.

[Hatton, Edward]. *A New View of London.* 2 vols. London, 1708.

Haugaard, William P. *Elizabeth and the English Reformation: The Struggle for a Stable Settlement of Religion.* Cambridge, 1968.

Heath, James. *A Brief Chronicle of the Late Intestine War in the Three King-doms.* London, 1663.

[————]. *Flagellum, Or the Life and Death, Birth and Burial of Oliver Cromwell.* London, 1663.

Heathcote, Evelyn D. *An Account of Some of the Families Bearing the Name of Heathcote.* Winchester, Eng., 1899.

Helms, M.W., and Leonard Taylor. "Thomas Clarges." In Basil Duke Henning, ed., *The History of Parliament: The House of Commons, 1660–1690.* 3 vols. London, 1983.

Henry, Philip. *Diaries and Letters of Philip Henry.* Ed. Matthew Henry Lee. London, 1882.

Herrick, Robert. *The Poetical Works of Robert Herrick.* Ed. Percy Simpson. Oxford, 1921.

Hibbard, Caroline. *Charles I and the Popish Plot.* Chapel Hill, N.C., 1983.

Hill, Christopher. *The Experience of Defeat: Milton and Some Contemporar-ies.* New York, 1984.

————. *God's Englishman.* New York, 1970.

————. *Milton and the English Revolution.* New York, 1977.

An Historical Account of all the Tryals and Attainders of High-Treason, From the Beginning of the Reign of King Charles the First, Chronologically Digested. London, 1716.

Historical Manuscripts Commission. *Reports.*

The History and Present State of the British Islands . . . and More Particularly of the County of Middlesex, and City of London. 2 vols. London, 1743.

Howell, Roger. "'That Imp of Satan': The Restoration Image of Cromwell." In Richardson, *Images of Cromwell.*

Hughes, Ann. *Politics, Society and Civil War in Warwickshire, 1620–1660.* Cambridge, 1987.

Hunt, William. *The Puritan Moment: The Coming of Revolution in an En-glish County.* Cambridge, Mass., 1983.

Hutchinson, Lucy. *Memoirs of the Life of Colonel Hutchinson.* Ed. James Sutherland. London, 1973.

Hutton, Ronald. *The Restoration.* Oxford, 1985.

Hyde, Edward, Earl of Clarendon. *The History of the Rebellion and Civil Wars in England.* 7 vols. Oxford, 1849.

————. *State Papers Collected by Edward, Earl of Clarendon.* 3 vols. Ox-ford, 1767-86.

[Ireton, Henry]. *A Letter from the Lord Deputy of Ireland unto the Honourable William Lenthal Esq; Speaker of the Parliament . . . Together with the Articles Formerly Offered.* London, 1651.

Isselbacher, Kurt J., et al., eds. *Harrison's Principles of Internal Medicine.* 13th ed. New York, 1994.

Jesse, John Heneage. *London and Its Celebrities.* 2 vols. London, 1850.

J.G.M. to Editor. *Notes and Queries* 146 (Jan.–June 1924): 270–71.

Jones, Colin., Malyn Newitt, and Stephen Roberts, eds. *Politics and People in Revolutionary England: Essays in Honour of Ivan Roots.* Oxford, 1986.

Jones, J.R. "Booth's Rising of 1659." *Bulletin of the John Rylands Library* 39 (1956–57): 416–43.

Jones, J.R., ed. *The Restored Monarchy.* Totowa, N.J., 1979.

Josselin, Ralph. *The Diary of Ralph Josselin, 1616–1683.* Ed. Alan MacFarlane. London, 1976.

Keeton, G.W. *Lord Chancellor Jeffreys and the Stuart Cause.* London, 1965.

[Kennett, White]. *A Register and Chronicle . . . Faithfully Taken from the Manuscript Collections of the Lord Bishop of Peterborough.* London, 1728.

Kenyon, John. *The Popish Plot.* London, 1972.

———. *The Stuart Constitution, 1603–1688.* 2d ed. Cambridge, 1986.

Klaassen, Curtis D., ed. *Casarett and Doull's Toxicology.* New York, 1996.

Knott, John R., Jr. *The Sword of the Spirit, Puritan Responses to the Bible.* Chicago, 1980.

Le Goff, Jacques. *La naissance du purgatoire.* Paris, 1981.

Legouis, Pierre. *Andrew Marvell.* 2d ed. Oxford, 1968.

Lehmann, John. *Holborn.* London, 1970.

Lenihan, Maurice. *Limerick, Its History and Antiquities.* Dublin, 1866.

Lieb, Michael, and John T. Shawcross, eds. *Achievements of the Left Hand: Essays on the Prose of John Milton.* Amherst, Mass., 1974.

Lloyd-Jones, Hugh, Valerie Pearl, and Blair Worden, eds. *History and Imagination, Essays in Honour of H.R. Trevor-Roper.* London, 1981.

London and its Environs Described. 6 vols. London, 1761.

London County Council. *The Parish of St. Giles-in-the-Fields.* Vol. 3 of *Survey of London.* Part 1. London, 1912.

———. *The Parish of St. Giles-in-the-Fields.* Vol. 5 of *Survey of London.* Part 2. London, 1914.

Ludlow, Edmund. *The Memoirs of Edmund Ludlow, 1625–1672.* Ed. C.H. Firth. 2 vols. Oxford, 1894.

———. *A Voyce from the Watch Tower.* Part 5, *1660–1662.* Ed. A. Blair Worden. London, 1978.

MacArthur, Sir William P. "A Brief Story of English Malaria." *British Medical Bulletin* 8 (1951–52): 76–79.

MacLysaght, Edward. *Irish Life in the Seventeenth Century.* 1939. Reprint, Shannon, 1969.

Marshall, Alan. *Intelligence and Espionage in the Reign of Charles II, 1660–1685.* Cambridge, 1994.

Marvell, Andrew. *The Poems and Letters of Andrew Marvell.* Ed. H.M. Margoliouth. 2d ed. 2 vols. Oxford, 1952.

Masson, David. *The Life of John Milton.* 6 vols. London, 1875–80.

Mayer, Joseph, ed. "Inedited Letters of Cromwell, Colonel Jones, Bradshaw and Other Regicides." *Transactions of the Historic Society of Lancashire and Cheshire,* n.s., 1 (1860–61): 177–300.

Mead, Richard. *A Mechanical Account of Poisons in Several Essays.* London, 1702.

Meyer, Carl S. *Elizabeth I and the Religious Settlement of 1559.* St. Louis, 1960.

Milton, John. *The Poems of John Milton.* Ed. John Carey and Alastair Fowler. London, 1980.

The Montgomery Manuscripts, 1603-1706. Ed. George Hill. Belfast, 1869.

Morrill, John. *The Nature of the English Revolution.* London, 1993.

Mundy, Peter. *The Travels of Peter Mundy in Europe and Asia, 1608–1667.* Ed. R.C. Temple and L.M. Anstey. 5 vols. in 6. London, 1907–36.

Munk, William. *The Roll of the Royal College of Physicians of London.* 3 vols. 2d ed. London, 1878.

Murphy, Denis. *Cromwell in Ireland.* Dublin, 1885.

[Nedham, Marchamont]. *The Excellencie of a Free-State . . . Published by a Well-wisher to Posterity.* London, 1656.

Neve, Philip. *A Narrative of the Disinterment of Milton's Coffin, in the Parish-Church of St. Giles, Cripplegate, on Wednesday, 4ᵗʰ August, 1790; and the Treatment of the Corpse.* 2d ed. London, 1790.

Newton, Douglas. *London West of the Bars.* London, 1951.

Newton, E.E., to Editor. *Notes and Queries* 151 (July–Dec. 1926): 339–40.

Nicholas, Sir Edward. *The Nicholas Papers: Correspondence of Sir Edward Nicholas, Secretary of State.* Ed. Sir George F. Warner. 4 vols. London, 1886–1920.

Nicholl, Charles. *The Reckoning: The Murder of Christopher Marlowe.* London, 1992.

Noble, Mark. *The Lives of the English Regicides.* 2 vols. London, 1798.

———. *Memoirs of the Protectorate-House of Cromwell.* 2 vols. Birmingham, 1784.

Noorthouck, John. *A New History of London.* London, 1773.

Owen, John. *The Labouring Saints Dismission to Rest.* London, 1652.

Paracelsus. *Selected Writings.* Ed. Jolande Jacobi. New York, 1951.

Parker, William Riley. *Milton: A Biography.* 2 vols. Oxford, 1968.

The Parliamentary or Constitutional History of England: From the Earliest Times, to the Restoration of King Charles II. 24 vols. London, 1751–63.

Pascal, Blaise. *Pascal's Pensées.* Ed. Martin Turnell. New York, 1962.

Peachy, George C. "Thomas Trapham—(Cromwell's Surgeon)—and Others." *Proceedings of the Royal Society of Medicine* 24, no. 2 (1931): 47–55.

Pearson, Karl, and G.M. Morant. "The Wilkinson Head of Oliver Cromwell and Its Relationship to Busts, Masks and Painted Portraits." *Biometrika* 26 (1934): 269–378.

Pennant, Thomas. *Of London.* London, 1790.

Pepys, Samuel. *Diary of Samuel Pepys.* Ed. Robert Latham. 11 vols. Berkeley, Calif., 1970–83.

Petitfils, Jean-Christian. *L'affaire des poisons, alchimistes et sorciers sous Louis XIV.* Paris, 1977.

Phillips, Edward. "The Life of Mr. John Milton," In Darbishire, *The Early Lives of Milton.*

Phillips, Hugh. *Mid-Georgian London.* London, 1964.

Pierpoint, Robert. "The Carcasses of Cromwell, Ireton, and Bradshaw." *Notes and Queries* 146 (Jan.–June 1924): 227.

Potter, John Deane. *The Fatal Gallows Tree.* London, 1965.

Prestwick, John. *Prestwich's Respublica.* London, 1787.

Prestwick, Rev. John. "The Death, Funeral Order and Procession of His Highness." In John Towill Rutt, ed., *Diary of Thomas Burton.* 4 vols. London, 1828.

———. "John Prestwich MS." In *Diary of Thomas Burton,* ed. John Twill Rutt. 4 vols. London 1828.

———. "Rev. John Prestwich Ms." In Prestwich, *Respublica.*

Ramesey, William. *De Venenis: Or, A Discourse of Poysons, Their Names, Natures, & Vertues; with Their Several Symptomes, Prognosticks, and Antidotes.* London, 1663.

Ramsey, Robert W. *Henry Cromwell.* London, 1933.

———. *Henry Ireton.* London, 1949.

———. *Richard Cromwell, Protector of England.* London, 1935.

R.C. to Editor. *Notes and Queries,* 2d ser., 4 (July–Dec. 1857).

Rede, Leman Thomas. *Anecdotes and Biography.* London, 1799.

Richardson, R.C. *The Debate on the English Revolution.* London, 1977.

———, ed. *Images of Oliver Cromwell: Essays for and by Roger Howell, Jr.* Manchester, Eng., 1993.

Ridley, Jasper. *The Roundheads*. London, 1976.

Robbins, Stanley. *Pathologic Basis of Disease*. Philadelphia, 1974.

Rogers, P.G. *The Fifth Monarchy Men*. London, 1966.

Royal College of Physicians. *Certain Necessary Directions, As Well for the Cure of the Plague*. London, 1636.

Rugg, Thomas. *The Diurnal of Thomas Rugg, 1659–1661*. Ed. William L. Sachse. London, 1961.

Russell, Conrad, ed. *Origins of the English Civil War*. New York, 1973.

S. to Editor. *Notes and Queries* 151 (July–Dec. 1926): 226.

Saintsbury, George, ed. *Minor Poets of the Caroline Period*. 3 vols. 1905. Reprint, Oxford, 1968.

Salmon, William. *Pharmacopœia Bateana: Or, Bate's Dispensatory, Translated from the Second Edition of the Latin Copy, Published by Mr. James Shipton. Containing His Choice and Select Recipes*. London, 1694.

Scarisbrick, J.J. *The Reformation and the English People*. Oxford, 1984.

Scott, Sir Walter. *Chronicles of the Canongate*. 2 vols. Edinburgh, 1827.

Seaward, Paul. *The Cavalier Parliament and the Reconstruction of the Old Regime, 1661–1667*. Cambridge, 1989.

Sesek, Lawrence. *Images of English Puritans, A Collection of Contemporary Sources, 1589–1646*. Baton Rouge, La., 1989.

Sharpe, J.A. *Crime in Early Modern England, 1550–1750*. London, 1984.

Sharpe, Kevin. *The Personal Rule of Charles I*. New Haven, Conn., 1992.

Shawcross, John T. *John Milton, The Self and the World*. Lexington, Ky., 1993.

Sherwood, Roy. *The Court of Oliver Cromwell*. London, 1977.

Simms, J.G. "Hugh Dubh O'Neill's Defence of Limerick, 1650–1651." In D.W. Hayton and Gerard O'Brien, eds. *War and Politics in Ireland, 1649–1730*. London, 1986.

[Skiller, Cyriack]. "The Life of Mr. John Milton." In Darbishire, *Early Lives*.

Skinner, Thomas. *The Life of General Monk, Late Duke of Albemarle*. London, 1723.

Slack, Paul. *The Impact of Plague in Tudor and Stuart England*. London, 1985.

———. "Mortality Crises and Epidemic Diseases in England, 1485–1616." In Charles Webster, ed., *Health, Medicine, and Mortality in the Sixteenth Century*. New York, 1979.

Smith, Lacey Baldwin. *Treason in Tudor England, Politics and Paranoia*. London, 1986.

Solt, Leo F. *Church and State in Early Modern England, 1509–1640*. New York, 1990.

————. *Saints in Arms, Puritanism and Democracy in Cromwell's Army.* Stanford, Calif., 1959.

Spalding, Ruth. *Contemporaries of Bulstrode Whitelock, 1605–1675.* Oxford, 1990.

S.S.B. "To the Editor." *European Magazine* 55 (1809): 17–18.

Stanley, Arthur Penrhyn. *Historical Memorials of Westminster Abbey.* London, 1868.

Stannard, David E. *The Puritan Way of Death, A Study in Religion, Culture, and Social Change.* New York, 1977.

State Trials. Ed. T.B. Howell. 33 vols. London, 1816-26.

Stearns, Raymond P. *The Strenuous Puritan: Hugh Peter.* Urbana, Ill., 1954.

Stephen, James Fitzjames. *A History of the Criminal Law of England.* 3 vols. London, 1883.

Stone, Lawrence. *The Causes of the English Revolution, 1529–1642.* London, 1972.

Stow, John. *A Survey of the Cities of London and Westminster.* Ed. Robert Seymour [John Mottley]. 6th ed. 2 vols. London, 1734–35.

————. *The Survey of London.* London, 1633.

Strong, Roy. *Art and Power: Renaissance Festivals, 1450–1650.* Berkeley, Calif., 1984.

————. *Van Dyck: Charles I on Horseback.* New York, 1972.

Strype, John. *A Survey of the Cities of London and Westminster . . . Written at first in the Year MDXCVIII. By John Stowe.* 2 vols. London, 1720.

[Stuart, James]. *Critical Observations on the Buildings and Improvements of London.* London, 1771.

Sydenham, Dr. Thomas. "Febres Intermittentes." In Kenneth Dewhurst, *Dr. Thomas Sydenham (1624–1689) His Life and Original Writings.* Berkeley, Calif., 1966.

Taylor, A.A. "How the Proceedings of Parliament Are Recorded." *Pearson's Magazine* 3 (Jan.–June 1897): 42–46.

Thomas, Keith. *Religion and the Decline of Magic.* New York, 1971.

Thomas, P.W. "Two Cultures? Court and Country under Charles I." In Russell, *Origins of the English Civil War.*

Thornbury, George Walter. *Old and New London.* 6 vols. London, n.d.

Thurloe, John. *A Collection of the State Papers of John Thurloe, Esq.* Ed. Thomas Birch. 7 vols. London, 1742.

Trevor-Roper, Hugh. *Renaissance Essays.* London, 1985.

The Trials of Charles the First, and of Some of the Regicides. With Biographies of Bradshaw, Ireton, Harrison, and Others. London, 1832.

The True Manner of the Most Magnificent Conveyance of his Highnesse Effigies from Sommerset-house to Westminster. London, 1658.

Underdown, David. *Revel, Riot, and Rebellion: Popular Politics and Culture in England, 1603–1660.* Oxford, 1985.

———. *Royalist Conspiracy in England, 1649–1660.* New Haven, Conn., 1960.

———. "Settlement in the Counties, 1653–1658." In Aylmer, ed., *The Interregnum: The Quest for Settlement, 1647–1660.* London, 1972.

Vansina, Jan. *Oral Tradition as History.* Madison, Wis., 1985.

Varley, F.J. "Cromwell's Burial." *Notes and Queries* 164 (Jan.–June 1933): 334.

———. *Oliver Cromwell's Latter End.* London, 1936.

Varley, F.J., to Editor. *Notes and Queries* 176 (Jan.–June 1939): 323; 177 (July–Dec. 1939): 69.

Vaughan, Henry. *The Works of Henry Vaughan.* Ed. L.C. Martin. 2d ed. Oxford, 1957.

Verney, Margaret M. *Memoirs of the Verney Family.* 4 vols. London, 1892–99.

The Victoria History of the County of Surrey. Ed. H.E. Maldon. 4 vols. London, 1902–12.

Waller, Edmund. *The Poems of Edmund Waller,* Ed. George Thorn-Drury. 2 vols. London, 1901.

Warwick, Sir Philip. *Memoirs of the Reign of King Charles the First.* Edinburgh, 1813.

Watters, David H. *"With Bodilie Eyes": Eschatological Themes in Puritan Literature and Gravestone Art.* Ann Arbor, Mich., 1981.

Webb, Alfred. *A Compendium of Irish Biography.* Dublin, 1878. Reprint, New York, 1970.

Webster, Charles, ed. *Health, Medicine and Mortality in the Sixteenth Century.* Cambridge, 1979.

Wedgewood, C.V. *The Great Rebellion: The King's War, 1641–1647.* New York, 1959.

———. *Oliver Cromwell and the Elizabethan Inheritance.* London, 1970.

Weever, John. *Ancient Funerall Monuments.* London, 1631.

Weir, Alison. *The Princes in the Tower.* New York, 1995.

"What Became of Cromwell?" *Gentlemen's Magazine* 250 (1881): 553–64.

Wheatley, Henry B. *London, Past and Present . . . Based upon the Handbook of London by the Late Peter Cunningham.* 3 vols. London, 1891.

Whitelock, Bulstrode. *The Diary of Bulstrode Whitelocke.* Ed. Ruth Spalding. Oxford, 1990.

————. *Memorials of the English Affairs.* 4 vols. Oxford, 1853.

Williams, J.B. "Cromwelliana." *Notes and Queries* 4 (July–Dec. 1911): 3–4, 103–5, 262–64.

Willis, Thomas. *The London Practice of Physick.* London, 1692. Reprint, Boston, 1977.

Willson, D. Harris. *King James VI and I.* London, 1956.

Wood, Anthony. *Athenae Oxonienses.* 2 vols. London, 1721.

————. *The Life and Times of Anthony Wood.* Ed. Andrew Clark. 5 vols. Oxford, 1891–1901.

Woolrych, Austin. "Last Quests for a Settlement, 1657–1660." In Aylmer, *Interregnum.*

————. "Milton and Cromwell: 'A Short but Scandalous Night of Interruption.'" In Lieb and Shawcross, *Achievements of the Left Hand.*

————. "Putney Revisited." In Jones, Newitt, and Roberts, *Politics and People.*

Worden, Blair. "Classical Republicanism and the Puritan Revolution." In Lloyd-Jones, Pearl, and Worden, *History and Imagination.* New York, 1982.

Yale, D.E.C., ed. *Lord Nottingham's Chancery Cases.* 2 vols. London, 1957–62.

Yule, George. *Puritans in Politics: The Religious Legislation of the Long Parliament, 1640–1647.* N.p., 1981.

Zagorin, Perez. *A History of Political Thought in the English Revolution.* London, 1954.

Zaret, David. *The Heavenly Contract: Ideology and Organization in Pre-Revolutionary Puritanism.* Chicago, 1985.

$\mathcal{I}$ndex

**Western Suburbs
of
Seventeenth-Century London**